THE MOSAIC VILLAGE

AN ILLUSTRATED HISTORY OF WINNIPEG'S NORTH END

RUSS GOURLUCK

GREAT PLAINS
PUBLICATIONS

Great Plains Publications
345-955 Portage Avenue
Winnipeg, MB R3G 0P9
www.greatplains.mb.ca

Great Plains Publications gratefully acknowledges the financial support provided for its publishing program by the Government of Canada through the Canada Book Fund; the Canada Council for the Arts; the Province of Manitoba through the Book Publishing Tax Credit and the Book Publisher Marketing Assistance Program; and the Manitoba Arts Council.

Design & Typography by Relish Design Studio Inc.
Printed in Canada by Friesens

Library and Archives Canada Cataloguing in Publication

Gourluck, Russ
        The mosaic village : an illustrated history of Winnipeg's
North End / Russ Gourluck.

ISBN 978-1-894283-86-1

        1. North End (Winnipeg, Man.)--History. 2. North
End (Winnipeg, Man.)--Biography. 3. Winnipeg (Man.)--
History. 4. Winnipeg (Man.)--Biography. I. Title.

FC3396.52.G69 2010   971.27'43   C2009-906694-7

In honour of "The Boys" of Midland Fruit,
who taught their families the importance
of integrity and hard work...

■ The nine children of Ukrainian immigrants George and Mary Gowriluk grew up on their family farm in Gonor, Manitoba (south of Lockport along Henderson Highway). The times were hard and everyone shared in the work. Shown is a family portrait during the 1950s.
• Credit: Courtesy Diane Gourluck

ACKNOWLEDGEMENTS

SPECIAL THANKS TO:

- Abe Anhang, June Dutka, Gail Fine, Irma Penn, and Glenn Salter for helpful information and numerous interview prospects

- Mike and Frank Humniski for an information-packed driving tour of the North End

- George Smith and the late Ron Meyers for a nostalgic walking tour of their old neighbourhood

- Carole Kurdydyk and the members of the St. John's High School 100th Anniversary Reunion Committee for their valuable support and assistance

- John Crawshaw, Chris Dewar, Mary Kelekis, Olga Kucher, John Marczyk, Len Offrowich, Pat Panchuk, Ed Pascal, Ron Romanowski, Libby Simon, Sam Singer, Dan Skwarchuk, Peter Tittenberger, Mandy van Leeuwen, John Whiteway and Harriet Zaidman for a wealth of information and images

IMAGES AND COPYRIGHT:

Efforts were made to locate current copyright holders of images included in *The Mosaic Village* and to obtain permission for their use. The publisher welcomes clarifications from rights holders.

Images from the *Winnipeg Tribune* Collection are copyright the University of Manitoba and are reproduced with the permission of Archives and Special Collections.

Images from the Jewish Historical Society Collection at the Archives of Manitoba are the property of the Jewish Heritage Centre of Western Canada and are reproduced with the permission of both institutions.

The billboard photo in Chapter Two originally appeared in *The North End* by John Paskievich, published by the University of Manitoba Press in 2007 and is reprinted with the permission of John Paskievich and the University of Manitoba Press.

The poem "St. Nicholas and his Devil" in Chapter Two was published in 2004 in *Sweet Talking* by Ron Romanowski and is reprinted with the permission of Ron Romanowski.

Libby Simon's memories of St. John's Park and the accompanying photo in Chapter Five originally appeared in the Spring 2008 issue of *Geist* magazine. Both are reprinted with permission of Libby Simon and *Geist*.

Special thanks are extended to Ava Block-Super and Stan Carbone of the Jewish Heritage Centre of Western Canada; Sharon Foley of the Archives of Manitoba; and Shelley Sweeney of University of Manitoba Archives and Special Collections for their assistance in obtaining images for use in the book.

INTERVIEWS

The following individuals made major contributions to this book by generously sharing the stories of their families and themselves in individual interviews.

Michael Averbach
Earl Barish
Brenda (Gallis) Barrie
Julia Berschley
Sheila (Bass) Billinghurst
Heather (Weber) Borody
Larry Borody
Audrey Boyko
Todd Britton
Larry Brown
Sel Burrows
Annette Champion-Taylor
Jack Chapman
Myrna Charach
Lawrie Cherniack
Saul Cherniack
Gus Damianakos
Matt De Landes
Audrey Desmond
Pat Duseigne
Ron Devere
Ross Einfeld
Larry Fleisher
Doreen (Morrison) Geiszler
George Gershman
Pearl (Rosenberg) Globerman
Mel Goldenberg
Sid Green
David Gruber
Arthur (Fivie) Gunn

Bernie Gunn
Tom Halprin
Natalie (Berschley)
  Hemingway
Vera Hershfield
Andy Hill
Ben Hochman
Phyllis Hochman
Frank Humniski
Mike Humniski
Orysia (Krevesky) Jackson
Harry Kaplan
Nancy Kardash
Sam Katz
Steve Kiz
Bernie Klein
Tracy Konopada
Bill Konyk
Esther Korchynski
Millie Krause
Mike Krevesky
Julia Kurjewicz
Richard Kurtz
Eleanor Lazare
Harry Lazarenko
Roger Leclerc
Astrid Lichti
Ed Lichti
Gladys (Pearlman) Love
Gord MacDonald

Margaret MacDonald
Gord Mackintosh
Lorraine Maciboric
Sandra (Nezon) Magid
John Marczyk
Doug Martindale
Jason McDonald
Gord McTavish
Erhard Meier
Lillian Mendelsohn
Ron Meyers
Joseph Mindell
Rose Mindell
Betty (Dougloski) Murray
Mel Myers
Bob Naleway
Leslie Nepon
Arie Perlmutter
Danny Pollock
Joseph Presznyak
Walter Procter
Tracy Lynn Proctor
Mary Pytel
Vera Pytel
Carolyn Rickey
Dave Roman
Ron Romanowski
Phillip Rosen
Dennis Ruggles
Manly Rusen

Melanie Rushton
Morley Rypp
Shirley (Elhatton) Scaletta
Marcia Schnoor
Myron Shatulsky
Bill Shell
Sophie Shinewald
Roslyn Silver
Norman Silverberg
Colleen Simard
Libby (Klein) Simon
Sam Singer
Yale Singer
Lil (Grushko) Slonim
Betty Smith
George Smith
Fred Solomon
Phyllis (Oretzki) Springman
Sharon Staff
Catherine Thexton
Sylvia Todaschuk
Judy Wasylycia-Leis
Ken Werner
Wayne Whalen
Rita Winrob
Ted Wojcik
Mike Wolchock
Phil Young
Julie Zatorsky
Martin Zeilig

An early business (ca 1909) at 742 Flora

• Credit: Archives of Manitoba, Jewish Historical Society
Collection, 3145

PREFACE

One of the things I've learned about writing local histories is that, at a certain point, each book begins to determine its own direction. When I started gathering information for *The Mosaic Village*, I searched a number of archival sources and found some interesting historical data. But it was only when I began to interview current and expatriate North Enders that the story of the North End came alive and the direction of the book became clear.

This is a book about people who proudly call themselves North Enders, and many of their stories are related in their own words. Some have achieved a degree of fame, but most are regular people who have worked hard so they and their families could have good lives. Just as the North End is a mosaic of diverse individuals and cultures, this book is a mosaic of the stories of generations of people who have lived and worked in the North End.

As I interviewed men and women from across North America, it became clear that many people who grew up in Winnipeg's North End continue to regard themselves as North Enders regardless of where their lives have taken them. I suspect that one Winnipegger who grew up on Stella Avenue and now lives in West Kildonan isn't unique when he explains that he has a "compass direction" in his mind that finds him determining routes to any destination in Winnipeg with the intersection of Selkirk and Arlington as a starting point.

The very name "North End" tells its own story. Areas like St. Boniface, Fort Rouge, and the Kildonans, have names that reflect their roots in local history. Others, including such relative newcomers as Linden Woods, Waverley Heights, and Mandalay West, have names devised by developers or politicians to evoke images of genteel living. The name of the North End simply states where it is. That directness is a reflection of the down-to-earth character of the area and its people.

One early decision that needed to be made in writing *The Mosaic Village* was to clarify the limits of the North End. I've used the generally accepted boundaries of the Canadian Pacific Railway mainline on the south and the Red River on the east. For the northern boundary, I've taken the advice of a number of North Enders and regarded McAdam Avenue, the former boundary between the City of Winnipeg and the City of West Kildonan, as the dividing line.

The western limit proved to be the most unclear. Some older North Enders suggested that Arlington was the boundary, but most were willing to stretch the edge to McPhillips. Many Sisler alumni, however, were adamant that, whether they lived east or west of McPhillips when they went to high school, they were North Enders and their school was in the North End. So Sisler High School is included in the book.

Another aspect of the book that needed to be decided was its chronological parameters. In general terms, *The Mosaic Village* tells the story of Winnipeg's North End from the arrival of European immigrants in the 1880s until the present time. The main emphasis, however, is from the 1930s until the 1970s, in part because those can be seen as the glory days of the North

End, and in part because much of the information I received through interviews was from that period.

Although I've tried to verify the information in the book, there will undoubtedly be some errors of fact or interpretation, and those are my responsibility. Readers who notice problems or anyone who would like to contact me about any aspect of *The Mosaic Village* can reach me by email at russgourluck@shaw.ca or by mail in care of Great Plains Publications at 345-955 Portage Avenue, Winnipeg MB R3G 0P9.

The Mosaic Village represents the collective efforts of many people. More than 100 individuals whose names are listed in the acknowledgements participated in individual interviews and provided a treasure chest of fascinating information. Unfortunately, only a portion of that huge volume of information could be accommodated in the book. Most of the interviews were recorded and, where interviewees have given consent, the recordings have been donated to the Winnipeg Public Library and the Jewish Heritage Centre of Western Canada so that this wealth of oral history can be accessed by the public for many years to come.

I want to thank Gregg Shilliday and Catharina de Bakker of Great Plains Publications and the talented people of Relish Design for transforming a collection of files and images into a real book. Special thanks go to Glenn Marquez for his support and critiques, and to Miko the Pug, who facilitated the process by sleeping on the sofa.

Most of all, I want to thank the many North Enders who proudly shared the stories of their parents and grandparents as well as their own experiences. Without their help, this book could not have been written.

Russ Gourluck, June, 2010

CONTENTS

Holy Trinity Ukrainian
Orthodox Cathedral, 2009
• Credit: Photo by Russ Gourluck

PROLOGUE
NEW HORIZONS
IN A NEW WORLD

Immigrants arriving at the CPR station in 1927 • Credit: Archives of Manitoba, Foote Collection 466, N2066

A CITY OF DREAMS

Winnipeg in the 1880s was a place of unbounded optimism. The arrival of the Canadian Pacific Railway created a wealth of opportunities, and soon the city's predominantly British citizens were joined by waves of immigrants with very different cultural and religious backgrounds. By 1921, Winnipeg's population had grown to nearly 180,000, largely the result of the arrival of immigrants from eastern Europe.

■ The Manitoba Immigration and Colonization Office at 439 Main Street (near Bannatyne) in 1916 • Credit: Archives of Manitoba, Winnipeg-Buildings-Business-Bird Block 2, Foote and James Photographers

A Time of Rapid Growth

Winnipeg in its early days was a place of great aspirations. In 1873 – despite a population of only 1,869, no waterworks or streetlights, and no paved roads or sidewalks – the tiny community was incorporated as a city. When the Provincial Legislature dared to reject the first incorporation bill, irate townsfolk accosted the Speaker of the House and bathed him in tar. The new city's crest optimistically featured a railway locomotive, even though no railway had yet reached Winnipeg.

The boundaries of the new city were the Assiniboine River on the south, Maryland Street on the west, the Red River on the east, and a line slightly north of what was later named Selkirk Avenue on the north.

The 1880s were exciting times for Winnipeg. A short-lived real estate boom early in the decade saw land values soar. The long-anticipated arrival of the Canadian Pacific Railway in 1885 established Winnipeg not only as the CPR's western headquarters but also as the "Gateway to the West," a place through which people and goods on their way to the western part of Canada had to pass. The city's population of fewer than 8,000 in 1880 more than doubled to 20,000 by 1886.

Attracted by the torch of Winnipeg's growth (its flames fanned by the boosterism of local businessmen), manufacturers established factories in the city, and the CPR shops became a major employer.

Eager to demonstrate to people down east that "The Chicago of the North" was more than just a frontier town, Winnipeg's political and business leaders (many of whom had moved from Ontario) took pride in the establishment of cultural and educational institutions, religious facilities, and a large number of political, fraternal, and sports-related organizations.

The British Establishment

The majority of Winnipeggers in the 1880s were proudly British in origin and primarily Protestant in religion. Much of the British presence was the result of an influx of settlers from Ontario after Manitoba entered Confederation in 1870. Other Manitobans of English and Scottish origin were employees of the powerful Hudson's Bay Company. Some were the offspring of Selkirk Settlers who first arrived in 1812.

There was no question that the people who held positions of authority in Winnipeg were virtually all British. The civil service was dominated by the English, the police force by the Scots, and the fire department by the Irish. Names like Ashdown, Bannatyne, and McDermot ruled business and politics, and the anglophile Manitoba Club was the site of many momentous discussions.

Members of this Anglo-Saxon establishment, and especially its wealthy and powerful elite of fewer than 400 people, were not inclined to be tolerant of different cultural practices or religious beliefs. But to continue the growth in which they took such pride, and to fill the thousands of jobs that resulted from the presence of the CPR mainline, immigration needed to draw on more than Ontario and the United Kingdom.

The Arrival of the "Foreigners"

Immigration to Manitoba from Europe began on a relatively small scale in the early 1870s with the arrival of Mennonites and Icelanders who settled in rural areas of the province.

In 1896, a major federal government policy was implemented to recruit immigrants from eastern and central Europe. The main emphasis of this permissive policy was to attract immigrants with farming experience by offering free land and the opportunity to start new lives in a free society. Immigration Minister Sir Clifford Sifton described this new kind of immigrant as "a stalwart peasant in a sheepskin coat, born on the soil, whose forefathers have been farmers for ten generations, with a stout wife and a half-dozen children..." Many English-speaking Canadians, however, disagreed with the plan lamenting, as one journalist said, the influx of "illiterate Slavs in overwhelming numbers."

Some of the new arrivals, particularly Jews, chose to settle in urban centres. Winnipeg was especially attractive because it offered apparently limitless opportunities to work for the railway or in manufacturing, or to establish businesses to serve the city's exploding population. Between 1886 and 1916, Winnipeg's population boomed from 20,000 to 163,000.

Slavic Immigration

The offer of the Canadian government was particularly appealing to Ukrainians who were eager to escape oppression, a lack of religious freedom, and a severe shortage of land.

Galician Immigrants

■ Ukrainian immigrants were often referred to by the names of their regions of origin, ca 1912 • Credit: Archives of Manitoba, Immigration Collection 1, N7926

Jewish welfare institutions in Winnipeg in 1932 included an orphanage and an old folks home • Credit: Archives of Manitoba, Jewish Historical Society Collection, 10

The first wave of Ukrainian immigration to Canada that began in the 1890s saw approximately 170,000 people arrive in Canada. Many Ukrainians (who were often called Ruthenians, Galicians, Bukovinians, and other names that reflected the regions in which they had lived) chose to accept the Canadian government's offer of free land and to pursue farming in various parts of the province, including the Dauphin area and the Interlake region. Others, however, opted to live in Winnipeg where work – generally railway jobs or the construction of roads and buildings – was available, and many of them settled in the area north of the CPR mainline. In 1912, Winnipeg had a population of about 3,500 Ukrainians, approximately ten percent of the Ukrainians in Manitoba.

■ (BELOW) Immigrants received thorough medical inspections on departure and arrival. • Credit: Courtesy Sam Singer

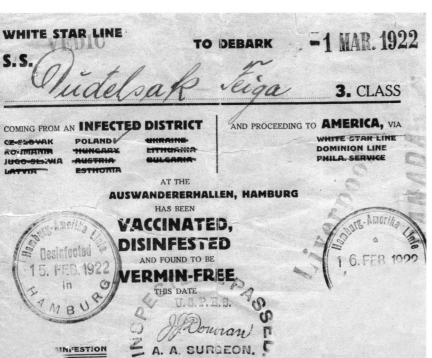

Despite their impoverished living conditions and the need to do exhausting physical labour, Ukrainian immigrants by the 1920s were active in politics, had built several churches, were publishing Ukrainian language newspapers, and had established a variety of cultural programs.

Similarly, immigration from Poland that began in the mid-1890s attracted Polish settlers to rural areas such as Hadashville and Polonia, while others found work opportunities in Winnipeg. Like their Ukrainian counterparts, Polish immigrants found basic labouring jobs and lived in the inexpensive housing of the North End. They too established their own cultural and religious institutions, including, in 1899, Holy Ghost Roman Catholic Church on Selkirk Avenue.

Most people of German origin who moved to Manitoba in the late 1800s didn't come from Germany. They were primarily ethnic Germans who came from eastern Europe and, to some extent, the American Midwest and Ontario. They and their descendants were scattered in several areas of rural Manitoba and Winnipeg, including parts of the North End and Elmwood.

Jewish Immigration

A few early Jewish immigrants came to Manitoba during the late 1870s and became involved in small business ventures (often as merchants, shopkeepers, peddlers, and tailors) in Winnipeg. By 1881, there were 21 Jewish families in Winnipeg and an overall total of about 100 people in the province.

■ Rabbi Israel Kahanovitch (standing, ca 1907), tended to the spiritual needs of the largest Orthodox congregation in Western Canada at Beth Jacob Synagogue, located on Schultz Street, just north of Jarvis. • Credit: Archives of Manitoba, Jewish Historical Society Collection, 326B, N21266

■ David Pascal came to Winnipeg in 1903, and his wife Feige Rochel, above, arrived from Romania with their children the following year. • Credit: Courtesy Ed Pascal

A year later, a party of 267 Jewish men, women, and children arrived in Winnipeg, part of a mass exodus of Jews from Russia as the result of the oppressive anti-Semitic policies of Russia's Czarist government. Barred from owning land, from higher education, and from many professions and occupations, the Jews also found themselves the targets of the vicious pogroms that threatened their lives. Most lived in the ghetto-like Pale of Settlement – the western provinces of Russia, including Belarus, much of Poland, and sections of Ukraine.

When the first party of immigrants arrived, they were welcomed by the existing Jewish community with food, employment assistance, and translation help. By mid-June 1882,

MOTHER

■ Fanny Klein waited to board a ship in Poland in 1928 with her two sons (note arrow). Two more sons and daughter Libby (Simon) were born in Winnipeg. • Credit: Courtesy Libby Simon

there were 340 Russian-Jewish immigrants. Some found jobs in rural Manitoba, including laying tracks for the CPR, and others (despite a lack of agricultural experience) were involved in farming. Most Jewish immigrants preferred to stay in Winnipeg, however, where jobs and business opportunities were plentiful and where Jewish worship, education, and social activities were available.

A second wave of Jewish immigration began in 1905 after a quashed Russian revolt. In contrast to the original Jewish settlers, many of whom had established themselves in the community and lived comfortably in the southern part of the city, the later arrivals were often destitute, arriving with little more than the clothing on their backs. In many families, the father made the journey to Canada alone to find work and accommodations, and then sent money or tickets for boat and train passage so his wife and children could join him. By 1912, twelve synagogues with three full-time rabbis were functioning, along with several Hebrew free schools and some Jewish social agencies.

Aaron Klein sometimes told of men on horseback beating people – especially Jews – who got in their way, invading homes and pillaging Jewish homes. He left everything behind in Russia to escape with his life to Vilna, Poland, where he met and married his wife Fanny and where their first two sons were born. They were able to escape while "Hitler was in the wings" but most of the relatives who remained behind were killed in the Holocaust. Because of the quotas on Jewish immigrants, refugees went to any country that would take them. One of Fanny's sisters found refuge in South Africa, the other in New York. The Kleins settled in North End Winnipeg where Chief Rabbi Kahanovitch had arranged for Aaron to teach at the Talmud Torah School.

A Long and Difficult Journey

The journey from the Old Country to Canada was, for many, a long and difficult experience. The sea voyage itself generally lasted two or three weeks. Steamship companies often crammed as many passengers on board as possible, due in part to a bounty-like incentive offered by the Canadian government of $5.00 for the head of an immigrant family and $2.00 for each family member. Passengers were often accommodated on cramped narrow bunks in noisy and sweltering areas below decks. Food and water were frequently inadequate. When passengers became ill and vomited, the stench remained. The cost per person was approximately $100.00.

But before families even boarded the ships, they had to make their way to the seaports. For some, this meant a railway trip, where narrow benches in overcrowded cars were quickly filled and many passengers sat on their luggage. For others, walking was the only way to reach the coast. Border checks by unscrupulous agents, medical examinations, means tests, and passport inspections made many wonder if they would even make it to their ship.

When passengers disembarked in Canada (usually in Halifax or Quebec), their rail trip westward was on specially-designated "Colonist Cars," where conditions were relatively comfortable. These cars included wooden seats that converted into beds, washrooms, heaters, and even cook stoves. And the trip was free of charge.

Bill Shell arrived from Russia in 1924 when he was nine years old with his mother and father, one brother, and one sister. "My parents were running away from Russia during the pogroms," Shell explains. "It took us two or three years. We were in hiding. The Bolsheviks were killing a lot of the Jews. We ran away with just our clothes."

He remembers that they travelled in a cattle boat and were at sea for 30 days. "It wasn't really a passenger boat," he points out. "The cattle were in the bottom part of the ship."

A particularly vivid memory that has stayed with Shell is that his family was required to change ships twice in mid-ocean by walking on planks precariously placed between two vessels. The steamer that finally brought them to Halifax was a passenger ship.

He recalls that as one of the ships passed some small islands, boats came out to peddle various items. That was the first time his family had seen bananas. "We didn't know what to do with them, and we were told to peel them and eat them."

When the Shell family first arrived in Winnipeg, they lived in the Immigration Hall (on Higgins Avenue adjacent to the CPR depot) for a period of time before arrangements were made for them to move to a house at 252 Jarvis.

■ British immigrants arriving in Halifax in 1912.
• Credit: Archives of Manitoba, Immigration Collection 10, N20750

Vera Hershfield, who was born in Russia, came over with her family when she was seven years old in 1930. She spoke only Russian, but she and a little English-speaking girl of the same age formed a friendship on the ship and played together, communicating with gestures. They arrived in Halifax and travelled to Winnipeg by train.

One of the most unusual tales of how a family came to live in Winnipeg is shared by Danny Pollock. His grandfather, Sheftel Malinsky, went to New York City in 1917 to collect payment for a shipment of grain that had been sent by the family business in Ukraine. After being told that the shipment had been sold by the purchaser to someone in Winnipeg and that he'd have to collect the payment there, he travelled to Winnipeg. Malinsky was paid for the grain, but before he was able to begin his journey home, the Russian Revolution broke out. A telegram from the family advised him not to go home but to stay in Winnipeg, start a business with the cash he'd received for the grain, and send passage for his wife and three children.

Malinsky opened a furniture store and was able to send steamship tickets to his wife. Unfortunately, due to the devaluation of the Ukrainian currency, she needed money before she and the children could begin their journey. She opened a restaurant where, ironically, most of her customers were Cossacks, and accepted only gold coins because of their stable value. Eventually she and the three children were able to begin their long walk to the seaport of Marseilles, France. The trek, which took almost a year, included sneaking across borders and paying off border guards with the gold kopeks. When they finally reached Marseilles, Mrs. Malinsky had run out of money and had no way to contact her husband, so she sold her hair to buy food for the children. When they finally arrived in Halifax, the family was refused entry by Canadian Immigration officials for not having the $25 entry fee. Luckily a cousin was on the ship and paid the fee and their train fare to Winnipeg. The cousin, Noah Witman, later became a well-known member of Winnipeg's Jewish community.

Norm Silverberg's parents were born in separate small villages in Russia. Around 1920, both of their fathers coincidentally emigrated to Canada to find jobs and places for their families to live, and then sent for their families. During a stopover in Poland, Silverberg's maternal grandmother died and a sixteen-year-old sister undertook to look after her siblings all the way to Canada. Fortunately that family met the family of Silverberg's father, and that mother took the children of both families into her care. The two families, including the boy and girl who would grow up to become Norm Silverberg's parents, travelled to Winnipeg together. At that point, the boy's family settled in Winnipeg, the girl's family went on to live in Saskatchewan, and it was ten years later when the two, then grown up, were reunited and eventually married.

Rose Mindell came from Poland in 1929 when she was ten, living on Dufferin and then on Stella. She had never seen chewing gum before ("I couldn't understand why people were chewing.") Her father had been here for three years before sending for his wife and three daughters. In the meantime, he

The First North End Mayor?

Some publications have described Stephen Juba, who was Mayor of Winnipeg from 1957 to 1977, as a resident of the North End. There's no question that Juba, arguably Winnipeg's most colourful and controversial mayor, possessed many of the personal and political attributes that North Enders admire and that he received strong support from the North End. According to his biographer Michael Czuboka, however, Juba grew up in the Town of Brooklands and attended Brooklands School. His business, Keystone Supply, was on Keewatin Street. And while he was mayor, Steve and Elva Juba lived at 858 William Avenue, between Tecumseh and Arlington.

■ Stephen Juba, 1960 • Credit: U of M Archives, Tribune Collection, Personality Files

had brought over about six other relatives because he knew he couldn't help others once his family arrived. Those he didn't bring perished in the Holocaust.

Many years later, Chaim and Zena Katz arrived in Winnipeg with their sons David and Samuel and virtually nothing in material possessions. It was 1952, and both of the older Katzes had survived the Holocaust that had taken almost all of their family members. They chose Winnipeg because friends had told them it was a place of opportunity and would be a good place for them to bring up their two children. Chaim (who was known to most as "Hymie") had been a soap maker in the old country, but in Winnipeg he found a job carrying heavy bags of flour at a bakery. He learned the trade and became a baker at Main Bakery and City Bread. Neither parent spoke English when they arrived, and Hymie, who spoke five other languages, never did learn English. Zena taught herself basic English while working as a sales clerk at Tasty Bread on Main Street where she was also able to chat with customers in Polish, Ukrainian, Yiddish, and Hebrew.

The Katz family settled in the North End, renting apartments on Dufferin and then on Burrows. After a few years they were able to purchase their own home at 267 Cathedral Avenue and, like many other North End families, they later moved to West Kildonan. As a child, their son Sam attended Champlain School and enjoyed playing on the boulevards and riding his bicycle with his friends. Although Zena encouraged Sam to become a dentist (in part because Jewish dentists and doctors had been spared in concentration camps) he graduated from university with a Bachelor of Arts in Economics and became a businessman. On June 22, 2004, Sam Katz was elected Mayor of Winnipeg, becoming the city's first Jewish mayor and the first to have grown up in the North End.

1

LIFE IN THE MOSAIC VILLAGE
THE FIRST GENERATIONS

■ The CPR Yards
near the Salter Bridge

■ A circus parade made its way south on Main Street in 1921 towards the CPR underpass.
• Credit: Archives of Manitoba, Foote Collection 360, N1460

NORTH OF THE TRACKS

The CPR mainline in Winnipeg symbolized the aspirations of Winnipeggers, but it also became a barrier that divided the city into two distinctly different sections. By the early 1900s, the North End had become a mosaic of diverse cultures, religions, and languages.

The Main Street underpass (shown in 1910) enabled pedestrians and vehicles to cross under the CPR tracks. The centre portal was for streetcars. The building on the right was the elegant Royal Alexandra Hotel.
• Credit: Archives of Manitoba, Winnipeg-Streets-Main, N10924

The CPR Mainline

The Canadian Pacific Railway mainline represented the hopes of political and business leaders to establish Winnipeg as a thriving city that channelled goods and services to all of western Canada. It also became a boundary that segregated Winnipeg's residents along socio-economic, ethnic, and religious lines.

On Main Street, the tracks (north of present-day Higgins Avenue) were often an impenetrable barrier for northbound and southbound vehicles and pedestrians. Until an underpass was built in 1904, the level crossing was routinely blocked for hours by freight cars. Because streetcars didn't cross the railway tracks, passengers were required to walk across – when they could – and transfer. The CPR's marshalling yards (in the vicinity of present-day Arlington and Salter Streets) had nearly 200 kilometres of track and enough room to accommodate 10,000 railway cars.

Even the residential area of Point Douglas, the once-prestigious neighbourhood of some of Winnipeg's wealthiest and most powerful families, became the site of industries that sprang up close to the railway tracks such as Vulcan Iron Works, Ogilvie Flour Mills, and several saw mills. By the late 1890s, most of its upper-middle-class residents had moved southward and been replaced by working-class people.

Residents in the vicinity of the vast railway yards lived in an environment dominated by the smoke, soot, smells, dust, and noise generated by trains, railway activities, and the manufacturing and commercial operations located near the mainline.

By 1900, there were an estimated 3,500 railway workers, and most of them lived in the area north of the tracks.

■ ■ ■ ■ ■ ■ ■ ■

■ Views from Sutherland Avenue both east and west of Main in 2009 demonstrate that the CPR tracks continue to be a formidable barrier between the North End and the centre of the city. • Credit: Photos by Russ Gourluck

■ Many of the homes of immigrant families in "New Jerusalem" (shown in 1904 at the corner of King and Dufferin) were little more than shacks. • Credit: Archives of Manitoba, Winnipeg-Streets-Dufferin 2, N7962

The Foreign Quarter

As European immigrants continued to arrive into the early years of the 1900s and to settle in Winnipeg, a distinct community began to emerge. "North End" is the name that has endured, but in its early days the area was also known, often disparagingly, as "The Foreign Quarter," "CPR Town," "New Jerusalem," and even "Jew Town." It was populated almost entirely by immigrants and working-class families.

To accommodate the recent arrivals, developers – often at considerable profits – built houses quickly and cheaply along streets like Jarvis, Dufferin, and Stella, in close proximity to the CPR tracks and the nearby industries where most of the men worked.

The homes were small and the lots were narrow, usually 25 or 33 feet in width. There was little provision for parks or recreational space, and few of the homes were initially connected to the city's water and sewer system. In 1904 and 1905, a major epidemic saw Winnipeg experience more cases of typhoid and smallpox than any other North American city, with most of the cases occurring in the North End. At that time, 80 percent of homes in the southern part of the city had waterworks, but fewer than 45 percent in the North End had that service. Living

■ Milk delivery in 1910 in the Foreign Section
• Credit: Archives of Manitoba, Winnipeg-Streets 2

conditions were frequently overcrowded because the tiny homes often lodged more than one family. It was reported by *The Winnipeg Telegram* in 1909 that houses built to accommodate seven people were actually lodging 25 to 30 people.

In 1913, the infant mortality rate in the North End was a dramatic 248.6 deaths per 1,000 births, compared to 173.1 in the core of the city and 116.8 in the western and southern areas. Children were often undernourished because their families couldn't afford food.

Although the influenza epidemic of 1918-1919 was probably sparked by returning World War One soldiers and first affected Winnipeggers in the relatively affluent South End, it soon spread to the North End. Crowded housing conditions, poor sanitation, and inadequate water and sewer services contributed to a disproportionately high death rate among North Enders. According to statistics of the time, there were 6.73 deaths per 1,000 residents in the North End, compared to 4.02 deaths per 1,000 in the South End. More dramatically, once patients contracted influenza, 90 per 1,000 died in the North End compared to 46 per 1,000 in the South End.

(RIGHT) Immigrants were criticized for crowding into homes previously occupied by affluent Winnipeggers (1909 photo). • Credit: Archives of Manitoba, Immigration Collection 21, N7940

ONCE ONE OF WINNIPEG'S FINEST RESIDENCES. AFTERWARDS IT BECAME CRAMMED WITH GALICIAN LODGERS

Despite poverty, crowded living conditions, and deplorable sanitation, the North End continued to flourish. To meet the needs of this emerging and distinctive community, a commercial district soon developed, particularly along Selkirk Avenue. Stores operated by Jewish and Slavic merchants offered foods and clothing that were familiar to European customers, and storekeepers were often able to communicate in several languages.

Different socio-economic groups tended to reside in different sections of the city. Residents of the West End were primarily middle class, while South End residents were generally wealthier. The North End, located close to many of the workplaces of labourers, became the home of the working class. In 1906, the North End accommodated 43 percent of the population of Winnipeg even though it covered less than one-third of the city's geographic area. The 1911 census revealed that, of all Canadian cities, Winnipeg had the largest percentage of Slavs and Jews and the lowest percentage of Anglo-Saxons.

Chickens and Eggs

Many North End homes had small backyard gardens to provide fresh, inexpensive produce for summer eating and fall preserving. As late as the 1950s, some families had backyard coops for chickens and pigeons to provide eggs and the key ingredient of countless pots of stew and soup.

By 1913, the North End housed 87 percent of the Jews, 83 percent of the Slavs, 67 percent of the Scandinavians, and 22 percent of the Germans in the City of Winnipeg.

Residents of British extraction, however, were such a large percentage of the city's population that, even though only 20 percent of them lived in the North End, they still outnumbered each of the other groups.

Facing Intolerance

In 1901, foreign-born residents of Winnipeg comprised 38 percent of the population; by 1911, they represented more than 55 percent. During the period of European immigration from 1896 to the beginning of World War One, immigration accounted for approximately 80 percent of Winnipeg's population growth. The new arrivals not only performed back-breaking, dirty, and necessary jobs, they also brought substantial economic advantages to the businessmen of Winnipeg through real estate sales and retail business.

Although most of the immigrants from Europe arrived with very little money, few possessions, limited (or no) English skills, and very different cultural backgrounds, there were few organized efforts to assist with their transition to a new and different way of life. Some religious groups and private agencies tried to provide orientation and practical assistance, but the city's powerful elite preferred to channel their altruistic energies into more fashionable causes like foreign missionary work, women's suffrage, and the temperance movement.

Prejudice was prevalent and overt, particularly towards Jews and Slavs, who were maligned by critics as "the scum of Europe" and "the unfortunate product of a civilization that is a thousand years behind the Canadian." Their languages, cultural practices, religious beliefs, clothing, and food preferences were ridiculed and condemned as inferior.

Jewish people faced scorn not only from established Anglo-Saxon Canadians, but also from some Slavic immigrants who had imported attitudes of intolerance from Europe. For the first few decades of the twentieth century, some faculties of the University of Manitoba enforced "quotas" to limit the number of Jewish students admitted, and a number of professions shunned Jews. Many financial institutions and insurance companies would not knowingly hire Jewish employees, and the affluent suburb of Tuxedo honoured a "gentlemen's agreement" to exclude Jewish residents.

Polish and Ukrainian immigrants often found that job opportunities were limited to manual labour, and some Canadian-born children of Slavic immigrants anglicized their names to increase their chances of career promotions. World War One saw increased hostility to German immigrants and the classification of people of Austro-Hungarian background (including Ukrainians) as "Enemy Aliens."

The 1917 Russian Revolution was seen as a threat to Anglo-Saxon civilization around the world and aggravated prejudice against Winnipeggers of Slavic origin. Unemployed returning soldiers resented the fact that Ukrainians and Germans were occupying jobs at the end of the war, and some demanded their deportation. In January of 1919, a group of veterans went on a rampage in the North End, smashing store windows, breaking into homes, and demanding that people they considered "foreigners" kiss the Union Jack.

Although the key organizers of the 1919 Winnipeg General Strike were not "foreigners," many of the participants were, and some opponents of the strike demanded that the "Alien Enemy" be deported.

The process of assimilation of the children of immigrants was hampered by a multi-lingual school system. Manitoba's Public Schools Act, originally intended to permit instruction in French and English, didn't disallow instruction in other languages. By 1907, students in Manitoba schools were receiving instruction in thirteen different languages. Because the Act didn't make school attendance compulsory, the children of many immigrant families didn't attend school at all, and others attended private schools. A unilingual school system and compulsory attendance were established by a newly-elected Liberal government in 1915.

■ Many opponents of the Winnipeg General Strike demanded the deportation of "foreigners." • Credit: Archives of Manitoba, Winnipeg Strike 4, 4 June 1919

MEMOIRS OF SAUL PASCAL

■ Saul Pascal lived at 764 Bannerman (at Arlington) until he was 12. His father raised the house and dug a basement by hand to install a gravity-fed coal furnace, an innovative system at the time. • Credit: Courtesy Ed Pascal

■■■■

In 1988, Ed Pascal gave his father Saul Pascal a surplus computer, some instructions on how to use it, and the suggestion that the elder Mr. Pascal write his memoirs. At the time, Saul Pascal was 77 years of age and had never used a computer. The machine he was given was an early model with no hard drive; two 5 ☐" floppy disc drives served as program and data storage. After Saul Pascal's death in 1996, Ed found a manuscript of nearly 17,000 words that his father had written. Other than some corrections in spelling and punctuation and the addition of some photos, the manuscript has been left as Saul Pascal wrote it. The following excerpts are reprinted with the permission of Ed Pascal. The entire manuscript is available in Winnipeg at the Jewish Heritage Centre of Western Canada.

I was born on Saturday February 18th 1911 in Winnipeg. The house was in a working class new area where all the European immigrants were congregated. This area has since aged and had become a slum. The house that I was born in was in the second block west of Main on Jarvis Avenue in the north end.

I was the youngest of four children. There were originally two more but they died in infancy. The oldest was Aaron who was twelve years older than me. Then there was Jack, then Ella who is four years older than I am.

I was given two names. Moishe after some long dead relative, and Sholem, which translated from the Hebrew means peace. This name apparently was given to me as was generally the custom and still is among some people to signify some hope for peace. There was considerable persecution against the Jews in Romania and other eastern European countries, and wherever possible the Jews were streaming out to America and Canada or anywhere else they could to escape the murderous persecution.

The Jews were considered second rate citizens and were not allowed to own land, nor ply a regular trade. All that was left for them to do to make a living was to do business, as it was considered beneath the dignity of others to handle money. My father's father was allowed to sell wine in a wine store, something like a local bar, and my father was listed in the records as a clerk in that store.

My mother was the oldest of five children, three girls and two boys, and was a very distant relative of my father. Even though there was an attraction to each other, the only way for them to become a pair was when it was properly arranged through a marriage broker as was the custom.

Even though the Jews were not real citizens so to speak, nevertheless they were subject to the military draft the same as all other young men. Every family was compelled to deliver to the army the oldest son. At military age my father was already married so his second oldest brother took his place on the draft list, and my father prepared to escape from Romania.

■ Saul Pascal (standing at rear, second from left) attended grade six at Ralph Brown School in 1928.
• Credit: Courtesy Ed Pascal

■ ■ ■ ■

At this time (the turn of the century) there was a great movement to try and reach any country that needed immigrants. There actually were groups of three or four or more setting out on foot, walking through fields, valleys and mountains gathering others, and the groups grew larger and larger till they reached the coast. These groups were called 'foosgayers' or footwalkers and together with my uncle Ben, my mother's younger single brother, my father joined them and travelling through Bulgaria and other Balkan countries finally reached the sea. Travelling and working their way as they went they were able to arrive at Rotterdam. There was an agent of the Canada immigration department who arranged for them to set sail for Canada. (Canada needed farmers to develop the land). This was an inspiration of the then Liberal party. They assumed that the immigrants out of gratitude would vote for them when they became citizens of the country. When they arrived in St. John, they learned that Canada also needed to build the Canadian Pacific Railroad. They joined the work force on the railroad. My uncle Ben learned the trade of tinsmith and my father became a carpenter. (Learning a trade was forbidden for a Jew in Romania).

After working on the railroad back and forth for a few months my uncle continued onward at his trade and remained with the company. But my dad being a married man decided to settle down and bring the family to Canada. Picked Winnipeg, which was exploding in size at the time. He rented a small house and sent for my mother and her two sisters and her mother (my grandmother Zelda) as well as three children, one of which died soon after arriving in Canada. One child had died as a very small infant in Romania before my father had left. My father having left the C.P. then went to work as a carpenter, for himself. This was the year 1903.

My mother tells us the story of her arrival. She of course could not speak the language, but to save her embarrassment, she was taught to pronounce the words 'I don't know' when spoken to in English. When she answered 'I don't know' to every conversation, she was admired by her fellow travellers. saying that she has already learned to speak the language.

■ ■ ■ ■

■ Saul Pascal as an adult
• Credit: Courtesy Ed Pascal

It was the strongest desire of the new immigrants to own their own home and as soon as possible. Our family after living on Burrows Ave. when my sister Ella was born, he (sic) had rented temporarily the house on Jarvis Ave. where I was born. My parents, as all immigrants, had a boarder, a young man named Winestock. He was single at the time and became almost a member of the family. He later married a Russian Jewish girl named Brida and they had three children, two boys and a girl. Their daughter Dora Kohm, herself a grandmother now and living in Toronto are still our very good friends.

Now my father went all out and put a down payment on a cheap cottage without a basement out of the city so to speak. This was at the corner of Bannerman and Arlington. There were only eight houses in the six blocks on Arlington from Mountain and eleven houses in the three very long blocks on Bannerman from McGregor to our house. Ours was the very last house on the edge of the prairie. I can still recall the low and deep music of the wind through the tall grass singing me to sleep. Standing at the front door you could see the horizon to the north and also to the west. My father had anticipated that the street cars running down Arlington Street and turning on Mountain Avenue would continue on Arlington to Bannerman and then go on Bannerman to McGregor and join up with the McGregor and Bannerman street car. He had hoped that this way the street car would pass our house in the future. Our nearest Jewish neighbours were many streets away.

The cottage had five rooms containing two bedrooms, a living room, which we used as a bed room, a front room which we almost never used, a bathroom which did not have a bathtub for many years. We had a large tin tub which we filled with heated water from the top of the coal and wood stove. We did not have any hot water heater and therefore no hot water. We also had a kitchen, which actually became our living room. It had a kitchen table and the coal and wood stove which kept us warm. And we had a 60 watt light hanging from the ceiling under which we all read and which we kids did our homework.

■■■■

I made friends with some kids two or three streets away but they weren't Jewish. The kids that I played with were the descendants of Scotch or Irish with one or two Scandinavian and a couple of French Canadians. I was the only Jew. We would call on each other and go for hikes. We learned to slide on slippery ice as if we had skates. We played hockey with broomsticks and road apples (frozen horse droppings) and would kick the can for a block or so. Then we started school and we then began to play soccer and baseball. Everything was fine for a number of years, until they would start talking on Mondays about the previous day's Sunday School sessions in their church. I of course could not enter this type of conversation. I was challenged many times to come to their Sunday school too. But of course this was not to be. Gradually the togetherness grew apart as our interest began to differ. I will say this. I was never called a dirty Jew. And even though my mother had a very heavy accent she was also never looked down upon. She used to hand out special Jewish tidbits like strudel, homantashen, and even pieces of matzos to my gentile friends and they loved her for it.

The Apartment Blocks

It was common for North End families, particularly during the 1930s and 1940s, to rent suites in apartment blocks until they were able to afford to buy (or at least rent) houses. Some, however, lived in apartments on a long-term basis.

Gord MacDonald's parents, Clarence and Catherine MacDonald, moved into the Redwood Apartments at College and Main when Clarence became the caretaker in the mid-1930s. They lived there until 1962. The two parents, Gord, and his four sisters, Eleanor, Audrey, Kathy, and Gwen, lived

■ The Redwood Apartments in 2009
• Credit: Photo by Russ Gourluck

in the building's only basement apartment, a two-bedroom suite. There was also a spare room that they used for visitors, but it later became a full-time third bedroom for the family. They called it "the other room." MacDonald explains that the residents of the Redwood Apartments and the Stratford Hall apartment building behind it were like a "community within a community." Many residents lived in the Redwood for long periods of time, some for 20 or 25 years.

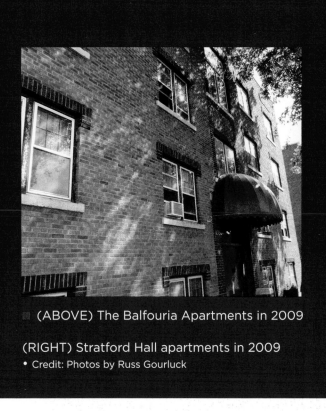

(ABOVE) The Balfouria Apartments in 2009

(RIGHT) Stratford Hall apartments in 2009
• Credit: Photos by Russ Gourluck

Brenda (Gallis) Barrie and Phillip Rosen first met as very young children in the mid-1940s when their families lived across the hall from each other in the Renfrew Apartments, which were owned by Rosen's grandfather George Filkow. Barrie's family moved out when she was four and the war had ended, but Rosen lived there from birth to age 16. Suites in the building at Mountain and Powers housed a number of other relatives. One of the advantages of the location of the Renfrew Apartments was that children could watch the Santa Claus Parade from their suites.

Manly Rusen grew during the 1930s and 1940s in the Balfouria Apartments at Cathedral and Main. It was later renamed Balfouria Manor, he explains, an attempt "to characterize it with a little more class." The neighbours consisted of several inter-related families, including his cousin Monty Hall (Halperin).

Ron Meyers' family lived in Suite 2 of the Harrison Block at Main and Jarvis in the early 1940s. Each floor had a single bathroom to serve three or four apartments. His family paid $18.00 per month for their apartment, which had two rooms – a bedroom and a kitchen. There was no living room. His parents had the bedroom, and he and his brother slept in the kitchen. Meyers explains that, while he was a child, his family moved six times. "You moved wherever you could afford to live."

■ The MacDonald family were long-term residents of the Redwood Apartments. • Credit: Courtesy Gord MacDonald

St. John's Avenue, east, Winnipeg.

There were a number of apartment blocks near Main Street in the area of Jarvis and Dufferin, including the La Salle, the Continental Block, the Harrison Block, King's Court, and the Crump Block.

Moving Around

North End families, especially during the 1930s, moved frequently. Some moved when they could afford something better. Others moved because they could no longer afford what they had – quietly, at night, and without informing the landlord.

Mary and Vera Pytel grew up during the 1930s and had six addresses, all in the North End. Their family's first home, after they arrived from Europe at ages 3½ and 5, was a house on Selkirk near Parr that was shared with three other families. Each family was allotted one room "no matter how many kids they had."

Bernie Klein's family also moved frequently. One of their first homes, in the 1930s, was in a house behind a Chinese laundry at the corner of Boyd and Charles. He thinks their accommodation was probably the original living quarters and that a

■ (ABOVE) The area east of Main Street featured many elegant homes. • Credit: Courtesy Dan Skwarchuk

(BELOW) Streetcars provided transportation in the early days. • Credit: Courtesy Gord Mackintosh

laundry section was added to the front later. The Chinese men who operated the laundry slept there and rented out the rest. Klein explains that their rooms were warmed by a space heater, the chimney pipe left uninsulated to radiate heat. At times, the four Klein brothers slept together in one double bed, their heads alternating so they'd fit.

Myron Shatulsky and his parents lived on Pritchard Avenue near Artillery Street in a three-room shanty with a kitchen, a living room, a bedroom, and no basement. A dugout served as a root cellar. There was a sink in the kitchen and small room off the kitchen with a toilet.

Living North, Living South

As families' financial situations improved, they were able to move from rented accommodations to their own houses. During the 1920s, Jewish families who had lived on streets in the southern part of the North End, such as Jarvis and Dufferin, became financially able to relocate north of Redwood into newer, larger homes on attractive streets like Boyd, College, and St. John's, east of McGregor. Their previous houses were occupied by more-recently-arrived Ukrainians, Poles, and Germans. The area east of Main Street, and especially along St. Cross and Scotia, became the site of large, expensive homes where affluent families resided. During the 1920s, many Ukrainian immigrants bought homes in the area between Selkirk and Mountain west of Main Street. Over the next few decades, the North End gradually expanded northward to the city boundary of McAdam Avenue and westward to McPhillips Street and beyond.

In the period of optimism and financial comfort that followed the World War Two, Winnipeggers, like their counterparts in

■ By the early 1950s, many Winnipeg families owned cars and were more mobile. • Credit: Courtesy Dan Skwarchuk

■ An All People's Mission kindergarten group in 1904
• Credit: Archives of Manitoba, Winnipeg-Churches-All People's Mission-Maple Street Church 3, N13261

other North American cities, began moving to the bungalows of the suburbs. Families who didn't previously have the money (or the confidence) to purchase cars bought them and acquired a new-found mobility. Streetcars and trolley buses were supplemented by increasing numbers of diesel buses that were able to travel wherever roads were built.

Many of the people who left the North End were the children and grandchildren of the original European immigrants. These generations, with the benefits of higher education and rewarding careers, were able to fulfill the dreams that had motivated their parents and grandparents to leave Europe many decades earlier.

Families of Slavic origin tended to move to East and West Kildonan and Transcona; during the decade of the 1950s the North End's Ukrainian population dropped by 10 percent. Many German families moved to North Kildonan or parts of the West End, while Anglo-Saxons dispersed throughout the city. North End houses left behind were snapped up by landlords who were often more concerned with making a profit than with maintaining the dwellings.

Jewish families in large numbers moved north to West Kildonan, although others joined the long-established Jewish residents of the South End. During the 1950s, the North End's Jewish population decreased by almost one half, from approximately 12,000 to around 6,000. In 1941, only 2.4 percent of Winnipeg Jews lived in suburban areas like West Kildonan, River Heights, and Tuxedo. Twenty years later, that percentage was 44.2.

Making Ends Meet

Although newly-arrived immigrants were able to find jobs in Winnipeg in the early 1900s, the pay was far from adequate. Most of the men worked in factories, for the railways, or in other manual labour jobs. Women were often employed as domestic help in the home of affluent Anglo-Saxon families or found other ways to supplement the family income. Many children sold newspapers or did odd jobs and gave their earnings to their parents to help put food on the family table. In some families, children left school before graduation and entered the workforce.

A 1913 study by social activist and clergyman J. S. Woodsworth determined that a basic annual income of $1,200 was needed for a family to maintain a reasonable standard of living.

Many working men had incomes in the range of $500 to $600. All People's Mission, founded by the Methodists in 1898, was originally intended to save souls, but under the direction of Woodsworth it began operating kindergartens, recreational facilities, and night classes to help new immigrants cope and assimilate.

Ironically, the immigrants themselves, rather than inadequate wages, were often blamed for their wretched living conditions. The Associated Charities Bureau in 1912 attributed the majority of applications for relief on "thriftlessness, mismanagement, unemployment due to incompetence, intemperance, and immorality." One 1912 publication described people who lived north of the tracks as "not of a desirable character."

Historically the North End has always been populated largely by families with relatively low incomes. Yet, when North Enders look back on earlier years, they don't recall perceiving themselves as being poor. As Libby (Klein) Simon observed, "Everybody lived in poverty then. Nobody had money, so you didn't feel poor." Nancy Kardash's recollection is similar: "We were poor but it never really struck us that we were poor."

Coping with the Great Depression

Jack Chapman experienced the Great Depression as a child in the North End. "I guess I survived the tough times," he says, "but I don't remember them as being tough. You know, you eat, and you have clothes, and you make guns out of pieces of wood and inner tubes."

Roslyn (Weisman) Silver graduated from St. John's Tech in 1938 and couldn't go on to university because of the Depression. She remembers that men who hopped trains as they travelled west sometimes approached North End homes to ask for food. One young man in particular remains in her mind after seven decades. He knocked on their door and politely asked, "Can you please give me something to eat?" She gave him some food and the address of her father's confectionery because, "He was one who never turned anybody away."

■ Aaron and Ann Grosney welcomed customers to their delicatessen ca 1951. • Credit: Archives of Manitoba, Jewish Historical Society Collection, 2975

SHOPPING IN THE NORTH END

Many North End families did almost all of their shopping in the North End. Corner stores conveniently provided day-to-day grocery needs, but Selkirk Avenue, which has been described as "the heart of the North End," was the destination of most North End families.

■ (LEFT) Selkirk Avenue in the 1960s offered a variety of services. • Credit: Vogue Studio photo by Dmytro Harapiak ca 1960, courtesy Peter Tittenberger

(BELOW) Dufferin Avenue was a shopping destination for many Winnipeggers in the 1960s. • Credit: U of M Archives, Tribune Collection, 18-6261-181

■ At its peak, the North End had bank branches on all major streets. (TOP) The Bank of Montreal had branches at 606 and 804 Selkirk Avenue. • Credit: Archives of Manitoba, Jewish Historical Society Collection. Banks on Main Street included the Royal Bank at the corner of Mountain and the Bank of Montreal at 1386 Main at Bannerman. • Credit: Archives of Manitoba, Jewish Historical Society Collection, 2847 and 2853

Corner Stores

Into the 1950s, small grocery stores were located on street corners throughout residential areas of Winnipeg, and some intersections had more than one store. The families who owned and operated them often lived behind or above the stores.

It was a laborious and competitive business. Corner stores stayed open when larger grocery stores were closed, and family

■ Grocery stores, such as these at 347 Aberdeen and 471 College, could be found on almost every street corner in the North End during the 1930s and 1940s. • Credit: Archives of Manitoba, Jewish Historical Society Collection, 2848 and 2850

members – including children – worked long hours. Because they could purchase only in small quantities, smaller stores paid higher prices to wholesalers than their larger competitors.

In addition to the convenience they provided in an era when few families had cars, the stores generally followed the European practice of extending credit, allowing neighbourhood families to "run a bill" and pay the money owed at the end of the month. Although most customers conscientiously settled their accounts, some simply reached their limit in the hand-written records of one store and moved on to another, leaving behind an uncollectable debt.

A typical corner store had floor-to-ceiling wooden shelves stocked with cans, boxes, and bottles of various household needs. This was not an invitation to self-service. Even though customers might walk right by items they wanted, they were expected to go to the counter, which was usually near the back of the store, and ask for them. The storekeeper would then go and retrieve the articles. To reach items on high shelves, many

■ Doreen (Morrison) Geiszler's father built a house behind the family grocery store at Bannerman and McGregor in 1942 at a cost of $5,000. They burned the mortgage five years later. It had two bedrooms (one of which Geiszler shared with her grandmother) and a door from the living room opened directly into the butcher area of the store. N.O. Morrison Grocery was staffed primarily by Nils "Oscar" Morrison and his wife Marjorie, with their daughters helping out on Saturdays. The store was open from 8:00 a.m. until 6:00 p.m. on weekdays, but, like most North End retailers, it closed Wednesday afternoons and Sundays.
• Credit: Courtesy Doreen Geiszler

stores had a device that resembled a broomstick with a claw-like "grabber" on one end and spring-loaded handles on the other.

Brenda (Gallis) Barrie, whose family operated P. Gallis and Sons Grocery Store on Mountain Avenue from the 1920s to the 1950s, recalls the technique that her father, Max Gallis, used. "I used to think my father was incredibly brave because he didn't use the claw very often. Mostly he would knock it off the shelf and catch it. Even corn syrup – which was a big heavy thing – and Mazola Oil. He would just knock it off the shelf and catch it."

Many stores offered more than just canned and boxed groceries. The Gallis store had a full butcher counter with a German butcher who made sausages on the premises. Their extensive delivery service included such far-flung areas as Transcona and St. Boniface. The staff consisted of "my grandfather, and my father, and my uncle Oscar, and the butcher, and usually one clerk." Brenda's mother did the books. Like most North End businesses, the store was closed on Wednesday afternoons. The family sold the store in the late 1950s after hearing that a Safeway store might be built at Mountain and Salter.

Pearl Globerman's family's grocery store – she's not sure it had a name – at Andrews and Manitoba opened in the 1930s and closed in the mid-1950s. Located in a former house, the grocery area occupied the living room, and one bedroom was the meat area. The family lived in the remaining rooms behind the store. Even though the father was away four days a week working as a cook on CPR trains, the parents were the only staff. The grandmother, who lived with them, looked after the children. There was another grocery store just two doors away, several kosher butcher shops were nearby, and Altman's Hardware was across the street.

When Gord MacDonald was a boy in the 1940s, and 1950s he was often sent to Gurvitch's Grocery Store (Goodwill Grocery at 1148 Main near Boyd) with ration coupons and a note for butter, sugar or other scarce items. He was usually instructed to tell the storekeeper to "put it on the bill." A long stalk of bananas dangled in the store's front window, and the owner cut bunches off for customers on request.

The arrival of grocery giants Safeway, Loblaws, and Dominion Stores and smaller supermarkets like Shop-Easy, Tom Boy, and Jewel Stores in Winnipeg spelled the beginning of the end for many small stores. Some banded together to achieve the price advantages of quantity purchases and operated under such names as Red and White and Lucky Dollar, but as more families acquired automobiles and were able to travel to spacious well-stocked stores with lower prices, business for corner stores declined.

One of the first Safeway stores in the North End was at Mountain and Salter, where the General Sir Sam Steele Legion is presently located. It was later replaced by a newer Safeway at

■ (ABOVE) The Rosner family owned Atlantic Grocery at 347 Atlantic from 1960 to 1982.

(AT RIGHT) Mina and Michael Rosner in 1963.

Mountain and McGregor, the former site of the Tower Theatre. Another Safeway opened at Main and Luxton in the early 1950s, and there was a Jewel Store at Main and Bannerman. Natalie (Berschley) Hemingway remembers how she and her childhood friends were impressed by the sparkling new supermarkets. "When we were kids we'd go to Safeway and walk up and down the aisles and gawk at how much there was."

The Krevesky family bought Square Deal Groceteria at Cathedral and Arlington in 1949, operating it under the banner of Red and White and then as a Lucky Dollar affiliate.

Initially business was good and the small store, open seven days a week from 7:00 a.m. to midnight, employed a butcher and two clerks. Mersil Krevesky, his wife Pauline, sons Mike and Boris, and daughter Orysia lived behind the store in a two-bedroom residence, working in the store virtually every day except for Wednesday afternoon, when the store closed and

■ The Rosners closed their store and took down their sign as competition from larger stores became overwhelming.
• Credit: Courtesy Cecil Rosner

7•UP

ATLANTIC GROCERY

■ Mirsil Krevesky and previous owner John Smadyla posed outside Square Deal Grocery at Cathedral and Arlington after Krevesky bought the store in 1949. • Credit: Courtesy Orysia Jackson

The Square Deal Red & White Store raffled off a brand new Chevy in 1956. The winner was "a very diminutive lady who didn't drive." • Credit: Courtesy Orysia Jackson

Mr. Krevesky went to their wholesaler, Western Grocers, to replenish the stock. The Kreveskys sold the store in 1962 after a larger competitor opened on Polson Avenue.

Selkirk Avenue

Although concentrations of stores were located along Main, Salter, McGregor, Mountain, and other streets, it was Selkirk Avenue that, by the 1920s, became the commercial centre of the North End. At times the sidewalks were so crowded there was barely room to move. Its variety of shops and services clearly illustrated the ethnic diversity of the area.

Arthur "Fivie" Gunn, was born on Selkirk Avenue next door to the bakery his father founded in 1937. "In the early days, Selkirk Avenue was like a North End Portage Avenue," he explains. "You could go to Clifford's. You could go to Oretzki's.

You could buy your bread; you could buy your fish; there were I don't know how many butchers. There was a shoemaker, grocery stores on every corner, a bowling alley, barber shops, tinsmiths. You could live and die on this street."

Tom Halprin, who remembers shopping on Selkirk with his family in the 1950s and 1960s, says, "You could shop on that street in any language." Many storekeepers were able to conduct business in languages such as Yiddish, Ukrainian, Polish, Russian, and German.

■ Streetcar routes 90 and 96 served Selkirk Avenue. The 90 cars turned north onto McGregor, while the 96 route went farther west towards McPhillips. In the 1940s, tickets were 5 cents. Sid Green grew up at Selkirk and Parr. When he first moved to Machray Avenue at the age of 22, he had trouble falling asleep at night because he could no longer hear the streetcars. • Credit: Archives of Manitoba, Jewish Historical Society Collection, 2756, 1950

Ben Zaidman recalls that at the foot of Selkirk Avenue on the east side of Main Street there once stood a red cast iron watering trough for horses. Nearby was a "Public Comfort Station," as public washroom facilities were discreetly called. And the Times Theatre, a movie house that began its life as a live theatre named the Royal and closed in the early 1950s, stood nearby at 959 Main.

The first few blocks of Selkirk north of Main offered a number of photography studios over the decades, including Charach's, Shapiro's, Charles, Kline's, Vogue, and Liberty. Joseph Presznyak, owner of Liberty Studios until it closed in 2005, reports that there were seven studios on Selkirk Avenue as late as 1970.

The first few blocks also included blacksmith shops, the iconic Hebrew Sick Benefit Hall, the popular White House Restaurant, and Saidman's, the source of millions of sunflower seeds that were nibbled and spat out by generations of North End teenagers.

Despite competition from Eaton's and the women's clothing stores along Portage Avenue, many fashion-conscious (and bargain-conscious) women shopped for clothing on Selkirk Avenue. Probably the best-known ladies' store on Selkirk was Clifford's, but the Original Shop, Brody's, Belle Rykiss, and the

■ The Public Comfort Station – as Winnipeg's public washrooms were discreetly called – at the southeast corner of Main and Selkirk (pictured in 1975) was a welcoming refuge in more ways than one. Because the facilities were located underground, they were pleasantly cool on sweltering summer days. • Credit: Archives of Manitoba, Winnipeg-Buildings-Municipal-Public Lavatory/Selkirk 1

landmark Oretzki's were popular places to purchase fashions. One of the most popular milliners was Debbs. Misha Pollock's sold infants' and children's clothing. Mittleman's and Stalls were clothing manufacturers, and Ben Jacob and John Crowley started their successful women's garment manufacturing business on Selkirk Avenue with just six sewing machines.

W. Grushko Meat Market

Located at 452 Selkirk Avenue across from the White House, W. Grushko Meats was one of five or six kosher butcher shops along Selkirk during the 1940s and 1950s. William Grushko, who had arrived in 1921 from an area now known as Ukraine, spoke Yiddish, Ukrainian, Russian, Polish, Hebrew, and some German.

His daughter Lil explains that the family lived behind the store. Her mother and father and a "young delivery boy" were the staff. Sometimes the delivery boy was her brother Ben who rode his bicycle to make deliveries – even in winter – until he turned 16 and was able to drive the family car. Their father made deliveries to the South End by car twice a week and went back to collect for the orders on Sunday morning. Saturday evening was a particularly busy time at the meat market, and the parents often worked until 3:00 or 4:00 a.m. The store remained in business for approximately 50 years, closing in the 1970s.

During the 1940s, there were three grocery stores on Selkirk Avenue near Grushko's. The busiest was Star Grocery, owned by Henya Wertlib, who later opened a store at Main and Cathedral.

■ (RIGHT) A shoe repair shop at Selkirk and McKenzie, ca 1930s • Credit: Archives of Manitoba, Jewish Historical Society Collection, 2846

(BOTTOM RIGHT) Namak's (shown ca 1938) was one of several beauty parlours and barber shops on Selkirk Avenue. • Credit: Archives of Manitoba, Jewish Historical Society Collection, 2839

Many North End Jewish families visited kosher meat markets along Selkirk Avenue on Saturday evenings. Once the Sabbath ended, parents with children in tow made the trek to replenish their supply of meat (purchased in small quantities in the days before home refrigerators) and to chat with neighbours and friends. Roslyn Silver's family went to Zipursky's Market on Saturday evenings during the early 1930s. She recalls that Mr. Zipursky always wore a white apron and a white coat and that the floor of the butcher shop was covered with sawdust.

Natalie (Berschley) Hemingway's family lived on Redwood Avenue during the 1950s. Every Saturday morning her mother woke the kids up so they could walk to Selkirk Avenue. Her family shopped at Barabash Grocery, which was owned by her brother's godfather. Barabash's, located on Selkirk between Parr and McKenzie, had its own smoke house in the back. Hemingway describes the avenue as "a North End mecca" on Saturday mornings, a time to buy clothes for the kids from Oretzki's and for mom from Clifford's.

Sam Nezon was the owner of Sam's Fish Market, located across from the Palace Theatre on Selkirk Avenue. The market specialized in fillets from Lake Winnipeg that he picked up on ice from the Farmers' Market on Main Street, along with occasional

Glimpses of Selkirk Avenue in the mid 1960s • Credit: Archives of Manitoba, Architectural Survey Collection, Selkirk Avenue

HOUSE OF 1001 SPECIALS

BIG 4 SALES LTD.

HOUSE OF 1001

■ Selkirk Avenue
businesses in 1981
• Credit: Jewish Heritage
Centre, JM 2309

■ (ABOVE) Sam Nezon delivered fish by truck every day or two. Whitefish and pickerel fillets were especially popular with Jewish families. • Credit: Courtesy Sandra Magid

■ Sybil, Abe, and Sherman Grosney posed in front of their delicatessen at 407 Selkirk Avenue in 1941. • Credit: Archives of Manitoba, Jewish Historical Society Collection, 2785

barrels of live fish. Sam and his wife Anne both worked in the store, along with one employee remembered only as "Jinx," who wore high black rubber boots as he scaled and filleted in the wetness of the back room.

For general grocery shopping there was Soloway's Supermarket and a number of other grocery stores. The two department stores on the Avenue were Oretzki's and Woolworth's. Oretzki's was a locally-owned emporium, while Woolworth's was part of a multinational retailer. Both attracted North Enders in droves.

The sometimes-infamous Merchants Hotel at Selkirk and Andrews began its life in 1913 as the Steiman Block, owned by the family of hardware merchant Robert Steiman until

A Long Walk for Some Small Fish

John Marczyk bought his first goldfish at Woolworth's on Selkirk when he was seven and walked home with it to 108 Cathedral. The fish cost 15 cents, and the bowl it came in was a dollar. The store clerk, probably thinking the boy had only a block or two to walk, poured about an ounce of water in the bowl, and, in keeping with the ethics of the 1960s, John "didn't want to correct them because they were adults." By the time he reached home, most of the water had splashed out of the bowl and the fish were desperately flipping about on the bottom.

Johnny Pollock of Clifford's

When Gladys (Pearlman) Love was a growing up in the 1930s, she remembers that her mother often saw a young man pass by their house, carrying suitcases as he walked to Selkirk Avenue to catch a streetcar. One day while hanging laundry on the clothesline, Mrs. Pearlman called out in Yiddish, "Young man, what are you carrying in those suitcases all the time?"

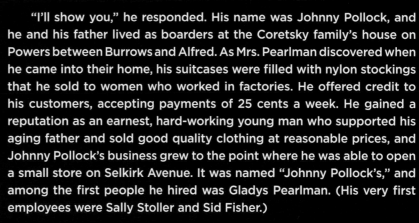

"I'll show you," he responded. His name was Johnny Pollock, and he and his father lived as boarders at the Coretsky family's house on Powers between Burrows and Alfred. As Mrs. Pearlman discovered when he came into their home, his suitcases were filled with nylon stockings that he sold to women who worked in factories. He offered credit to his customers, accepting payments of 25 cents a week. He gained a reputation as an earnest, hard-working young man who supported his aging father and sold good quality clothing at reasonable prices, and Johnny Pollock's business grew to the point where he was able to open a small store on Selkirk Avenue. It was named "Johnny Pollock's," and among the first people he hired was Gladys Pearlman. (His very first employees were Sally Stoller and Sid Fisher.)

A few doors down, Clifford Rusen had a women's wear store named "Clifford's," and when Rusen rejoined his family in their wholesale fruit business, Pollock bought Clifford's and retained the name. Johnny Pollock's nephew Misha took over Johnny's first store, renamed it "Misha Pollock's," and specialized in children's clothing.

approximately 1926. An upstairs hall once accommodated wedding celebrations. Despite a clear condition in the original building permit that no part of the premises was to be used for residential purposes, the building became a hotel in 1933.

Vogue Studios, one of several North End photo studios that served the ethnic community, was founded in 1921. Owned and operated by Dmytro Harapiak from 1958 until 1971, the business was originally located at 691 Selkirk Avenue and later moved to 567 Selkirk.

Harapiak was born in Ukraine in 1927, and many of his clients were Ukrainian families in the North End and surrounding rural communities. Much of the studio's work involved wedding photography, with Harapiak and his assistants sometimes shooting as many as five weddings on a Saturday. He also did portrait photography and some commercial photography.

Harapiak followed a familiar pattern when he photographed weddings, and, because of the limitations of the camera equipment of the 1950s and 1960s, most shots were carefully posed. The bride was generally photographed at her parents' home before the wedding in several standard situations: a formal portrait with her gown carefully arranged; pinning a corsage on her mother; having her engagement ring admired by the bridesmaids; and coyly revealing her garter.

A more comical approach was generally used in photographing the groom, portraying him as harried, disorganized, and even somewhat reluctant. Standard shots included being helped to put on his formal attire; looking at his wristwatch to determine if he could make it to the church on time; or pretending to be dragged out of the car and into the church.

Photos after the ceremony generally showed the bride and groom emerging from the church in a shower of confetti. At the reception, basic shots often included the wedding dinner; presentation; the couple's first dance; cutting the cake; and turning the groom upside down to empty the money from his pockets.

Vogue Studios

■ (ABOVE) The bridal garter shot was one of Harapiak's favourite poses.

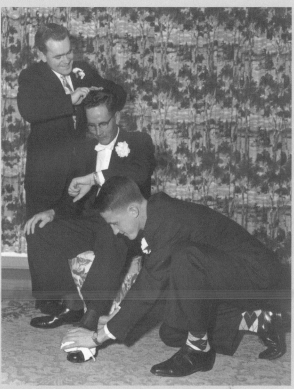

■ (ABOVE) The groom was portrayed as disorganized and needing help from the groomsmen.

■ (LEFT) And where are the holubchi?

(BELOW) The happy couple were framed by a frost shield.

• Credit: Vogue Studio photos by Dmytro Harapiak ca 1950, courtesy Peter Tittenberger

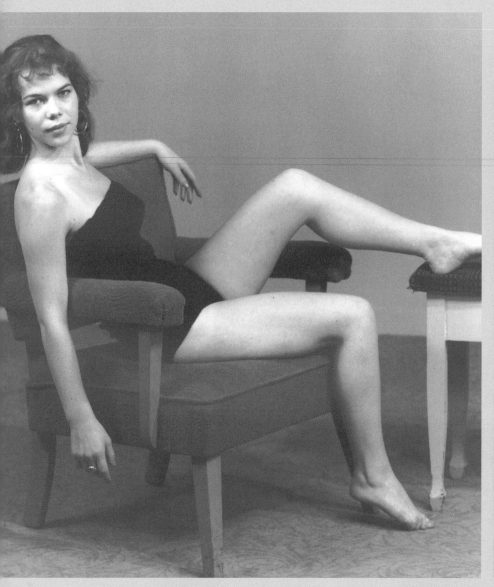

■ (TOP LEFT) Glamour portraits were often influenced by Hollywood stars and sometimes bordered on the risqué.

(TOP RIGHT) Family portraits were carefully posed. • Credit: Vogue Studio photo by Dmytro Harapiak ca 1950, courtesy Peter Tittenberger

(LEFT) Dmytro Harapiak (rear) posed with his parents and two younger brothers. He was considerably older than his siblings. • Credit: Vogue Studio photo by Dmytro Harapiak ca 1950, courtesy Peter Tittenberger

■ Louis Dolgoy supplied fruit and vegetables to small grocery stores.
• Credit: Courtesy Esther Korchynski

MAKING A LIVING

In most immigrant families, the fathers were the primary breadwinners, often working in factories or for the CPR. Some opened small wholesale, retail, or manufacturing businesses. A few made a living by breaking the law.

■ The Dolgoy family posed at their home at 689 Selkirk Avenue in 1921 with Louis Dolgoy at the gate.
• Credit: Courtesy Esther Korchynski

Peddlers

Many Jewish immigrants became peddlers, some selling various goods to households or small grocery stores, others buying and selling old clothing and glass bottles as they made their way along streets and back lanes. Although many of the peddlers confined their business to the North End, some travelled north to sparsely-populated West Kildonan, and others ventured south of the tracks.

Some specialized in supplying restaurants and the hundreds of corner grocery stores across the city. Esther Korchynski tells of her father Louis and his brothers Max and Leon (Lazer) who formed Dolgoy Brothers Fruit and Vegetables. In the days before refrigeration, many stores and restaurants needed to place small orders for produce virtually every day on a small scale that major wholesalers were reluctant to provide. Dolgoy Brothers (and others like them) combined the orders of many of these smaller businesses, purchased the produce from wholesalers, and delivered. Louis Dolgoy continued in the business until he was more than 70 years old, not taking a day off for 45 years except for Yom Kippur and Rosh Hashanah.

Not long after Bill Shell's family arrived in Winnipeg in 1924, six or seven people including three Shell relatives formed the Achdus Free Loan Society at their home. "It was a society for loaning money to each other on Sundays to get going. I don't know where the name came from, but it started in our house," he explains.

That loan enabled his father to purchase a horse and wagon and establish his business as a fruit peddler. Each morning he purchased a quantity of fruit on credit from Rusen and Solomon, a wholesaler located right next door to their home on Jarvis Avenue. The next morning, he returned to the wholesaler, paid for the previous day's purchase, and picked up his order

for that day. Each day he drove along the streets of the North End selling apples, oranges, and bananas in Yiddish, Russian, and eventually some English. After six or seven months he was able to lend some of the profit to other members of the free loan society. "They all became quite successful," Shell points out.

Morley Rypp's father peddled fruits and vegetables in the West End during the 1930s and 1940s and, although he had previously spoken only Yiddish, he learned English quickly. Every morning he got up at 4:00 a.m. so he could purchase choice fruits and vegetables on Fruit Row (Ross Avenue). Although Mr. Rypp did some house-to-house sales, most of his customers were grocery stores and restaurants. He continued to use a horse and wagon until he bought a truck after World War Two. Mr. Rypp took great pride in the fact that he never went on relief.

■ Alexander Weber built four brick homes (shown in 2009) near Lansdowne and McKenzie in 1944. His father, who had come from a German-speaking area of Russia in 1911, established a construction business that installed sewer and water lines, and Alexander left school at the age of 14 to work with him. Weber built the 1½-storey homes, despite wartime shortages of materials, for his own family, his parents, and other family members.
• Credit: Photo by Russ Gourluck

Small Businesses

Bill Shell's father became a dry goods jobber by purchasing merchandise below wholesale prices at sales in Eaton's basement. The Eaton's prices were so low that Mr. Shell was able to resell to country merchants at a profit.

Mel Goldenberg's father had City Hay and Feed Supply, which he describes as "a filling station for horses," on Jarvis Avenue. Oats and hay were stored in a large galvanized garage behind their house, along with a wagon and two horses that understood Yiddish but not English. Part of their business was a livery stable with five horses that they rented out to peddlers. Goldenberg's father died when he was just two years of age, but his mother and his older brother Ben carried on the business.

■ Menorah Catering was a kosher catering service at Main and Redwood.
• Credit: Courtesy Jack Chapman

Home Businesses

Because the incomes of many fathers in North End households weren't adequate to meet their families' needs, various types of home businesses were quite common until the 1950s and 1960s brought better economic times.

Many North End families with empty rooms in their houses offered rooms, board, or both to single individuals, and life-long friendships often resulted. Julie Zatorsky, who moved to Bannerman Avenue in 1949, explains that she and her husband turned their house into a temporary duplex to be able to make the mortgage payments, as did many of their neighbours.

Esther Korchynski tells of her aunt, Basheva Levin, who was born in Ukraine and came to Canada with her husband and three children. From the 1920s until the 1940s, she operated a kosher restaurant and catering service in her boarding house at 331 Manitoba Avenue. The house had a large kitchen on the main floor and a dining room spacious enough to cater small events. Unusual for its day, especially in a house, was a walk-in wooden-walled refrigerator in the kitchen. Levin was well known in the community for hand-made strudel stuffed with Turkish delight. One of the boarders at Levin's boarding house was "Cheerio" Osterley, who acquired the nickname because of his cheerful disposition and inevitable use of "Cheerio!" as a greeting. Osterley was especially popular with children because of the candies and chewing gum he regularly dispensed.

Jack Chapman's mother, widowed in 1939, also started a pioneer kosher catering business from her home. Left virtually penniless during the Depression, Katie Chmelnitsky took in boarders, did cooking for others, and, in their small College Avenue house, arranged some dinner parties. These ventures developed into a business named Menorah Catering service, located at Main and Redwood across from Kelekis Restaurant.

Women with sewing and tailoring skills often set up small dress sales businesses in their homes, particularly during the 1930s. They obtained dresses from factories, sold them to neighbours, friends, and family, and altered them to fit. This helped to supplement the incomes of their husbands and provided a potential source of employment if they should ever be widowed.

One elderly North End woman was forced to compensate for her family's lack of retirement income by bootlegging. Her husband was a CPR employee who participated in the 1919 Winnipeg General Strike and, like other strikers, was told by the CPR when he returned to work that his pension benefits were cancelled. He retired after 40 years of service, and, true to their word, the CPR provided absolutely no pension. To supplement the meagre income they received from the government's Old Age Pension plan, the man's wife became one of the North End's many bootleggers, selling beer from the family home. Some of her regular customers were police officers who dropped by after their shifts.

The Dairy Farms of West Kildonan

Until the expansion of West Kildonan began in earnest in the 1950s and 1960s with the development of Garden City, much of the area remained rural in appearance. Filkow Dairy was owned by George Filkow, who emigrated from Ukraine in 1905. A bay in The Maples is named for him. The dairy was a 16-acre operation located in the area now in the vicinity of Sinclair Street between Jefferson and Leila Avenues. Phillip Rosen recalls accompanying his grandfather as he drove around buying cattle and feed during the early 1950s. There were several other family dairy operations in the same general area, including the Chochinovs, the Zipurskys, and the Pudavicks.

Gamblers and Bootleggers

In the decades before Manitoba's gambling laws were liberalized, the only legal form of gambling centred on horse racing at Polo Park Race Track. This meant that most of the gambling in the province took place illegally.

In the North End, Selkirk Avenue was the site of numerous card games in various businesses over the decades. Manly Rusen recalls that several "clubs" on Selkirk near Salter had ongoing card games.

Probably the best known of all North End gamblers was Stanley Zedd. Born in Ukraine in 1899, Zedd (whose surname was anglicized from Zarawiecki) organized floating craps games throughout Winnipeg and surrounding rural areas during the 1940s and 1950s. Zedd generally rented private homes or empty garages as one-time-only locations for gambling activities. Gambling tables were set up during the day and quietly taken down and carried away when games ended in the wee hours of the morning. Prospective players (who were

■ Stanley Zedd wore tailor-made suits and smoked expensive cigars.

often prominent city businessmen and lawyers) were directed to specific locations (the White House Restaurant on Selkirk Avenue was one of the most popular) and told to wait for cars to pick them up. They were kept unaware of their destinations until they arrived.

Stanley Zedd became somewhat of a folk hero, a Runyon-esque character who wore dapper custom-tailored suits and stylish fedoras. He smoked and handed out the finest of cigars and was often chauffeured around in a black Cadillac. Zedd was respected for the honesty of his games, and the police left him alone unless they felt pressured by complaints from the public. Winners were paid immediately and were free to leave when they wished. Losers were given a few dollars and transportation home. His Osborne Street business, the Margaret Rose Tea Room (named for Princess Margaret) served as a front for his operations.

A boxer in his younger days, Stanley Zedd supported local sports, and was instrumental in setting up the ManDak Baseball League, using some of the profits of his gambling operation. His own team, the Winnipeg Buffaloes, was made up entirely of players from the disbanded Negro League in the United States.

Similarly, until Manitoba's liquor laws were liberalized in the 1960s, bootlegging took many forms throughout the province. Restaurants provided "set-ups" of ice and mix to complement brown-paper-bagged bottles stashed under tables. Many houses, particularly in the North End, were open for drinks on the premises or provided bottles to go after the dingy men-only beer parlours closed. And millions of gallons of homebrew were distilled for home consumption or sale.

One of Manitoba's most ambitious Prohibition-era bootlegging operations was run by Bill Wolchuk, a resident of Boyd Avenue. During the 1920s he became a major exporter to the United States of overproof booze (94% pure alcohol) that was produced in two huge Winnipeg stills as well as several satellite operations in rural Manitoba. Wolchuk was jailed for five years in 1940. After his release, he helped found Capital Lumber at 92 Higgins.

Two Dollar Bet

When Danny Pollock was 10 or 12 years of age, he and his brother chipped in a dollar each to bet on a horse race at Polo Park. Acting on a hot tip, the boys approached a bookie at a Main Street hangout and made a Daily Double wager. The horses (he still remembers their names – "The Farmer" and "Bee Air") won, and the bet was paid promptly by the bookie with an unquestioning "Here you are, kid."

■ The General Monash Legion marching band took part in a parade along Main Street, ca 1950. The North End was (and remains) the home of several Royal Canadian Legion branches associated with specific ethnic groups. • Credit: Courtesy Ed Pascal

(OPPOSITE) House parties and socials were popular and inexpensive social events for North Enders. • Credit: Vogue Studio photo by Dmytro Harapiak ca 1950, courtesy Peter Tittenberger

STAYING IN THE NEIGHBOURHOOD

North Enders who had originally come from Europe generally stayed close to home. For most wage earners, work was not far away, and most of a family's shopping needs could be met within a few blocks of home. Religious and social activities were found in the many churches and synagogues in the area and through a variety of ethnically-based clubs and cultural organizations. The North End was the home of people who shared similar lifestyles, beliefs, and traditions. They felt comfortable there.

"We Never Left Stella"

As children in North End families grew up and married, they often chose to live close to their parents. In many cases, they bought or rented houses or apartments within a few blocks, maintained close ties with their parents, and had the advantages of nearby Babas as babysitters.

In Mike Humniski's case, the move was, as he says, "three feet away." After he and his wife Stefanie were married in 1940, Humniski built a house at 767 Stella Avenue in 1948, right next door to his parents' home at 769 where he'd grown up. He did most of the construction himself. Mike and Stef brought up their three sons in the modest home, and Stef established a catering service from the home kitchen, specializing in fancy sandwiches and many kinds of perogies. She was devoted to her sons, sometimes delivering their *Star Weekly* newspapers when they couldn't and, in one incident that saw her sons subsequently bar her from their games, she marched onto a football field to tend to the injuries of one of her boys.

■ John Marczyk Sr. often sat pensively in his car at the rear of their house when he arrived home from work. His son John Jr. later became the proud owner of the 1956 Chevy and, he recalls, "It opened up the entire North End to me." • Credit: Courtesy John Marczyk

An engineer for the CPR, Mike often just hopped off a train and walked home. The Humniskis usually shopped at a nearby store known simply as "Sophie's." "Sophie carried people," son Frank explains. She wrote each transaction in a book and customers settled their accounts at the end of the month. No interest was charged. Mike and Frank can still name all of the families who lived on their block of Stella. As Mike puts it, "We never left Stella."

Cocooning with Others

Displaced Persons like the Marczyk family typified the tendency of new immigrants to stay close to familiar people and practices. They arrived in Winnipeg from Poland in 1959 after

■ The Marczyk family were able to purchase their own home at 108 Cathedral after years of hard work.
• Credit: Courtesy John Marczyk

seeing their relatives scattered by World War Two, with Elizabeth Marczyk's Germanic family spending time in Russian Prisoner of War and United Allied Forces relocation camps. They escaped to the West under rifle fire as the Iron Curtain was lowered and arrived in Canada with dreams of living in a sanctuary that offered freedom and the opportunity to work hard and prosper.

Living conditions were very basic at first, living above a corner store at Church and Aikins. Their son John describes them as "kind of at the poverty level." He recalls, "My Mom was washing dishes in the bathtub for many years." Eventually they had their own house on Cathedral and found friends with similar backgrounds and interests at Holy Ghost Roman Catholic Church on Selkirk Avenue for John Marczyk Sr. and the children, and at a Lutheran Church for Elizabeth Marczyk.

They had failed to anticipate the intolerant attitudes of some of the more-established immigrants and their Canadian-born children, who frequently labelled them as "D.P.'s" (Displaced Persons). At work, Mr. Marczyk was often the butt of "Polish jokes" inspired by Archie Bunker in *All in the Family* and compounded by the fact that he spoke little English. His work ethic was resented by some of his co-workers at Motor Coach Industries on Wall Street, especially when the appreciative managers rewarded his productivity at Christmas time with expensive toys for his children.

When Mr. Marczyk arrived home from work and parked behind their house, he sometimes spent a solitary half hour sitting silently in his car before going into the house. Asked by his wife why he did this, he simply said it was because he missed the old country.

The Marczyks, like many immigrants, took refuge from homesickness and the intolerance of others by associating with people like themselves. They formed close friendships with the Polish and Galician Austrian families who attended their churches and socialized at Polish clubs and legions in the North End. As John Jr. observes, "This was a new country where the sky was the limit, but day to day life could be hard and sometimes cruel. Cocooning amongst other families with similar old world histories in the North End was often the only way to make it through a bad day, week, month, or year."

Neighbourhood Safety

The North End has always had the reputation of being "tough" – especially among Winnipeggers who don't live there. But from the perspective of North Enders themselves, there was little cause for concern, at least during the 1940s, 1950s, and 1960s.

The front doors of many North End homes were left unlocked during the day to admit Eaton's drivers, milkmen, and the children who lived there. Kids routinely left their bicycles unlocked in the front yard with little fear of theft.

Teenagers of that era were generally able to walk home safely after dark along sidewalks and even back lanes, although Larry Fleisher concedes "there was the odd fight going to Hebrew School at night." When trouble did arise, most children knew most adults in their own neighbourhoods and could find a safe haven in virtually any house.

Arie Perlmutter, whose parents lived in the same house on Inkster Boulevard for 48 years, acknowledges that the North End was "a rough neighbourhood, but it wasn't dangerous." While growing there up in the fifties and sixties, he says, "You might have got pushed around a little bit here and there. But when you went out, you expected to come home. You didn't expect to end up in the hospital."

Richard Kurtz, whose family has owned Valley Flowers at Mountain and McGregor since 1947, reports that he often left his convertible parked overnight in the late 1960s with the top down and money on the dashboard. Nothing was disturbed the next morning.

Going to the Show

North Enders didn't have to travel far from home to be entertained. Although some ventured south (usually on foot) to the cluster of Main Street movie theatres near Logan that included the Fox, the Regent, the Colonial, the Starland, and the Oak, many frequented the North End's own movie houses.

The Deluxe (Hyland) Theatre

The Deluxe Theatre at 1525 Main south of Matheson was the most northerly of the North End movie theatres. It was opened by Leon and Cecilia Asper in the late 1930s and featured a lunch bar with a separate entrance. Many North Enders recall that the Deluxe was always immaculately clean and that Mrs. Asper was often the ticket seller. Roland Penner, in his book *A Glowing Dream: A Memoir* also remembers sneaking in through the back door of the theatre.

Walter Procter and his friends liked to attend movies at the Deluxe because it was closer to his McAdam Avenue home and the admission (10 cents before 6:00 p.m. and 12 cents after 6:00) was cheaper than the College. During wartime, children were admitted to some Saturday matinees for free with donations of scrap grease, rolled up tinfoil, or old aluminum pots for the Patriotic Salvage Corps. For Heather Borody and her

■ Residents east of Main experienced severe flooding in 1950. Luxton School served as a headquarters for police and navy personnel and boats were able to dock at the front door. • Credit: Courtesy Dan Skwarchuk

13 ST. JOHNS DISTRICT WINNIPEG MAN

friends in the early 1950s, the admission was 10 cents and, once inside, a flavourful pink pillow of Double Bubble Gum cost just two cents.

In later years, the Deluxe became the Hyland Theatre, then closed as a movie theatre in the early 1980s. The building is currently the home of Talmud Torah Beth Jacob Synagogue.

The College Theatre

The College Theatre at Main and Church was a large movie house with a seating capacity of approximately 1,000. Vera Hershfield and her friends attended Saturday matinees when they were little girls in the early 1930s, waiting in line before it opened at noon and not leaving until supper time. The ten cent admission charge provided two features, serials, cartoons, trailers, and shorts.

A decade later, Danny Pollock and his chums paid twelve cents for a matinee. When the lights went on at 5:00 p.m., incentives were sometimes offered to clear the theatre of its young patrons. Pollock tells of promotion for a movie serial titled *Jungle*

■ The former College Theatre building was a church in 2009. • Credit: Photo by Russ Gourluck

Raiders. As the children left the theatre, each was given a card with a pair of letters, and the object of the contest was to collect a set that spelled out both words of the title. Winning sets were to be taken to Hershfield's Hardware at Mountain and Main to claim a prize. Many kids, including Danny Pollock, soon figured out that, although most of the letters were plentiful, the "ID" combination was somewhere between rare and nonexistent, and they decided to counterfeit a card with those letters. Being the boldest of the bunch, young Danny volunteered to take the

bogus card to Hershfield's. The ruse worked once, and a sceptical clerk handed the boy a flashlight. When greed prevailed and the boys tried a second time, they were told: "Forget it, kid!"

Gord MacDonald remembers a rag drive during the 1940s with shiny new bicycles as prizes. John Marczyk recalls that matinee admission in the 1960s was 25 cents, that Jerry Lewis comedies were the movies of choice, and that kids threw popcorn in the air and made visors from the boxes. "It was a free-for-all," he chuckles. "We drove the owners nuts." After the show, he and his friends sometimes went to the nearby car dealerships and took new car brochures. His dad drove an older car that they could still barely afford, and he and his friends looked at the shiny new models with their mouths open.

Phil Young managed the College Theatre for Winnipeg-based Western Theatres from 1949 to 1956. Because television was quickly eroding movie theatre attendance, chinaware giveaways were initiated and Young recalls arranging for "Cactus Jack" Wells to act as an auctioneer in a "Bonus Buck" promotion. Lena Horne once visited the theatre for an autograph session when one of her movies was playing.

Young also explains that, while younger children attended Saturday matinees, Friday night was favoured by teenagers. "I think every teenager in the North End used to go to the College Theatre on Friday nights. They were a good bunch of kids, but adults soon learned not to go to the theatre that night." He tried hiring a "bouncer" to patrol the aisles with a flashlight and threaten especially unruly teens with eviction. That was just a bluff, he now admits. At worst, offenders were relocated to seats some distance away from their friends.

After closing in the mid-1960s as a motion picture theatre, the College Theatre building later became a meeting place for religious organizations.

The Palace Theatre

The larger of the two movie theatres on Selkirk Avenue, the Palace, which opened in the mid-1920s, was a favourite of many North Enders until it closed in the mid-1960s. As a child in the late 1930s, Morley Rypp accompanied his chinaware-collecting mother to the Palace every Friday night. "It didn't matter what they were showing," he chuckles. "Eventually she got a set of dishes."

Gladys (Pearlman) Love explains that patrons weren't required to leave when features ended, so some would stay and watch the same movie over and over again. In the early 1930s, her sister, Luba often paid the five cent Saturday children's matinee admission at noon and would leave only when a family member came to retrieve her at 8:00 p.m. "By then, she knew all the words to the musicals," Love jokes. Gladys's daughter Sharon could have been admitted to the Palace for free as a youngster in the 1950s – the Miles family who owned the theatre were cousins – but she usually paid because ticket stubs were drawn for prizes at the Saturday matinee. Admission then was 20 cents. A box of popcorn was five cents.

Nellie (Merkel) Zaidman, like many movie-goers in an era before outside food was barred from theatres, spent countless happy hours noshing at the Palace. "You took your lunch and your supper in a paper bag and you ate corned beef sandwiches and you watched a double movie. And sometimes they would even have a little vaudeville act on the stage."

Located at 501 Selkirk near Powers, the Palace closed as a theatre in the mid-1960s, housed a Big 4 variety store for a period of time, and is currently vacant.

The Leland (State) Theatre

The Leland (later known as the State) Theatre was at 572 Selkirk, on the south side between Andrews and McGregor. In some ways it was the poor cousin of the larger and classier Palace. Ron Meyers and George Smith, childhood friends in the 1940s, joke that the Palace got the second-run movies, but the State got the third run.

The smaller theatre did, however, offer some advantages. Norm Silverberg points out that Saturday matinees in the early 1940s were six cents at the State, compared to 12 cents at the Palace. Some children cashed in pop bottles at corner stores to raise the necessary funds. The shows began at 11:00 a.m., but kids were lined up at 10:00 with their lunches. They'd stay until 4:00 or 5:00 p.m. (or until their mother came to get them) watching double feature cowboy movies, cartoons, and serials. Libby Simon, whose mother packed a big lunch and sent the kids to spend Saturday afternoons at the State, recalls that, to clear the theatre before the next showing, the management gave exiting children photos of movie stars.

■ The empty Palace Theatre in 2009
• Credit: Photo by Russ Gourluck

The Twentieth Century Baseball League

From the late 1940s until the early 1950s, a uniquely North End baseball league drew thousands of spectators to the Aberdeen School playground on spring and summer Sunday afternoons. It was an era before television, and before sports, movies, and shopping were permitted on Sundays.

As Robert T. Diamond reports in his nostalgic account of the league, *Kings of the Diamond*, the two small sets of bleachers could accommodate only a couple of hundred people each, but as many as 8,000 fans crowded into the grounds. The league was founded by Mickey Bass, Aaron Goldman, and Laurie Mainster. Some of the players went on to become well-known: Leible Hershfield, Charlie Krupp, Sam Minuk, Ed Parfeniuk, Charley ("Doc") Rusen, and Chick Zamick. Hershfield was a centre fielder who caught fly balls bare handed.

Many of the players were veterans of World War Two or young men with ambitions of turning professional. The teams included the Margaret Rose Maroons sponsored by Stanley Zedd, the Maxwell King Whirlaways sponsored by Max Freed, and a team from the Northern Hotel. Post-game beer sessions were held at the hotel, which was owned by the Diamond family. There were weekday games, but it was the Sunday double headers that attracted the biggest crowds. With a PA system illicitly rigged to a nearby City Hydro pole, wagons and trucks that vended soft drinks, chips, and, of course, Saidman's sunflower seeds, the Aberdeen grounds had most of the features of the best baseball venues.

■ Baseball fans flocked to the Aberdeen School grounds to watch Twentieth Century League games.

Mickey's Bowling Alley

The sign out front displayed only the letters "M. A. C.", (which stood for Maroon Athletic Club), but many North Enders knew the establishment as "Mickey's Bowling Alley."

The M. A. C. Alleys at 430 Selkirk Avenue was opened in 1930 by brothers Mickey, Teddy, and Louis Bass. Mickey was the older brother, and Teddy was a star athlete who had played soccer and lacrosse, including senior lacrosse at the age of 16. In addition to its ten five-pin bowling lanes and eight billiards tables M. A. C. was known for organizing and sponsoring sports teams, competitions, and trophies. The teams that bore the Maroons name competed in softball, soccer, and lacrosse.

Another name that was attached to Mickey's was the Twentieth Century Bowling Club, revealing its connection to the baseball league. The basement housed the Twentieth Century Credit Union.

Unlike many other North End teenage hangouts, Mickey's was the gathering place of young people with an interest in sports. Many went on to become outstanding athletes, and many boy-girl friendships that began there blossomed into marriages.

■ Teddy Bass (shown in 1971) was a star athlete as a youth.
• Credit: Courtesy Sheila Bass Billinghurst

(BOTTOM) Maroons Athletic Club sponsored many outstanding athletes and teams • Credit: Courtesy Sheila Bass Billinghurst

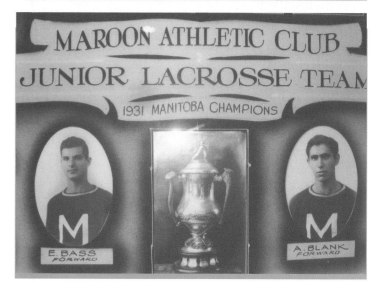

MAROON ATHLETIC CLUB
JUNIOR LACROSSE TEAM
1931 MANITOBA CHAMPIONS

E. BASS
FORWARD

A. BLANK
FORWARD

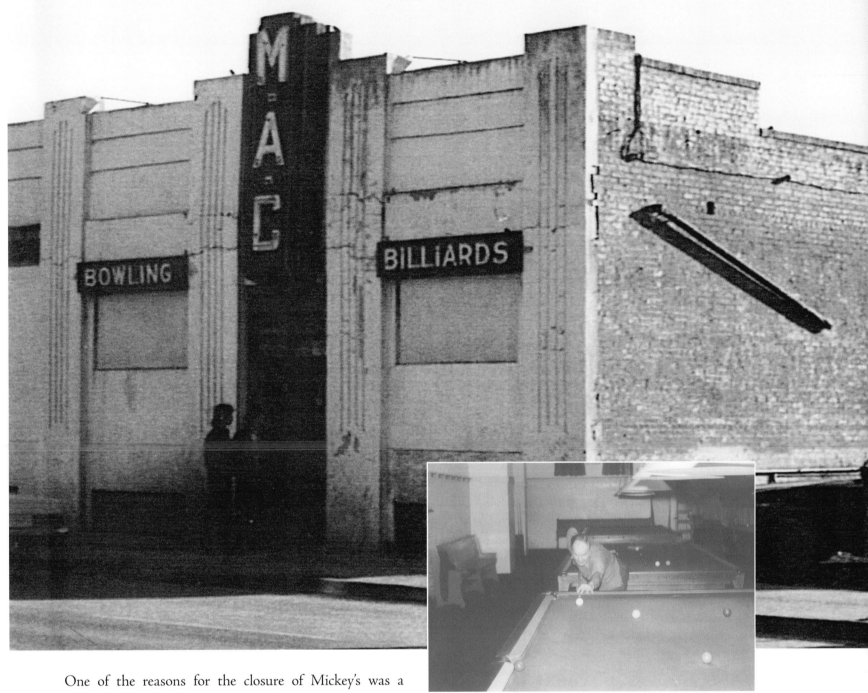

One of the reasons for the closure of Mickey's was a shortage of pinsetters. The lanes never had pinsetting equipment installed, and over the decades many North End boys who went on to become businessmen, doctors, lawyers, and judges learned the importance of moving quickly and avoiding fast-moving projectiles. The building later became an Italian and then a Sicilian social club.

■ (INSET) Louis Bass at one of the M.A.C. billiard tables • Credit: Courtesy Sheila Bass Billinghurst.

(ABOVE) M.A.C. was more than a bowling alley and pool room. It was the hub of numerous sporting activities. The building later became a private club.
• Credit: Courtesy Sheila Bass Billinghurst

■ The boys slicked down their hair and put on their best clothes and the girls wore their tunics for their grade 9 class photo at Machray School in 1952. • Credit: Courtesy Ed Pascal

2

GROWING UP IN THE NORTH END

THE NEXT GENERATIONS

STILLWATER BEVERAGES LTD.

Phone 57 288   WINNIPEG   1588 Main St.

≡ 5 ≡
LARGE
GLASSES

Delicious and Refreshing

KIK

SERVE ICE-COLD

_____ 194__

Sold to
M _____

Address _____

SOLD			CHARGE	AMOUNT	
Cases	12 Oz.	30 Oz.		$	c.

■ The original bottling plant of Kik Cola was located on Pritchard, just west of Main. The Bell Bottling Company, situated on Selkirk Avenue just east of McPhillips and founded by the Boroditsky family in 1918, produced Wynola, Suncrest Orange, and Nu-Grape. Kik and Wynola were colas and, because they came in larger

■ Boyhood chums Ron Meyers (left) and George Smith pause at the site of Smitty's Chip Stand, which was operated by Smith's uncle. Both grew up in the neighbourhood, which Meyers describes as "our whole world." • Credit: Photo by Russ Gourluck

NEIGHBOURHOODS

For children growing up in the North End, the immediate neighbourhood became the stage on which most of the events of their young lives played out. Their friends, their favourite places to play, and their schools were usually within a few blocks of home. Kids felt comfortable and secure in these familiar surroundings and there was rarely any need to venture away from them.

An annual reunion in Vancouver attracts some of the thousands of North Enders who have moved west.
• Credit: Courtesy Mike Krevesky

"This was our world..."

As Ron Meyers and George Smith stroll down Main Street near Jarvis in a hot July afternoon in 2009, they're looking beyond the pawn shops and panhandlers that now dominate the area. They're seeing their old neighbourhood as it used to be. They grew up one block from each other and were playmates before they began grade one at David Livingstone in 1940. Meyers went on to become a lawyer and then a judge, while Smith established a successful inter-city trucking firm. Neither has forgotten his North End roots.

"Our whole world was that area between Sutherland and Selkirk, from Main to around Salter," Ron Meyers gestures. He explains that they were reluctant to cross over to the east side of Main or to venture into Point Douglas, sticking to "our side of Main Street." Ron's first summer job when he was 12 or 13 was at the People's Book Store on Main Street, owned by Saul Miller's parents. He oiled floors and moved crates for $5 a week.

Ron's father worked on the railroad and also operated as a bookie out of the barber shop in the Manor Hotel as a sideline. In those days, many of the shoeshine parlours and barber shops had small gambling operations. George's mother was a maid for the family who owned Wolch's Department Store at Main and Euclid. The Wolches lived on Machray east of Main in what Smith calls "the ritzy Jewish part."

Knowing the Neighbours

The Krevesky family's neighbourhood during the 1950s centered around their grocery store at Arlington and Cathedral. It was a working-class neighbourhood, primarily populated by Ukrainians, Poles, and Jews, along with a few families with English, Scottish, or German roots. There were few visible minorities. Orysia (Krevesky) Jackson recalls that the Sumpters on Cathedral and the Williams on Machray were among the few Black families. Singer Maxine Ware lived on Parr.

■ One of the few Japanese-Canadian families in the North End in the 1950s, the Mizobuchis lived on Boyd Avenue. John (shown with his sister Sachi Guilbert) joined the Department of Immigration and was posted to India, Korea, Japan (where he was Deputy High Commissioner) and the Philippines. • Credit: Courtesy Orysia Jackson

■ (ABOVE) Michael Klym grew up to be a drummer with the D-Drifters. • Credit: Courtesy Orysia Jackson

(LEFT) Dan Dowbenko grew up to be a judge. • Credit: Courtesy Orysia Jackson

"I know your mother..."

Not only did children in typical North End neighbourhoods know the adults and the other children, the adults knew the kids. Natalie (Berschley) Hemingway, who grew up at 697 Redwood in the 1950s and 1960s explains that this provided a kind of control mechanism. Because both parents in many families worked weekdays, the neighbourhood, says Hemingway, "was run by kids" during the summer holidays. Most children knew that if they acted up, there was often an adult in the vicinity who could issue the most dreaded of threats: "I know your mother."

Memories of Growing Up

Reminiscing through the decades, North Enders share a few of their childhood memories.

At the age of four or five, Esther Korchynski often accompanied her mother to her aunt's home on Manitoba Avenue. Although she was sometimes allowed in the kitchen to watch her aunt make strudel for her catering business, she was usually expected to sit alone for several hours in the living room, to be quiet, and not to touch anything. She looked forward to the arrival home of her cousin Sally because the family had a Victrola and Sally would put on their only phonograph record. It was Lily Pons singing *The Bell Song*. During most visits she was expected to pay dutiful visits to the third floor with her mother to say hello to her aunt's aged and bedridden mother-in-law.

The Cathedral Avenue neighbours included the Snyders (commercial painters who raised pigeons), the Schwartzes (construction contractors), the Sopinuks (Mrs. Sopinuk modelled for Eaton's), the Kravetskys (son Murray, now a lawyer, had an impressive comic book collection), and the Schans (plastering contractors.) Alderman Slaw Rebchuk lived on Cathedral near McGregor. Orysia became a teacher, and her brother Mike joined the RCMP.

Some of their Machray Avenue neighbours included the Zelmers (son Larry became an art curator in Vancouver), the Shaleys, and the Miruses. The Lewickis and their cousins the Jasts lived next door to each other.

Stanley and Adelaide Zedd (they had no children) lived on the corner of Arlington and Machray. Orysia remembers them as a "kind-hearted and friendly couple." She enjoyed delivering groceries to the Zedds, and there was often a treat or a coin or two as a reward. Mike remembers Zedd's green 1951 Cadillac sedan, a lumbering barge of a car with no power steering or power brakes. Stanley Zedd ran illegal card games.

■ Ed Pascal (age 4) and his dog Peanuts in front of their home at 454 St. John's Avenue in 1941 • Credit: Courtesy Ed Pascal

■ Alex Finkelstein (shown ca 1950 at age 18), who grew up on Bannerman, and graduated from St. John's Tech, won a hockey scholarship to the University of North Dakota and became a journalist for several US newspapers. • Credit: Courtesy Ed Pascal

Shirley (Elhatton) Scaletta grew up at 128 Inkster in the 1930s. During the winter, her father flooded a skating rink on the empty lot they owned next door, attracting many of the neighbourhood kids. There were very few organized sports, so most children played on the street or in their front yards, knowing that when the street lights went on it was time to go home. Their kitchen had both a wood-burning stove and an electric stove – the wood stove was used in the winter because it provided additional heat for the house. They were one of the first families in the neighbourhood to own a radio.

Dr. R. T. Ross grew up at 188 Scotia and received a cocker spaniel puppy named Timmy for Christmas in 1929. Timmy was a good dog but, as he grew older, he developed a habit of wandering away at night in search of companionship. It became the duty of Dr. Ross's father to "find the dog." He found that the most effective approach was to wait at the bus stop for the Cathedral bus to come along and to ask the driver if he had noticed a gathering of panting dogs somewhere along the route, assuming that these would be male dogs (including Timmy)

that had found a female in heat. If the driver named a location, Mr. Ross would change from his bathrobe and pyjamas and walk to retrieve Timmy.

Nellie (Merkel) Zaidman tells of her friend Jeannie who wasn't allowed to drop by Nellie's house on the way to school during Passover because her mother had told her that during Passover Jews ate matzah made with the blood of Jesus Christ. After Passover, Jeannie resumed the twice-daily routine of meeting up with Nellie at home on the way to school.

Larry Fleisher and his friends played street hockey on winter evenings. There were no skates or other equipment, and frozen horse manure served as the goal markers. Sometimes on a Saturday afternoon they walked south across the tracks to the Fox or Starland for matinees that cost a dime.

Marcia Schnoor, who grew up in the 1940s, remembers taking a streetcar downtown by herself when she was eight years old. Her mother stocked up on canned goods and home-preserves and stored them on shelves in the basement.

Mel Myers grew up on Boyd Avenue near Powers in what he describes as "a polyglot community of Ukrainian, Jews, Ukrainians, Germans, Poles, and Anglo Saxons" with a syna-gogue, two Jewish grocery stores, and two kosher butcher

■ Dressed in their stylish "drapes" are (from left) Phil Rubin, Bernie Gunn, Sherwin Desser, and Ed Pascal, age 14, ca 1951. • Credit: Courtesy Ed Pascal

shops nearby. He and his father often walked from home to the Olympic Rink at Charles and Church to watch church league hockey on Sunday evenings.

Audrey Boyko's parents didn't want her to learn the Ukrainian language. The reason they gave was that they didn't want her to speak English with an accent, but her theory, as she told her brother as a child was, "They just want to talk about sex and money and we won't know."

One day in 1939 Ron Meyers and his father walked to the relief office to get a winter coat for Ron. They were handed a girl's coat. "He threw it back at them," Meyers says. On their way home they stopped at a theatre and saw *The Wizard of Oz*.

Mary and Vera Pytel remember that a special treat on Sundays was cornflakes instead of porridge. Three huge boxes were only a quarter at the corner store. During the Depression, their mother bought cracked eggs from the cold storage plant at the foot of the Salter Bridge. A nearby store sold loose cookies. When only pieces were left, their mother struck a bargain "We had cookies. They didn't have to be whole ones," they explain. When their sister got her first job as a housekeeper and came home with her monthly pay of $8.00, their mother took her shopping on Selkirk Avenue and they came home with her complete winter outfit: a coat, boots, and mitts. "Mother could wheel and deal," the sisters laugh.

Walter Procter grew up on McAdam Avenue during the 1940s. His family first lived at 94 McAdam, a four-bedroom two-storey house with a basement that had a floor that was mostly soil. His father once used a shovel to kill a rat in the basement. The house had an octopus-like coal-burning furnace in the basement as well as a wood-burning stove in the kitchen. "The lot between 94 and 90 McAdam was an odd shape (tapered somewhat) and was unsuitable for a house," Procter tells. "We squatted on it and used it for a garden (to support a large family) in the summer, and in the winter Dad and the older boys would make a toboggan slide and a bit of a skating rink." In the summer of 1941, they moved across the street to 91 McAdam. "When moving day came, I can recall that Dad hired Stevenson's Moving (a half-ton truck) to bring the cook stove across the street. Everything else moved on coaster wagons, trip

after trip. I was only five, so I got to watch, and keep my brother David in tow. It was no smooth journey from one house to the other, as the street was a gravel road," Procter says.

Betty (Dougloski) Murray enjoyed going to the Times Theatre on the east side of Main Street near Selkirk Avenue, where the price of admission was only 11 cents when other theatres charged 15 cents. The Times had popcorn but no soft drinks. The most memorable movies she saw there were *Red River* with John Wayne and *The Jolson Story*. Al Jolson is still her favourite singer.

Libby (Klein) Simon had four brothers. They played a game they called "tippie sticks" that involved placing one stick in a hole in the ground, then using a second stick to flip the first one out of the hole and hit it before it fell to the ground. "I don't recall how we kept score, but it kept us busy and didn't cost anything, she laughs." They also played hide and seek, kick the can, and, of course, hockey. "They'd stick me in goal and then they'd shoot pucks. I developed good co-ordination and fast reflexes."

When Mother's Day came along, Lillian Mendelsohn and her brother often shopped for gifts at St. John's Drugs. If they'd saved enough money, they'd purchase a bottle of the most popular scent of the 1950s, Evening in Paris. If they were short of money, they'd gather pop bottles, cash them in at the corner store for two cents each, and buy a bottle of Jergen's Hand Lotion for their mother.

■ Einar Anderson with his black Mercury Christmas 1940 • Credit: Courtesy of John and Alice Crawshaw

(RIGHT) In the dining room with "Auntie Gert" and "Uncle Einar" in the dining room, Christmas 1940 • Credit: Courtesy of John and Alice Crawshaw

(BELOW) Crawshaw (shown in 1944) joined the Air Cadet Corps of Canada, an experience that led to his career in Britain's Royal Air Force. • Credit: Courtesy of John and Alice Crawshaw

The Boy from England

John Crawshaw was one of thousands of English children evacuated to Canada and other parts of the Commonwealth from the London area because of the bombing during the Second World War. He and 350 other children left Glasgow on August 10th, 1940 by ship and arrived in Halifax on August 21st. He was 11 years old and knew no one else on the ship. He remembers little of the voyage but does recall the long train journey from Halifax to Winnipeg because of the "strange scenery and the unusual taste of Canadian bread." On arriving in Winnipeg, he and other children were taken to the School for the Deaf to meet their temporary guardians. He admired a sleek Mercury sedan in the driveway and was pleased to find out that it was owned by the family with whom he'd be spending the next five years.

Crawshaw describes Mr. and Mrs. Anderson, who soon became his "Uncle Einar" and "Auntie Gert", as "lovely people who treated me as their own and involved me in their families." The Andersons, who had no children of their own, lived at 152 Bannerman (later to become the home of Mrs. Rhoda Cummings and her son Burton.) John Crawshaw attended grades 7, 8, and 9 at Luxton School and grades 10 and eleven at St. John's Tech. Many decades later, he fondly recalls several of his teachers at Luxton, particularly Miss Pybus and Miss McBeth, as well as Mr. Johnson, Miss Cummings, and the principal Mr. Reeves at St. John's. He still has his Torch yearbooks.

As he grew into his teenage years, John Crawshaw enjoyed dances at St. John's and Cokes, apple pie, and hot dogs at This Is It. "I have never since enjoyed such relish as they served with their wieners," he comments. He learned to ski and snowshoe along the Red River. He joined the 175 Squadron of Air Cadets of Canada, which met at the St. John's Cathedral Hall, and credits that experience with influencing his decision to pursue a career in the Royal Air Force. He recalls delivering The Winnipeg Tribune and spending summers working at Eaton's and Vulcan Iron Works.

Although he has never returned to Canada, John Crawshaw considers himself to be "half Canadian, over sixty years later," and is still able to sing O Canada in both English and French.

Mendelsohn remembers bundling up in multiple sweaters and scarves to watch Eaton's Santa Claus Parade with her friends as it made its way along Salter to climb the bridge. In one of the parades her brother was dressed as an upside-down clown and appreciated the generous hot meal that Eaton's provided after the frigid march. "I was never tall enough," Lillian points out. "He was the only one in our family that actually marched in the parade."

Harry Kaplan once delivered a nine-foot-long roll of linoleum flooring on his bicycle from his parents' general store on Dufferin to a customer in Point Douglas, managing not to stop traffic as he crossed Main Street. He once rode his bike to the Rupert Avenue Police Station to pay a fine his parents owed for keeping the store open on a Wednesday afternoon.

At Cooper Mosienko Lanes, many boys found jobs as pinsetters during the 1940s and 1950s and could occasionally earn some extra money by bowling. Gord MacDonald explains that when evening adult leagues needed spare bowlers, they frequently enlisted teens at the alleys. The kids were usually able to bowl for free and some teams would even bid against one another to recruit the best bowlers. The compensation was generally only a quarter, but, as MacDonald points out, "That was big money in those days. You could buy a drink and a bag of chips and a chocolate bar." When he was in junior high school he and a couple of his friends sometimes went to the Quality Grill after church on Sundays and ordered more Chinese food than they could possibly eat for around $4.00.

During summer holidays, MacDonald and his friends often watched craftsmen apply the finish to tables at Cramer's furniture factory, across from the Redwood Apartments where he lived. Many of the workers were Europeans who spoke little English but they and the boys managed to communicate as the workers explained what they were doing. "They always had smiles on their faces. Even though we were small kids, they tried out their new-found English on us to see if we could understand it."

For John Marczyk's family, a typical meal included a big boiled sausage from one of the Polish butchers on Selkirk Avenue, steaming whole boiled potatoes, and sauerkraut. "I'd be given a buck every day to go to City Bread and get some rye bread warm out of the oven," Marczyk relates. "We ate only rye bread. There was no fluffy white toast in our house."

Frank Humniski remembers a shoemaker shop near his home on Stella where he often noticed people sipping a clear liquid. It was years before he realized that it was homebrew.

Len Offrowich reminisces, "There was a barber in a tiny shop on Mountain Avenue just before Arlington where I remember having one of my first haircuts and the wonderful white hair cream that came in a glass bottle that he would use and which my dad also had at home. It was called Wildroot Cream Oil and it made your hair sleek and shiny."

Lillian Mendelsohn can still picture her itinerant piano teacher Miss Provisor, who boarded with a family in a house in West Kildonan and walked from there after school to the homes of her students in the vicinity of St. John's Avenue.

In the early 1940s Norm Silverberg's family lived in a triplex and had no bathtub. He went to his aunt's home for baths or bathed in a galvanized wash tub at home. "My dad would get the water first, and then my brother and I would go in. It was the same water." He and the other kids helped chop wood for the wood-burning stove in the kitchen. He recalls that, when he and Lenny Kubas were six years old, they went to Children's Hospital on Redwood to get their tonsils taken out at same time.

Walter Procter enjoyed visiting King's Confectionery on Main between Inkster and Lansdowne. At the soda bar, milkshakes were 12 cents – or 15 cents with an extra scoop of ice cream. There was a huge Hires Root Beer keg on the counter. Mr. King tolerated the reading of comic books from the rack for only a limited period of time before asking, "Are you gonna read it or are you gonna buy it?"

Len Offrowich remembers that the McGregor Armoury was the starting point for Eaton's Santa Claus parades and that the floats arrived there overnight in order to not spoil the surprise for children. He and his friends enjoyed playing "Knock Knock Ginger," a game that involved knocking on someone's door and then running and hiding to watch the reaction of whoever came to the door to find no one there. He and his friend walked everywhere, even on bitterly cold nights in the dead of winter; their parents didn't drive them. And he reports that they had the first television set on their street and, as a result, a living room full of visitors every evening.

Like many children from German and Ukrainian families, Heather (Weber) Borody took accordion lessons at Kent's Accordion College at Bannerman and McGregor in the late 1950s.

Poetry of the North End

Ron Romanowski grew up on Polson Avenue, the son of a native North Ender and her newly-arrived Polish husband. After attending Inkster and Faraday Schools, he graduated from St. John's High School in 1972. Romanowski became a track athlete at St. John's and, as an adult, was a marathon runner until injuries forced him to give up running. Wanting to find an activity "as intense as marathon running," he turned to poetry. Describing the North End as "a template with which to measure the world," Ron Romanowski has had three books published.

One of his poems, "St. Nicholas and his Devil," tells of the annual visits of St. Nicholas to children's Christmas parties at Polish social clubs in the North End. Clad in a bishop's attire (not the red costume associated with contemporary Santa Clauses) the revered figure was often accompanied by an evil sidekick. In keeping with Polish tradition, children often jeered at this "devil" and threw objects at him. And, in keeping with the same tradition, the devil retaliated.

ST. NICOLAS AND HIS DEVIL

In those North End Polish halls
I remember St. Nicolas and his devil
deep in the hearty basement bosom of parents and friends
music, gifts and merriment

We tormented that devil
and he fought back against the buzzing swarm of children
but we revered the old saint
in his bishop's robes and crosier
for we were certain to be gifted by him
(no matter how we behaved)
just because we were kids

Close up St. Nicolas might look familiar
like a club member we might know
the soft side of a veteran of Africa or Monte Casino
the Polish Corps at ease
in a ritual of cartoons, sweet treats and raucous play

At thirteen I remember being cut off
welcome to the feast but too old for toys
and how I silently wished on the verge of manhood
I could turn back time to be a child again

Now the devil takes me older still
and I don't laugh at him
(I may meet him face-to-face soon enough)
but I remember carefree days in North End halls
when St. Nicolas was my generous friend
and snow lay sparkling on the ground

—Ron Romanowski
(Reprinted with permission from *Sweet Talking*)

GROUP OF PUPILS AT ABERDEEN SCHOOL, WINNIPEG, CANADA
First Row, left to right:
Mary Mosurinjohn, Roumanian; Jennie Kaleka, Ukranian; Clayton Spanier, English, Sally Dziurdziewicz, Polish; lily Yurechko, Portugese; Monty Binder, Jewish; Alice Vandal, French; Lorne Shepp, German; Billie Lusanko, Russian.
Second Row:
Allen Luxa, Bohemian; Janet Anderson, Scotch; Grace Charkes, Cuban; Kenneth Weppler, Swiss; Bitil Buzun, Lithuanian; Rosaline Stachowicz, Ruthenian.
Third Row:
Nickolas Zunic, Croatian; Joseph Fabri, Italian; Leslie Rogers, Irish; Stephen Vukets, Hungarian; George Dvorak, Bohemian; Tom Janakas, Greek;
A. W. Muldrew, Principal.

■ The diverse backgrounds (described as "21 nationalities") of students at Aberdeen School were illustrated in a 1938 photo. Their names and national origins were typed on the back. • Credit: Archives of Manitoba, Foote Collection 1569, N2664

SCHOOL DAYS

In many ways, the public schools of the North End served as equalizers that brought together children of diverse backgrounds and provided them with the basic skills and knowledge to succeed in Canadian society. Although some officials believed that the role of the public schools was to "Canadianize" the children of immigrants by eliminating their "foreign" culture, the actual result was that young people learned to live in a multi-cultural microcosm that prepared them for the society in which they would function as adults.

The Schools of the North End

The divisive Manitoba Schools Question of 1890 saw the replacement of separate Protestant and Roman Catholic school systems in Manitoba with a non-sectarian public school system. Under the leadership of Superintendent Daniel McIntyre, the formerly-Protestant Winnipeg School District built a dozen new schools throughout the city between 1890 and 1900. Unlike the small wood-frame school buildings that preceded them, most of the new schools were large multi-storey structures sturdily constructed of brick and stone.

Between 1900 and 1913, student enrolment in Winnipeg schools jumped from 7,500 to 22,000, largely as a result of immigration. During the same period, the number of teachers increased from 119 to 527 and the number of school buildings grew from 16 to 38. Although additional schools were constructed in the other parts of the city, the rapid growth of the North End necessitated several new school buildings.

Some of the earliest schools in the North End were located in Point Douglas. It's believed that one of them, named Central School, was located in a rented two-room store in 1882. Six

■ (ABOVE) Luxton School (shown in 1910) is an example of the multi-storey brick and stone schools that were built in Winnipeg in the early 1900s. • Credit: Archives of Manitoba, Winnipeg-Schools-Luxton 1, N16596

(BELOW) The 1892 Norquay School building • Credit: Archives of Manitoba, Winnipeg-Schools-Norquay 4, N8667. Norquay School in 2009 • Credit: Photo by Russ Gourluck

rooms were added in 1888, and the entire school was destroyed by fire in 1890. The replacement school, built in 1892 and named for Manitoba Premier John Norquay, was a modern three-storey structure, and Norquay School Number Two was built in 1920. The present building opened in 1971, with an addition constructed in 1992.

One of the earliest schools in Winnipeg was named for Archbishop Robert Machray. The original Machray School opened in 1884 in a rented house on Main Street in response to requests from local residents Alex Polson and Robert McKay, both of whom had large families. In 1886, a new wooden building was erected on a site at the corner of Charles Street and Mountain Avenue and later replaced by a brick structure. By 1913, increasing population required an addition. In 1921, as students continued to stay in school longer, Machray became the second junior high school in Winnipeg with the opening of Machray School Number Two. The present Machray School was built in 1975.

■ Aberdeen School in 1903 • Credit: Archives of Manitoba, Winnipeg-Schools-Aberdeen 1

Named for Lord Aberdeen, the Governor General of Canada, the first Aberdeen School was built in 1893. Aberdeen Number Two (which had fireproof stairwells instead of the silo-like spiral fire escapes of some other schools) was built in 1910, and Aberdeen Number Three was constructed in 1920. Reflecting the large number of Aboriginal families in the North End, there are now two schools on that site with an Aboriginal focus. The former Aberdeen School building at 450 Flora Avenue is now Niji Mahkwa School (nursery to grade 8), and Children of the Earth High School (grades 9 to 12) is located at 100 Salter Street. Along with Sisler High School, Children of

■ (BELOW) Machray School in 2009
• Credit: Photo by Russ Gourluck

■ Strathcona school is named for Donald A. Smith, who also has a downtown street named after him.
• Credit: Photo by Russ Gourluck

the Earth has been rated among Canada's Top Ten Schools by *Maclean's Magazine*.

Named for fur trader, rail baron and politician Donald A. Smith (Lord Strathcona) the ten-classroom Strathcona School opened in 1905, and an additional ten rooms were constructed in 1911. At that time, the school accommodated 900 students, of whom only ten percent were English-speaking. The school's first principal (1905 to 1920) was William James Sisler. The present 12-classroom Strathcona School at 233 McKenzie Street was built in 1962.

Luxton School opened in 1907 on Polson Avenue. Constructed of Tyndall stone and "Manitoba Pressed Brick," Luxton was built at a cost of $84,661 and contained 14 classrooms with a total enrolment of 338 pupils and eight teachers. The basement had two classrooms and a "manual training room," and the large main hallways on the second and third floors were designed for "physical exercises," which in other

schools had taken place in classrooms. Five of the upstairs rooms were utilized as a technical high school from 1909 until St. John's Technical High School was completed in 1912. There was an 8-room addition in 1915, and an auditorium was added in 1919. A new gymnasium opened in 1989. The school was named for William F. Luxton, Winnipeg's first public school teacher and the first editor of the *Manitoba Free Press*.

St. John's Technical High School welcomed the first students to its new building at 480 Salter Street in March, 1912. That building (an architectural twin to the original

■ The Luxton School building is an example of early multi-storey schools. • Credit: Photo by Russ Gourluck
(LEFT) A school with an Aboriginal focus
• Credit: Photo by Russ Gourluck

■ Named for the reigning monarch Edward VII, King Edward School, a brick building with 15 classrooms, opened in 1908 and included the innovative feature of showers. The King Edward Number Two building, with 24 classrooms, opened in 1914. The current building was constructed in 1976. King Edward Number One was demolished in 1973, and Number Two in 1977. • Credit: Photo by Russ Gourluck

■ St. John's Tech in 1928 • Credit: Archives of Manitoba, Winnipeg-Schools-St. John's Tech 1, N15577

Kelvin High School) continued in use until a gradual process of replacement began in the early 1960s. A new addition at 401 Church Avenue completed in 1960 accommodated the school's junior high grades. Further additions in 1964 and 1967 led to the movement of all students into new facilities. The original building was demolished in 1967. St. John's celebrated its 100th anniversary in 2010.

When William Whyte School opened in 1914, it was a three-storey building that accommodated 1,100 students and was named for railway executive Sir William Whyte. During some years of the 1930s and 1940s, William Whyte was an all-girls school in some grades. By 1973, wooden beams were being used to shore up hallways on three of the school's four floors

■ (LEFT) Domestic Science class for students of King Edward and William Whyte Schools in 1921 • Credit: Archives of Manitoba, Foote Collection 1584, N2684

(BELOW) In 1919, Lord Nelson School – named for the British naval hero – was built, with five classrooms and a boiler room. Four classrooms were added in 1922, and an additional seven classrooms and an auditorium were completed in 1949. A single storey annex with eight rooms was added on the north side in 1959.
• Credit: Photo by Russ Gourluck

■ Champlain School, named for explorer Samuel de Champlain, opened on Machray Avenue in 1920 in a 12-classroom room two-storey red brick building. Initially it accommodated the overflow student population from Luxton and Ralph Brown School and only five classrooms were in use. By October 1922, there were 508 pupils and a staff of 12. The present building at 275 Church Avenue opened in 1990 with 326 students and a staff of 22 and included 12 classrooms, a multi-purpose room, a daycare, and a lunchroom. • Credit: Photo by Russ Gourluck

and the building was condemned to demolition. The current building opened in 1976.

Named for a former Somerset School principal who died in action during World War One, the first Ralph Brown School was built on Andrews Street in 1918, and Ralph Brown Number 2 opened in 1920. The current building, which opened in 1989 and accommodates students in nursery to grade eight, includes a Ukrainian Bilingual program. It was designed to resemble the thatched-roof homes of early Ukrainian settlers.

Both Faraday and David Livingstone Schools opened in 1922 and were designed by the same architect, utilizing brick and stone in a Gothic style. Both had 14 classrooms and were constructed at costs of $89,838 and $79,989 respectively.

When Inkster School, named for the pioneering Manitoba family, was officially opened in 1949, a newspaper article lauded its "modern, up-to-date classrooms", indirect lighting, and tile flooring. After more than six decades, the brick building with its massive stone entrance remains one of the most impressive buildings in the North End. Inkster School

currently accommodates over 300 students from nursery to grade six, has integrated adaptive skills and autism programs, and includes an independent daycare centre and a parent-operated lunch program.

School trustee Joe Zuken was instrumental in having Andrew Mynarski School named to honour the war hero in 1955. Before World War One, the Winnipeg School Board had begun the practice of naming new schools in the North End after "men of eminence." For conservative school trustees, this meant distinguished Anglo-Saxons, and the result included schools honouring King Edward, Lord Aberdeen, Cecil Rhodes, and Lord Strathcona. Zuken's initial motion was defeated, and the school board chairman commented that the name Mynarski

■ (RIGHT) Margaret Scott School was built in 1920 as a temporary structure. It continued to be used until 1989, when it was declared unsafe, demolished, and not replaced. Margaret Scott Park has been built on the same site and includes a playground, a skate park, and a softball field. In the late 1800s and early 1900s, Margaret Scott established a program for delinquent young women, a lumberyard to provide jobs to unemployed men, and a nursing facility that was named the Margaret Scott Mission. She became known as "the Angel of Poverty Row."

(RIGHT) David Livingstone School in 2009

(FAR RIGHT) The original David Livingstone School building

(BELOW) When Isaac Newton School opened in 1921 it was the first school in Winnipeg to be designed and built as a junior high. The classic brick building with Tyndall Stone trim was immediately filled to capacity. By the 1930s, the school accommodated grades seven to 12. It returned to being a junior high when Sisler High School opened in October, 1957.

• Credit: Photos by Russ Gourluck

Isaac Newton Junior High School
WINNIPEG, MANITOBA
★
Closing Exercises

N

St. Giles United Church
Burrows and Charles
★
Friday, June 12th, 1959
at 2:00 p.m.

The entrance of Inkster School in 2009 • Credit: Photo by Russ Gourluck

1949

INKSTER SCHOOL

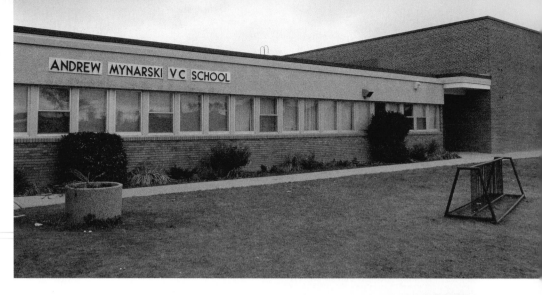

■ The name of Andrew Mynarski School includes the letters "V. C." to signify the Victoria Cross awarded posthumously to the war hero. • Credit: Photo by Russ Gourluck

"does not lend itself to the name of a school." A delegation of more than 50 people, including members of ethnic groups, war veterans, and some of Mynarski's former teachers presented a petition to the school board protesting the defeat of Zuken's motion and demanding that the school be named to honour Mynarski. The trustees recanted and agreed to the name. If the original decision had stood, it's likely that the school would have been named for former Governor General Baron Tweedsmuir (novelist John Buchan).

The Jewish Schools

Although most Jewish children in the North End attended public schools, many took after-school and evening classes in Jewish independent ("private") schools. Families who preferred that their children have a more comprehensive Jewish education chose to have them attend Jewish schools on a full-day basis. Initially, these schools provided a clear choice between a religious based education with an emphasis on the Hebrew language and a more secular approach with an emphasis on Yiddish.

■ Lansdowne School, which had been operating since 1954, faced closure in the early 1980s because of declining enrolment. The popularity of language programs at the time, however, saw the school reopen as Ecole Lansdowne, a French milieu school, in August 1984 with an enrolment of 88 students in kindergarten to grade 2. The school currently has a student population of 420 in nursery to grade eight. • Credit: Photo by Russ Gourluck

The first Talmud Torah School opened in 1902 adjacent to Shaarey Zedek Synagogue on Henry Avenue. It was named the King Edward Hebrew School in honour of the reigning monarch Edward VII and likely to demonstrate to Winnipeg's British majority the patriotism of the Jewish minority. The curriculum included the Hebrew language, the Talmud, and Jewish literature and history. In 1907, Rabbi Israel Kahanovitch established the Winnipeg Hebrew Free School – Talmud Torah at the corner of Dufferin and Aikins. The school relocated in 1912 to a larger building at the corner of Flora and Charles.

■ Currently the largest high school in Manitoba, Sisler High School was named for William Sisler, the Strathcona School principal who developed a practical and effective method of teaching English to immigrant students. The school opened in 1957 and received an addition in 1964. Grades 9 to 12 are offered. • Credit: Photo by Russ Gourluck

תלמוד תורה רעיר וויניפעג

■ A Hebrew Free School (Talmud Torah) class ca 1903 •
Credit: Archives of Manitoba, Winnipeg-Schools 3-Hebrew Free School

As might be expected, the sale of the building to the German Society of Winnipeg in 1952 elicited an outcry in Winnipeg's Jewish community. In 1944, Talmud Torah opened an English day school, and in 1952 the various branches of the school moved to a new building at the corner of Matheson and Powers. Joseph Wolinsky Collegiate opened in the late 1950s for English day students at the same site.

The Jewish Radical School was founded in 1914 and, in contrast to Talmud Torah, provided a secular program that focussed on the Yiddish language and on Jewish history and culture. The school's name was changed – and softened – one year later to honour the Yiddish writer I. L. Peretz, and it went on to offer such innovations as day school and kindergarten.

The I. L. Peretz Folk School began in two rented classrooms at Aberdeen School after regular school hours. As enrolment grew, the school moved to McKenzie and Pritchard, then to a house on Burrows Avenue, and then to a building near Salter and Aberdeen that it occupied from 1922 until 1950 before moving to a new building at 601 Aikins Street. The movement of many Jewish families to West Kildonan resulted in the opening of a second Peretz School on Jefferson Avenue in 1958.

By the late 1940s, much of Winnipeg's Jewish population was in the south end of Winnipeg, and this shift was reflected

■ Robertson School, with 14 classrooms and a gymnasium/auditorium was completed in 1952. A new gym, library, computer lab, and other facilities were added in 2009. • Credit: Photo by Russ Gourluck

Memories of School

Machray School inspired some happy memories in the mid-1940s for Eleanor Lazare. "I remember my kindergarten teacher. Her name was Miss Cowie or Mrs. Cowie — and I loved her." Eleanor also loved the taste of the white flour glue the children used.

Norm Silverberg attended William Whyte, Aberdeen, and St. John's during the 1940s and early 1950s. Most of his classmates were Jewish, and many were Ukrainian and Polish. He remembers only one Chinese kid, whose name was Wayne Pang,

■ Named for Robert Boyd Russell, one of the leaders of the 1919 Winnipeg General Strike, R. B Russell Vocational High School was built in 1966. Located on Dufferin Avenue near the Slaw Rebchuk Bridge, the school offers grades 9 to 12.
• Credit: Photo by Russ Gourluck

and one Black boy who was nicknamed "Snowball." Silverberg explains that the name wasn't meant to be derogatory, nor does he recall that it was taken that way.

In the early 1940s, Harry Kaplan was a boarder at the Jewish Orphanage on Matheson Avenue. His family lived outside of Winnipeg at the time and he attended Luxton School while preparing for his bar mitzvah at the orphanage.

When Betty (Dougloski) Murray attended Holy Ghost School on Selkirk Avenue during the 1940s, students were allowed to go to the store at recess. Most bought candies but she and her friends once bought a coconut so they could taste it. Charles Drug Store at Selkirk and Charles had what she remembers as "the very best toast and jam."

When Brenda (Gallis) Barrie attended I. L. Peretz Folk School during the postwar 1940s, some of her classmates were children from very poor Jewish families who lived on the older streets of the North End. She knew that they only spoke Yiddish and came from "the camps." She later learned that they had been in concentration camps and that their families were being financially supported by the Hebrew Sick Benefit and other free loan societies.

When Len Offrowich attended kindergarten in 1955 at Ralph Brown School, children took money to school to buy milk, which came in small waxed cardboard containers. He recalls, "It tasted so good. Not a bit like the identical article at home." After they finished their milk, the pupils lay down on mats on the floor for a short nap. He adds, "I still have one of my first objects made while in Kindergarten which (indicative of the times) was an ashtray (with handle) for dad, modelled from clay and painted with a red inside and a green outside, which was then lacquered by the teacher, Miss Hughes."

Steve Kiz attended Lord Nelson for grades one to nine and explains "It was all prairie out there." He recalls that a cow once decided to take a rest at the front door and the students couldn't get out for recess. The fire department removed the dozing bovine.

Larry Fleisher chuckles as he thinks back to his first day at David Livingstone. "I think I got strapped the first day of school because I wasn't standing straight in line."

The annual tea is part of Lillian Mendelsohn's memories of Machray School. It was a formal event to raise funds for the school. The girls, dressed in their tunics, were servers, and important adults in the community solemnly poured tea. She also remembers that there were two kinds of safety patrols. Stationary patrols were let out of class early to take up their positions at intersections. Mobile safety patrols walked the grade one and two children part-way home across busy streets.

Len Offrowich reminisces about field trips taken by Ralph Brown students during the 1950s. "Our field trips consisted of: a tour of the Coca Cola bottling plant (at the end we received miniature Coke bottles); a tour of the McGavin bakery (a miniature loaf of bread was a treasured souvenir and one which we handed over to mom and asked her to make tiny sandwiches for us), or the grandest trip of all which was either the trip to the Sandilands Tree Preserve or a ride on the Shoal Lake railway to see the source of Winnipeg's drinking water."

Larry Borody was "virtually the only Gentile" in his grade seven class at Machray School in the mid-1950s. Over half of the staff was Jewish. Kids were encouraged by some teachers to stay home on Jewish holidays, but, he recalls, "My parents wouldn't hear of it."

The Talmud Torah School at Flora and Charles (shown ca 1924) opened in 1912. The building was sold to the German Society in 1952.
• Credit: Archives of Manitoba, Jewish Historical Society Collection, 2804

in the opening of the Shaarey Zedek Religious School (later known as Ramah Hebrew School) in 1949. During the 1980s, some co-ordination of the operations of Talmud Torah, Ramah Hebrew School, and Joseph Wolinsky Collegiate took place through the Winnipeg Jewish Board of Education, and I. L. Peretz and Talmud Torah decided to amalgamate. Since moving to the Asper Jewish Community Campus in South Winnipeg in 1997, all of the existing independent Jewish Schools have combined under the name of the Gray Academy of Jewish Education.

Learning the Language

Many children of immigrant parents began to learn English when they entered grade one. Their parents, in many cases,

spoke only European languages, and that was what the children spoke at home. Those who arrived as pre-schoolers, however, often picked up some basic words and phrases as they played with English-speaking children in their neighbourhoods.

The ability of children to learn language skills outside of a school setting wasn't limited to English. Before Bernie Klein started grade one at Machray School in the late 1920s, he spoke mostly Yiddish and Polish, but he did learn some English from kids on the street. He also picked up some Russian from his parents, despite their strategy of using that language when they didn't want their children to understand them. Although many of the neighbours were Jewish, Klein had enough Ukrainian-speaking playmates as a child that he learned to swear in Ukrainian and, at age 84, he still can.

When children entered school in the early days, there were no special programs or resources to help them learn the English language. Although Morley Rypp was born in Winnipeg, only Yiddish was spoken at home. Aside from what he'd learned from neighbourhood children, his first experience with English was in grade one at William Whyte. "They just threw you in and you learned to speak English," he reports. Children who spoke little or no English were sometimes placed in kindergarten or grade one classes regardless of their age. Vera Hershfield remembers

■ The Joseph Wolinsky Collegiate building became a Christian independent school. • Credit: Photo by Russ Gourluck

being in a kindergarten class at Machray School when she was seven years old and feeling embarrassed when older students walked by, but she was able to catch up and to skip grade six.

Mike Humniski first attended Ukrainian School on Flora for the first three grades. When he entered King Edward School, he was put back two grades. He left school after grade six.

Adjusting to Canadian Ways

One of the primary functions of public schools, particularly during periods of extensive immigration, was to "Canadianize" the children of immigrants by teaching them English as well as Canadian (largely British-based) customs and values. In an area like the North End, these efforts were counterbalanced by family and community initiatives that encouraged children to retain their European heritage.

By bringing together children of different cultural and religious backgrounds, the public school system provided a setting where tolerance, respect, and understanding could be learned. As the Winnipeg-born children of immigrants became increasingly "Canadianized," they generally faced fewer instances of discrimination than their parents and grandparents.

Nonetheless, some of the prejudices their parents faced in the community found their way onto the playground and into the schools. When Norm Silverberg was about nine, a little girl across the street who had often been his playmate previously, solemnly announced, "Norman, I can't play with you anymore. When he asked why, she responded, "Because you killed Jesus." Norm's nine-year-old reaction was "What are you talking about? I didn't kill anybody!" Fortunately, the undoubtedly parentally-imposed boycott didn't last much more than a day or two.

Most of the time, however, children were oblivious to ethnic and religious differences as they formed friendships and played together. George Gershman declares, "We never knew about anti-Semitism in the North End in our time because the Jewish, Ukrainian, and Polish kids all played together."

■ Originally the Hebrew Free School from 1922 until the late 1940s, the building at 220 Andrews was Western Glove Works in the 1950s. • Credit: Photo by Russ Gourluck

Many instances of apparent discrimination can be viewed as the kind of name-calling that typically goes on amongst children. Morley Rypp sums it up: "We fought, but we got along. We called them names, they called us names, but it really wasn't taken as a slur. There was no political correctness then." As one of only two or three Jewish students in a class of 30, Sid Green recalls, "They let me know that I was a Jew, sometimes in a hostile manner. But it was more overt than it was hurtful."

There were, however, incidents that went beyond childhood name-calling. Libby (Klein) Simon vividly recalls one day when she and her brother Matty were walking home from King Edward School. She was in grade one, Matty in grade two, and they became separated at an intersection. When she looked back, Matty was on the ground, a group of children had gathered around, and Matty was being kicked and punched. Fortunately, a teacher came along and intervened. Their parents transferred them to Aberdeen School, where there many more Jewish children.

(OPPOSITE) The Quality Grill at 1142 Main, which opened in the early 1950s, had an attached duplex at the rear where the owners lived. The restaurant had a full Chinese menu as well as such contemporary favourites as hot beef and hot turkey sandwiches with chips. It was known for its coconut cream pie. Gord MacDonald and his friends from Machray School regularly went to the Quality Grill for chips and gravy. The booths had remote juke boxes, and he remembers that one of them, if hit in just the right spot, played tunes for free.

(ABOVE) In 2009 the former site of Nordic's sat vacant and the former Sportsman's building housed an electrical contracting business.
• Credit: Photos by Russ Gourluck

THE ERA OF HANGOUTS

North End teenagers from the 1940s through the 1970s had a wide range of places where they and their friends could meet, including pool halls, restaurants, movie theatres, and community clubs. No longer shackled by the poverty that had prevented their parents from participating in social activities, these were teens with some spending money and some leisure time. Although the North End had developed a reputation as the "tough" part of Winnipeg, most teens had little fear of coming and going.

Main Street Attractions

Even though North End teenagers were willing to venture farther than their younger brothers and sisters, most chose to hang out in locations that were not very far from home. The three main areas in which the teens of several decades generally congregated were Main Street, Selkirk Avenue, and the Mountain and McGregor area.

Larry Fleisher, who grew up on Flora and later on Inkster, describes the practice as "kind of a distinction in turf. Certain people hung out in a certain area, and the other side was dominated by another group." Arlington or McGregor were dividing lines that people generally didn't cross. "There were some rumbles. I remember one time they met in St. John's Park and cleared the air."

The Pool Halls: Nordic's and Sportsman's

"When you went in there in the evening, the smoke was so heavy you could barely see people," Ben Hochman says. Located at 1410 Main at the corner of Atlantic, Nordic Lunch and Billiards was a popular hangout for young North Enders. It was basically an "all-guy" environment; Nordic's was no place for girls. There were always sharks willing to play for money, with names like "Johnny Zoomball," "Booze" (Bill Rusen), and "Coke" Lander (who loved Coca-Cola).

Manly Rusen and his friends spent "an awful lot of time" at Nordic's, often playing for money. The minimum age for pool was 16, so many kids carried notes supposedly written by their parents. Rusen remembers one incident when he was 14 and saw the police coming. He tried to exit by a bathroom window, but it was too small. Others hid under the pool tables. He explains that, in those days, police just took kids home and handed them over to their parents. Rusen periodically visited his Uncle Charlie the dentist to borrow money, and once, at the age of 15, "mortgaged" his bike for a $5.00 loan to pay his gambling debts by leaving it as security at a bicycle shop. Manly Rusen grew up to become a lawyer and a judge.

Boys often skipped out of school to hang out at Nordic's. Tom Halprin explains that he attended St. John's but "my education really took place at Nordic's." He spent more time at the pool room than going to classes.

John Marczyk's parents wouldn't allow him to enter Sportsman's. "It was a place for evil bike riders and people of bad repute, and no women would ever be seen there."

Sportsman's Lounge was located at 1395 Main Street at the corner of Bannerman in a building that had previously served as an Eaton's Groceteria during the 1940s and a Jewel Store in the 1950s. Gord MacDonald explains that Sportman's had smaller tables than Nordic's "so if you played at Nordic's on the big tables and then went to Sportsmen's, you'd play like a pro."

For Men Only: Toph's

A typical Friday evening routine for North End teens during the 1940s and 1950s was to "go to the show" at the College Theatre and then to hang out at some of the nearby attractions.

One of the most popular was officially named The College Shop, but it was generally known by the name of its owner: "Toph's." A few doors north of the College Theatre, Toph's, like the pool rooms, was a strictly-male hangout. The College Shop was almost like a private club for older teens; young teenagers weren't admitted. Regulars were able to buy hotdogs, hamburgers, and sandwiches on credit by writing their purchases in Toph's little black book. The honour system apparently worked and it's said that Toph was always paid what he was owed.

Decades later, Toph's is fondly remembered as a place where cigarettes could be purchased for two cents each by regulars who couldn't afford to pay a quarter for a whole package. Teens could stay as long as they liked and read the magazines on the racks as much as they wanted. Bill Jewell loved to stand in the aisles and sing. Select regulars were able to place bets on the races at Polo Park and to visit an upstairs apartment where a man named Freddy sold whiskey and ran poker games.

Manly Rusen, who describes the place as his second home when he was a teenager, was one of a group of former Toph's regulars who held a reunion in the 1980s, complete with t-shirts.

A neighbour to the College Theatre and The College Shop was College Drugs, owned by sports enthusiast Ernie Nelko. Ben Hochman remembers 15 or 20 teens crowded around a small black-and-white television in 1954 watching Roger Bannister break the 4-minute mile. Also nearby was College Music Store, where Danny Pollock bought sheet music from a

clerk named Len Cariou who went on to a Tony-winning career on Broadway.

"See you at 'The It'"

Another legendary spot for teens was This Is It – more commonly known as "The It," a snack shop located near Main and Machray. During the 1950s, older teens from St. John's Tech frequented the popular spot, while their younger brothers and sisters were relegated to the Hop-Inn at Main and Polson. "The It" was one of many hamburger joints in the area, but the cafe and the sidewalk in front were often mobbed by teens. Harry Kaplan explains that most would go in and purchase a Coke or a milkshake. Those with a little more cash had their hands stamped to gain admission to an exclusive back room.

Yanks Lunch and the Good Earth

Located side by side and about a block north of Nordic's, Yanks was a delicatessen and the Good Earth (which opened in the 1950s) was a Chinese restaurant. Both were magnets for teenagers.

Some teens hung out inside Yanks, which offered corned beef sandwiches as well as nips and chips (as burgers and fries were then called.) Most of the hanging out at The Good Earth was on the front sidewalk. "They didn't like us to go in. We were just kids," explains Marcia Schnoor.

For Gail (Rosner) Fine and her friends, Yanks and The Good Earth were "the places to meet the guys." Usually they hung around outside the restaurants on Friday evenings to watch boys come and go from Nordic's and to see who was cruising Main Street in their cars. On colder evenings, they went inside The Good Earth or Yanks and, because they were expected to order food, they pooled their money to order a communal plate of chips.

On some Friday evenings, the hordes of teenagers on the sidewalk outside The Good Earth caused people in the area to fear an imminent riot and call the police. Most of the time, the kids were more interested in talking, laughing, and eating sunflower seeds than rioting. As one teenager of the era describes it, there were so many sunflower seed shells on the sidewalk that it was like walking on eggshells.

For those who did have the money to go inside, The Good Earth offered the usual 1950s Chinese food standards – chop suey, fried rice, and sweet and sour ribs. Consomme for takeout orders came in a mickey bottle. They also served a memorable Boston Cream Pie.

Other Main Street Hangouts

A favourite of Danny Pollock's was Jack Frost's, an ice cream shop on the east side of Main. It was owned by Mel Spigelman. Ice cream cones were a dime.

■ The snack bar at the Main and Luxton streetcar barns became a teen hangout.
• Credit: Manitoba Transit Heritage Association

The streetcar barns on the east side of Main and Luxton had a snack bar that was open late at night, primarily to serve the drivers, but night-owl teens were allowed in. The prices were reasonable, light lunches like soup and sandwiches were available, and it was a place to buy cigarettes at two in the morning. An Economart occupies the site today. Mel Myers, who went on to become a labour lawyer, remembers hanging around the snack bar when he was about fifteen years of age listening to his older brother and friends, including Larry Zolf, Norm Mittleman, Aubrey Tadman, and Bill Jewell discuss almost any topic and argue well into the night. "I learned a lot of things about debating and women and politics there," he explains.

The Salisbury House at Main and Matheson opened on July 1, 1963 and quickly established its reputation as a North End landmark. "The North End Sals," as it's often called, became a place where teenagers gathered and, especially when it was open around the clock, the destination of bar patrons after closing time. John Marczyk hung out there with other early teens in the 1960s. He explains that the Sals staff didn't mind kids hanging out. "They never hustled anybody out of there. If adults came in, the kids made room and doubled up at tables. Things were different then. Young people respected adults, and adults had a lot of time for kids."

Mountain and McGregor

The intersection of Mountain and McGregor had two landmarks that attracted teens from the surrounding area. Julia Berschley remembers that Connie's Place had booths and stools upholstered in red leatherette that reminded her of car seats. The tables and booths had small "satellite" juke boxes that were connected to the main jukebox.

Mike Krevesky says Connie's was "like *Happy Days* on television," especially in the late 1950s and early 1960s when a few

■ Ed Koranicki became a father figure to some of the kids who hung out at his pool room. • Credit: U of M Archives, Tribune Collection, 25-687-13

motorcycle owners in the pre-biker-gang era regularly parked their machines nearby. He and his friends called the place "Mrs. B's" because it was owned by the Bohonos family, and he still salivates over the "Connie's Special" – two cheeseburgers, fries, and a milkshake for 45 cents. Connie's closed around 1970, and a reunion was held in the mid-1990s.

Krevesky's group was loyal to Connie's, but the Hi-Spot across the street at 586 Mountain had its own following. Julia Berschley describes it as "a favourite hangout, a place where we all felt safe." It was smaller than Connie's, with a counter, stools, and only about five booths. In the mid-1960s teens would nurse a coke and chips, sit around listening to the latest hits, and discuss which bands were appearing at local community club dances. Berschley reports that when gangs started to take over, other kids moved to the Sals. Richard Kurtz's father owned 50 percent of the Hi-Spot, so, being a teenager, he hung out at Connie's.

A favourite spot for Orysia Jackson in the 1950s was Poppy's Cafe at Mountain and Arlington. She describes Poppy as "a friendly fellow with a buzz cut and glasses who always sported a muscle shirt and an apron."

Selkirk Avenue Hangouts

Eddy's Place was formerly known as Al's Billiards and Kuzma's Billiards, a place where Sid Green learned to play snooker. In 1955, Eddy Koranicki bought the pool room, renamed it, and went on to become a North End legend. Located at Selkirk and

McKenzie, Eddy's was a favourite place for Isaac Newton High School students. Teens who lived east of Arlington rarely went to Eddy's.

His daughter Tracy Konopada (now the owner of Luda's Deli) explains that her dad was a barber and that the attached barbershop had its own entrance. Koranicki cut hair between pool shots. At first, Eddy's had two large pool tables, three smaller tables, and small snack bar at front, but Koranicki removed the small tables and expanded the restaurant.

Wayne Whalen started hanging out at Eddy's around 1960 when he was only 13 years old. He and his friends were underage, and Koranicki sometimes had to tell them to leave, but Eddy's became like a second home for Whalen and his friends, many of them from families damaged by violence, alcohol, and abuse.

■ Across the street from the Dairy Dell, a landmark billboard with three-dimensional cows' heads fascinated generations of kids. The fibreglass heads, each about 2 metres in height, were mounted on the billboard around 1950 and were taken down in 1986. • Photo © John Paskievich

"I wouldn't call us a gang. I would call us just friends. But we really bonded, probably because of our environment, our home life," he explains.

Ed Koranicki became a father figure for the kids. When some of them broke the house rules by swearing too much or breaking a pool cue, they had to do penance by stripping copper wire or filling bags with sweeping compound – two sidelines Koranicki ran to help make ends meet. "He was great with us, but he sort of educated us too," Whalen says. "He taught us that nothing's for nothing and if you don't behave you're gonna pay a price."

■ The former site of Standard Dairies and Derry Dell became a used furniture store.
• Credit: Photo by Russ Gourluck

In return for his caring, the boys helped renovate the restaurant and provided a kind of adolescent protection service for the premises. "You couldn't come in there and cause any trouble because you were taken care of by us," Whalen recalls. The police once advised Koranicki to bar the boys, but Eddy reportedly said the kids offered better protection than the police.

After Eddy Koranicki died in 1992, Eddy's was taken over by his wife Marie until the year 2000. It has changed hands twice since then. Fellow Selkirk Avenue merchant Sylvia Todaschuk remembers that Christmas carollers who strolled the avenue always ended up at Eddy's. "He liked to play his accordion."

Other North End Attractions

Among the most popular gathering spots for teens in the 1960s were the community clubs (later redubbed community centres)

and church halls where sock hops and dances fledgling bands were the training grounds for kids who grew up to be rock 'n roll stars. "Teen canteens" attracted young people from across the city to CUAC (Canadian Ukrainian Athletic Club – later renamed Sinclair Park) and CPAC (Canadian Polish Athletic Club.) Young Richard Kurtz played in a band named "The Newtones" at the Tower Theatre and at canteens at Atlantic United Church, appearing with Burton Cummings and Randy Bachman.

Clubs with ethnic and religious affiliations became the centre of the social activities of other teens. Young Judea, (on Selkirk Avenue East and later at Redwood and Main) provided social and sports outlets for Jewish teens. Roslyn Silver joined Young Judea in 1931 at the age of ten and describes the organization as a major means of socializing during the Depression. In fact, that's how she met her husband. Other Jewish youth movements were the Habonim and Hashomer Zionist Clubs.

Rumble at The Good Earth

Phillip Rosen recalls one Friday evening in the mid-1960s when a "group of guys — probably from East Kildonan" came over to pick a fight with the Jewish boys outside the Good Earth. The Jewish teens had been forewarned, so as many as 300 of them were waiting outside the restaurant "to defend the Jewish reputation of not fighting." The intruders drove by and didn't come back.

The YMHA (on Albert Street and later on Hargrave) attracted large numbers of Jewish North End teens and often introduced them to South End Jewish teens who became life-long friends and even spouses. Ron Devere regularly took the Salter trolley bus from his home on McAdam to the "Y" on Hargrave. "I grew up there. I learned to swim, played basketball, joined clubs, and went to camp. My social life was there." Weekend dances brought together teenagers from across the city.

Dairy Dell became a weekend tradition for numerous North End families. The ice cream store, located in Standard Dairies at Salter and Flora, drew youngsters and parents for triple-headed cones topped with a multitude of flavours of ice cream. When their grandfather treated them to ice cream at Dairy Dell, Carolyn Rickey's brothers, sisters and cousins asked for rainbow, but Carolyn couldn't stand rainbow and always asked for chocolate. Marcia Schnoor remembers long lineups on Sunday afternoons while she waited for her favourite – Neapolitan.

Gangs of the North End

During the late 1940s and into the early 1950s, the Dew Drop Gang struck fear into the hearts of Winnipeggers. Named for the Dew Drop Inn at Parr and Manitoba, a restaurant where they congregated to the dismay of the owner, the Dew Drops were known for their dapper attire: highly-polished leather dress shoes, "drape" trousers with knees as wide as 30 inches and ankles as narrow as 15, and stylish grey fedoras. The members, mostly aged 18 to 22, were known for crashing teen dances en masse (as many as 50 or 60 of them) and picking fights. They armed themselves with switchblade knives, brass knuckles, and even nickel-plated revolvers. Major police roundups were initiated in 1950, and the Dew Drop Gang was effectively disbanded by 1953.

One spinoff of the Dew Drops was a fashion trend, as male teens throughout the city emulated their style of dress. Bill Konyk admits that he was one of them, but hastens to point out that he stayed clear of the law. There were also some imitator gangs, such as the Hi-Spots who hung out at the inn with that name.

Ben Hochman describes gang activity as "just a small part of what was going on. Whatever they had done was just something that we would talk about amongst ourselves, but we never really felt that this was a real problem. It was something that you heard about but it wasn't going to happen on your turf."

Growing Up Ruggles

"We were easy to pick out in a crowd, and we became targets," Dennis Ruggles explains as he reflects on his childhood in the North End. The Ruggles family had moved from Halifax to Winnipeg in 1952 when Dennis was six years old, and they were one of only two Black families in the area of King Edward School. He and his older sister Marlene came home in tears almost daily, complaining to their mother that they were being taunted and beaten up because of their race and because of Marlene's epilepsy.

Their father, Gordon Ruggles, worked for the CPR as a porter and a conductor. His job kept him away from home much of the time, so parenting in the Pritchard Avenue home was mainly the responsibility of their strong-willed mother, Marge. After too many tearful after-school reports, Marge decreed, "Don't come home crying to me anymore or I'll give you something to cry about myself. Stand up for your rights and fight back."

Rumbles in the Sixties

Richard Kurtz remembers that there were rumbles but "when you had a guy down and you had won, you left him. If somebody got shot or if there was dope around, that was a big thing back then."

As the oldest brother, Dennis (who was known as Butchie) accepted the responsibility of seeing that his brothers and sisters weren't picked on. He and his siblings learned to fight back and quickly established the reputation of the Ruggles children as people who shouldn't be pushed around. The family grew to the point where there were seven brothers and three sisters and, as Dennis says, "The reputation just grew and grew."

During the 1960s and 1970s the name "Ruggles" was feared in the North End and throughout the city, and some of the boys appeared to thrive on their notoriety as local legends. But people who really knew the brothers viewed them differently. One woman who went to school with some of the boys insists, "I grew up with these guys. I wasn't afraid of them."

One of the prices of the reputation the Ruggles brothers acquired was that it attracted challengers. Dennis calls it "the Jesse James Syndrome – when you're the fastest draw, everybody want to take you on." He remembers being in the North End Sals on Friday evenings and seeing groups of young males swagger in, hoping to pick a fight with a Ruggles brother. A former classmate observes: "They wouldn't go looking for trouble. Trouble would come to them."

Some of the brothers had serious encounters with the law and served time. Gordon died in 1977 at the age of 26 in a cell at the Public Safety Building. The official explanation was that he hanged himself, but he was the third young man – all had been friends – to die there under similar circumstances within a six-month period. More than three decades later, some family members and friends remain unconvinced that the deaths were suicides.

The reputation of the Ruggles family generally excluded the positive directions that the lives of most of the brothers and sisters took. Dennis was an outstanding athlete, playing baseball, hockey, and soccer, as well as football for the Winnipeg Hawkeyes and Weston Wildcats. After leaving left home at 19 and getting married at 22, he was a journeyman welder, worked in sales, and eventually retired after an 18-year career with Winnipeg Transit as a bus driver and as president and business agent of the Amalgamated Transit Union. He has been elected as a school trustee in his community and serves as a member of a provincial social services board. Richard (Dickie) retired after a lengthy career as an electrician with Winnipeg Hydro. One of the sisters has been a teaching assistant for more than 20 years, while another works with people with special needs.

■ North Enders came together in 1993
to keep the St. John's Library open.
• Credit: Courtesy Gord Mackintosh

3

SOCIAL ACTIVISM
POLITICS AND PEOPLE IN THE VILLAGE

The headquarters of the Manitoba branch of the Communist Party of Canada is on Selkirk Avenue. The front door and mailbox are painted red. • Credit: Photo by Russ Gourluck

A HISTORY OF POLITICAL INVOLVEMENT

Winnipeg's North End has a rich history of political involvement that began with the arrival of the earliest immigrants in the late 1800s. Over the decades, the area has been represented at various levels of government by a series of memorable figures, usually from the left side of the political spectrum.

■ From left, Ed Broadbent, Judy Wasylycia-Leis, reporter Gerald Flood, and David Orlikow on Main Street, ca 1985
• Credit: Courtesy Judy Wasylycia-Leis

The Cradle of Canadian Socialism

Although many of the early European immigrants arrived in Canada with few material possessions, they brought with them a tradition of political activism. Some had been involved in the Russian revolt of 1905, the Jewish workers movement, and other forms of political activity; others, after arriving in Canada, saw the need to become involved in politics to prevent the kind of persecution and oppression they had experienced in Europe; and still others shared an almost utopian vision of Canada's future and resolved to make their idealistic visions a reality. In most instances, the political philosophy that they embraced was socialism. Author Doug Smith, in his biography of Joseph Zuken, aptly refers to the North End as "the cradle of Canadian Socialism."

Reformists generally chose a relatively moderate approach, joining organizations like the Labour Party and the Independent Labour Party (ILP) that advocated increased government ownership of utilities, industry, transportation, and finance. The Labour Party and the ILP were the predecessors of the Co-operative Commonwealth Federation (CCF), and eventually of the New Democratic Party (NDP).

Those with more radical views supported such Marxist organizations as the innocuously-named Socialist Party of Canada, the Social Democratic Party, the Workers' Party of Canada, and the Communist Party of Canada.

Representatives in Ottawa

Although the name and the boundaries of federal ridings encompassing the North End have changed since the riding of Winnipeg North was first established in 1924, sections of the North End have been represented in the House of Commons primarily by a series of ILP, CCF, and NDP politicians.

Abraham Albert "A. A" Heaps

One of the leaders of the 1919 Winnipeg General Strike, A. A. Heaps was elected to the House of Commons in 1925 as a Labour Party candidate. Because the Liberals, led by William Lyon McKenzie King, were able to form only a minority government, Heaps and ILP MP J. S. Woodworth agreed to support them and, in return, the Liberals agreed to establish Canada's first old-age pension plan. As one of only a few Jewish Members of Parliament, Heaps tried to persuade the government to admit Jewish World War Two refugees.

Charles Stephen Booth

A lawyer and military officer, Charles Booth was elected as a Liberal candidate in 1940 to represent Winnipeg North.

Alistair McLeod Stewart

An accountant by profession, Scottish-born Alistair Stewart was first elected to represent Winnipeg North in 1945, then re-elected in 1949, 1953, and 1957, all as a CCF candidate.

Murray Smith

As the Conservative Party candidate in Winnipeg North, lawyer Murray Smith defeated Alistair Stewart in the 1958 federal election. This was part of the "Diefenbaker Sweep" that saw the Conservatives win a huge majority in the House of Commons.

David Orlikow

During a 43-year political career that evolved from the Winnipeg School Board to Winnipeg City Council to the Manitoba Legislature to the House of Commons, David Orlikow won 18 consecutive elections. He was first elected to the House of Commons in 1962 as a CCF (later NDP) candidate, where he served until his defeat in 1988. A pharmacist by profession, David Orlikow was born in the North End in 1918 and attended the Workmen's Circle (a Jewish secular school), St. John's High

School, and the University of Manitoba. Orlikow was respected by generations of North Enders for his dedication to constituency cases. He refused to delegate constituents' inquiries and problems to aides, insisting on personally making phone calls and writing letters. David Orlikow died in 1998.

■ David Orlikow, 1965
• Credit: U of M Archives, Tribune Collection, Personality Files

■ Coffee with a constituent • Credit: Courtesy Judy Wasylycia-Leis

Rey Pagtakhan

In the 1988 general election, David Orlikow was defeated by Liberal candidate Dr. Rey Pagtakhan, the first Philippine-born Canadian to be elected to the House of Commons. He was re-elected for Winnipeg North in 1993, and then for the redistributed riding of Winnipeg North-St. Paul in 1997 and 2000. A medical doctor by profession, Pagtakhan was named Secretary of State (Asia Pacific) in 2001, the first MP from North Winnipeg to become a cabinet minister in 75 years. He later became Minister of Veterans Affairs, the Senior Minister for Manitoba, and Minister of Western Economic Diversification.

Judy Wasylycia-Leis

Judy Wasylycia-Leis, who had been elected in Winnipeg North Centre in 1997, ran in 2004 against Rey Pagtakhan in Winnipeg North (the result of the redistribution of North Centre) and was elected. She was subsequently re-elected to Parliament in 2006 and 2008. Prior to moving to the House of Commons, Wasylycia-Leis was elected as the MLA for St. Johns in 1986, subsequently re-elected in 1988 and 1990, and served as Minister of Culture, Heritage, and Recreation in the government of Howard Pawley.

Members of the Legislature

Most of the North End is currently included within three provincial constituencies: Point Douglas on the southeast, St. Johns on the northeast, and Burrows on the west. As is the case with federal electoral ridings, a series of redistributions over the years has seen changes in the boundaries of constituencies.

The name "Point Douglas" was first applied to a provincial electoral constituency from 1969 until 1978. It was eliminated in 1978, then resurrected in 1989 with sections of Burrows, Logan, and

■ Manitoba's first Jewish MLA, Hart Green (shown in 1926) was elected at the age of 24 and represented the North End from 1911 to 1914. • Credit: Jewish Heritage Centre, JM 40

(LEFT) The political career of Saul Cherniack (shown in 1969) followed in the footsteps of his first cousin, David Orlikow, as a school trustee (Orlikow had followed Cherniack's sister Mindel Sheps), city council member, and MLA. A lawyer by profession, Cherniack represented St. Johns from 1962 to 1981 and served as Minister of Finance during the Schreyer years. He has been inducted into the Order of Canada and the Order of Manitoba.
• Credit: Archives of Manitoba, Saul Cherniack 1

(RIGHT) Gord Mackintosh was first elected to represent St. Johns Constituency in 1993. He was Minister of Justice and Attorney General with responsibility for the Manitoba Public Insurance Corporation from 1999 to 2006 and then was appointed Minister of Family Services. Mackintosh, a lawyer by profession, previously worked for both the Canadian and Manitoba Human Rights Commissions and as Deputy Clerk of the Manitoba Legislature.
• Credit: Courtesy Gord Mackintosh

St. Johns. During those periods, both MLAs were New Democrats: Donald Malinowski from 1969 to 1981, and George Hickes from 1990 until the present time.

St. Johns (which, unlike most other applications of the name, has no apostrophe) has elected CCF and NDP candidates consistently since its formation in 1958 – David Orlikow, Saul Cherniack, Donald Malinowski (after Point Douglas was eliminated), Judy Wasylycia-Leis, and Gord Mackintosh.

Burrows, since its establishment in 1957, has been represented primarily by a CCF/NDP MLAs (John Hawryluk, Ben Hanuschak, Conrad Santos, and, currently, Doug Martindale) but the constituency has had two Liberal MLAs:

Mark Smerchanski (1962-1966) and William Chornopyski (1988-1990).

Civic Politics

Through the decades, Winnipeg's North End has been represented by some of the most effective – and some of the most colourful – elected officials at the municipal level.

In the book *The Jews in Manitoba*, Rabbi Arthur Chiel reports that the first Jewish alderman to be elected in Winnipeg was Moses Finkelstein in 1904. He represented North Winnipeg and, in his campaign, emphasized sanitation and construction in the North End. He committed himself to work for more bridges and additional paved streets and sidewalks.

One the most colourful individuals ever to sit on Winnipeg City Council, Slaw Rebchuk became known as "the Mayor of the North End." A 1925 graduate of St. John's Tech, Rebchuk served at city hall from 1950 to 1978 and was a member of 68 committees. The former Salter Street Bridge was renamed in his honour in 1984.

First elected to the Legislature in to represent Burrows in 1990, Doug Martindale has served as NDP caucus chair and as Legislative Assistant to the Minister of Family Services and Housing. A United Church Minister, Doug Martindale worked for ten years at the North End Community Ministry (formerly Stella Mission.) • Credit: Courtesy Doug Martindale

■ (LEFT TO RIGHT) Jacob Penner, shown in 1955, was a highly respected city councillor. • Credit: U of M Archives, Tribune Collection, Personality Files

Joseph Zuken (undated photo) • Credit: U of M Archives, Tribune Collection, Personality Files

Slaw Rebchuk (shown in 1962) became known for "Rebchukisms" — mixed metaphors that encouraged listeners, including the media, to pay very close attention to everything he said. One example: "You've buttered your bread. Now lie in it." • Credit: U of M Archives, Tribune Collection, Personality Files

A North End tradition of electing far-left politicians to City Hall began in 1926 with the election of William Kolisnyk as an alderman. Believed to be the first Communist elected to any political post in North America, Kolisnyk, who had emigrated from Ukraine with his parents, was re-elected in 1928. He was an advocate for better transportation services for the North End, improved unemployment relief benefits, and the right – suspended after the Winnipeg General Strike – for civic employees to unionize. Kolisnyk made an unsuccessful bid in 1932 to win a seat in the Legislature as a Communist candidate, and was interred with other Communists by the federal government during World War Two.

One of the longest-serving and most respected city councillors was Jacob Penner. First elected in 1934, he served almost continuously until 1961. Penner, who was born in Ukraine and came to Manitoba in 1904, was involved in founding the Socialist Party of Canada and the Social Democratic Party. He joined the Communist Party in 1921. A distinguished figure, Jacob Penner was almost always seen wearing a conservative three-piece suit, a dress shirt and tie, a well-blocked fedora, and sometimes spats. His son, Roland Penner, who was elected to the Provincial Legislature to represent the Fort Rouge constituency in 1981 and 1986 and served as Attorney General and

Minister of Education, tells about growing up "Red" in Winnipeg's North End in his 2007 book *A Glowing Dream: A Memoir*.

Jack Blumberg

In one of the longest careers in Winnipeg political history, John "Jack" Blumberg was first elected as an alderman endorsed by the Dominion Labour Party in 1919. Later running as a CCF candidate, he served on City Council for a total of 37 years. Blumberg was born in England in 1892, stopped in Winnipeg in 1910 on his way to Australia, and stayed for the rest of his life.

■ Jack Blumberg, 1956 • Credit: U of M Archives, Tribune Collection, PC18-10032-006

■ (RIGHT) William Ross, 1976
• Credit: U of M Archives, Tribune Collection, Personality Files

(FAR RIGHT) During his unsuccessful campaign to become Mayor of Winnipeg in 1969, Joseph Zuken chartered a transit bus and had it run on a regular route so he could chat with voters.
• Credit: U of M Archives, Tribune Collection, PC18-10699-007, Ron Dobson photo.

He worked as a streetcar motorman for the Winnipeg Electric Railroad and became the chairman of the Greater Winnipeg Transit Commission. Jack Blumberg died in 1961. A municipal golf course bears his name.

Joseph Zuken

The political career of Joseph Zuken is remarkable not only because he served as an elected official for four decades but also because he continued to be elected as a Communist during the Cold War. In fact, in the early 1970s, Zuken was the only Communist to occupy an elected political position in North America.

Joe Zuken was first elected to the Winnipeg School Board in 1941 and he continued as a school trustee until 1961, championing such contentious innovations as kindergarten classes and free textbooks for all students. He was elected to Winnipeg City Council in 1961 and, until his retirement in 1983, Zuken fought for measures that he believed would benefit his low-income North End constituents, such as low-rental housing. Believing in the need for a hospital to serve the North End, he was a key figure in the lengthy campaign to establish the Seven Oaks Hospital. His life has been chronicled in *Joe Zuken, Citizen and Socialist* by Doug Smith.

Born in Ukraine in 1912, Joseph Zuken came to Canada with his family when he was two years old, living at the corner of Alfred and McGregor. He attended Strathcona and Isaac Newton Schools, as well as St. John's Tech. He was a lawyer by profession. His brother, Cecil Zuken changed his name to William Cecil Ross, adopting the surname of his wife Anne Ross for the safety of his family. William Ross was a two-term school trustee in Winnipeg and leader of the Communist Party in Manitoba from 1948 to 1991. Joe Zuken died in 1986, and William Ross in 1998.

Leave the Grandchildren

Saul Cherniack was born in the family home at 788 Flora Avenue in 1917, moving four years later to 326 College Avenue. In 1929, his parents built a three-storey house at 333 St. John's Avenue, and that house remained the home of Saul Cherniack until 2003. After he and his wife Sybil were married in 1938 and their sons Lawrie and Howard were born, they continued to live with his parents. One day Sybil Cherniack mentioned to her mother-in-law "We think we ought to move out." The joking reply was, "You can go, but leave the grandchildren."

The People's Co-op Creamery at 610 Dufferin and McGregor closed in the mid-1990s. • Credit: Archives of Manitoba, People's Co-operative Collection

(TOP) Home delivery was a popular service of People's Co-op. Pictured are an early horse and wagon (undated photo), drivers with a truck in 1936, and a driver and truck in 1952 at the creamery loading dock. • Credit: Archives of Manitoba, People's Co-operative Collection

A Dairy with a Difference

Although the People's Co-op was known by many Winnipeggers for its signature cream cheese and sour cream, it was much more than a dairy. It was a North End icon based on left-wing activism and the philosophy of the co-operative movement. People's Co-op began in 1928 as a small coal and fuel yard, later expanding into dairy products and lumber. The dairy initially offered only milk and cream, but soon buttermilk, sour cream, cottage cheese, and butter were added and proved to be particularly appealing to European immigrants. The cream cheese, introduced in 1936, was made from a recipe that plant superintendent John Krall brought from Switzerland, and was a favourite in cheesecake recipes and for serving with freshly-baked bagels. People's Co-op sour cream was considered by many to be the ultimate accompaniment for perogies.

In 1992, the assets of the co-operative were sold to the employees, but the free-enterprise competition that People's Co-op had faced for decades finally prevailed. The business was purchased by Dairyland in 1994. After more than six decades, the dairy was demolished and People's Co-op was no more.

The story of this unique blend of political idealism and everyday business has been told with affection by Jim Morochuk and Nancy Kardash in their book *The People's Co-op: The Life and Times of a North End Institution*. The records of People's Co-op are available at the Archives of Manitoba and include oral history interviews with employees, business records, and photographs.

■ Bill and Mary Kardash ca 1945 with son Ted and daughter Nancy. • Credit: Courtesy Nancy Kardash

William Kardash

Prior to becoming an elected official in Winnipeg, William Kardash participated in the Spanish Civil War as a member of the MacKenzie-Papineau Battalion, a group of Canadians volunteers who travelled to fight for the republican cause against General Franco`s fascist forces. Kardash lost a leg in the conflict.

William Kardash was the general manager of the People's Co-operative from 1948 to 1982 and served as the organization's long-time president. He was elected to the Manitoba Legislature in 1941 to represent the constituency of Winnipeg North, and then was re-elected in 1945, 1949, and 1953. As Doug Martindale, the MLA for Burrows observed in a tribute to Kardash following his death in 1997, "He was a member of the Communist Party and unabashedly a Communist. He would make no apology for that. He was proud of his political beliefs and stood by them and defended them throughout his entire life." William Kardash's records, including speeches, correspondence, and party literature, are available in the Archives of Manitoba.

Mary Kardash

Nancy Kardash describes her mother as "a modest and down to earth person" who enjoyed gardening, listening to music, household work, and trying new recipes. Mary Kardash, like her husband, was a Communist politician in North End Winnipeg, serving as a trustee on the Winnipeg School Board during the 1970s and 1980s. She was very active in the peace movement, involved in the women's movement, taught the Ukrainian language to children and the English language to immigrant women, helped organize children's summer camps, and wrote articles that were published in English and Ukrainian.

"I don't know how they did it," Nancy Kardash comments as she reflects on the amount of time her busy parents were able to devote to their children, exposing them to theatre, music, and cultural activities at the Ukrainian Labour Temple. To assist, grandparents and a circle of friends and acquaintances lived within walking distance of the Kardashes' Redwood Avenue home.

After Mary Kardash died in 1994, a child care centre on Polson Avenue was renamed in her honour.

Feeding Ferdele

During the 1950s, Co-op milk was delivered to homes by horse-drawn wagons. Lillian Mendelsohn and her friends sometimes fed their milkman's horse, which they had nicknamed "Ferdele" (a Yiddish diminutive for "little horse"). Mendelsohn recalls that the milkman was very protective of the horse, especially when some of the other neighbourhood kids teased it.

Becoming a Lawyer

Joseph Alter Cherniack had been a watchmaker in Russia, an occupation in which he continued when he first arrived in Winnipeg. It was a disagreement with his landlord at his place of business that inspired Cherniack to decide to become a lawyer. The dispute went to court and the lawyer who represented the landlord demonstrated such limited competence that Cherniack concluded that he too could be a lawyer. While he attended St. John's College to obtain a Bachelor of Arts degree, he sold insurance and kept books for storekeepers and his wife worked as a seamstress. Mr. Cherniack graduated in law in 1918.

• Credit: Jewish Heritage Centre JM1741

Growing Up in Politics

One vivid memory that Myron Shatulsky retains from his childhood is the visit he paid to his father in an internment camp in 1942. Matthew Shatulsky, a leader in the Ukrainian Labour-Farmer Temple Association, was one of many left-wing political figures jailed at the beginning of World War Two for alleged sympathy with Russia. Young Myron, only twelve years old at the time, travelled to Hull, Quebec in the care of the wives of some of the other detainees because his own mother was unable to get time off from work. He recalls meeting his father in a small office in the prison while a commandant sat nearby and listened. The entire conversation was in Ukrainian, so it's unlikely that the guard understood any of it. When the time of the short visit was up, the tearful boy approached the commandant and begged him, "Let my Daddy come home."

Asked how he first became involved in politics, Saul Cherniack matter-of-factly replies, "I was born into it." His

■ Myron Shatulsky with a bust of his father in the Ukrainian Labour Temple in 2008. • Credit: Photo by Russ Gourluck

The Sherbrook-McGregor Overpass

Although both were advocates for the North End, novice councillor Lawrie Cherniack and political veteran Joe Zuken found themselves disagreeing in the early 1970s over the issue of an overpass that would provide an additional traffic route across the CPR mainline by connecting Sherbrook and McGregor Streets. Zuken was adamant that failure to provide this corridor was yet another indication of the city's neglect of the North End. Cherniack described the plan as "giving up to the car and the suburbs." The controversial concept was eventually quietly dropped by City Council.

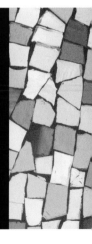

parents, he explains, were active socialists in Russia and were jailed for being at a meeting where contraband (socialist) literature was available. His father, Joseph Alter Cherniack, arrived in Winnipeg from Russia in 1905 and quickly became involved in community and political activities, including the establishment of the Jewish Radical School, the Jewish Welfare Fund, and the Winnipeg League for Yiddish. Saul Cherniack's own political career saw him elected to school board, city council, and the Manitoba Legislature.

Lawrie Cherniack spent many hours as a boy licking envelopes in the Main Street election rooms of MPs Alistair Stewart and David Orlikow. Shortly after he was elected as a city councillor in 1971 his father, Saul Cherniack, gave him some practical advice. "If you don't get a profession, then as a politician you will always do what people want you to do rather than what you should be doing." Realizing that he needed a profession to fall back on, rather than being driven by the fear of defeat, Lawrie Cherniack returned to university and became a lawyer.

Nancy Kardash remembers some advice she received from her mother as the daughter of not one but two self-declared Communists at the height of the Cold War in the 1950's and early 1960s. "You need to set a good example. People are watching you," Mary Kardash cautioned. As she reflects on her elementary school days, Nancy Kardash recalls occasional taunts like "Go back to Russia!" or "You Commie!" but, she explains, "We were just kids. We all got along, and I never felt any ostracism."

"The North End was ours."

As a child, Nancy Kardash loved to play in the People's Co-op fuel yard at Battery and Pritchard where her maternal grandfather, Myron Kostaniuk, was the manager. Her grandparents lived in a house on the same site, and her grandmother was constantly wiping away coal dust. On her block of Redwood between Parr and McKenzie there were a hundred children, and each evening as darkness began to descend, mothers opened the front doors and sang out the names of their children as a reminder that it was time to come in. Kardash recalls the sense of freedom that she and her friends enjoyed. "There was a sense that the North End was ours. We used to say that our yard went from our place on Redwood over to my uncle's place on St. John's and over to our grandparents' place at the fuel yard. That was our territory."

Northbound motorists on the Slaw Rebchuk Bridge are welcomed to the North End by a sign painted on the roof shingles of Nepon Auto Body. The business's message was supplemented in the late 1990s by a neatly-lettered piece of graffiti. The company's owner has left the difficult-to-remove socialist slogan and finds that some customers interpret it to mean that Nepon is a customer-centered business. • Credit: Photo by Russ Gourluck

NORTH ENDERS

By the 1970s, Winnipeg's North End had gained a new respect, not only among other Winnipeggers but also in the view of people in the outside world. By then it had become obvious that the children and grandchildren of the poor and uneducated immigrants who first settled in the North End had fulfilled their families' dreams of New World success.

Arts and Entertainment

Allan Blye

■ Allan Blye (shown in 1982) grew up on Selkirk Avenue. • Credit: Jewish Heritage Centre, JM2335

Born in Winnipeg in 1937, Allan Blye grew up in a small house on Selkirk Avenue near Gunn's Bakery and Saidman's Seeds. His career as a singer, which had its roots at Tamud Torah, Machray School, and St. John's Tech, blossomed when he appeared as the replacement for Bob Goulet on the CBC television show *General Electric Showtime*. But Blye became best known as a television producer and writer, with credits for such chart-toppers as *The Smothers Brothers Comedy Hour*, *The Andy Williams Show*, and *The Sonny and Cher Comedy Hour*.

Barney Charach

Barney Charach grew up in the house behind his father's barber shop at 228 Dufferin. At the time, six members of the Charach family were barbers in the North End but Barney chose photography as his career. He has been responsible for

University of Manitoba graduation photos for more than six decades and has photographed generations of grads at city high schools, including St. John's, as well as countless North End weddings. He was awarded an honorary high school diploma by St. John's High School in 2004.

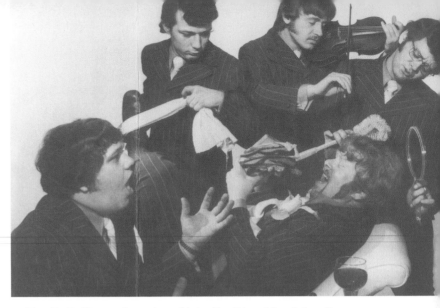

■ The D-Drifters played rock'n'roll with a Ukrainian flavour. • Credit Courtesy Dave Roman

The D-Drifters

The first bar that the D-Drifters played in Winnipeg was the Lincoln Motor Hotel on McPhillips. The group had just completed a late-1960s tour with the popular duo of Mickey and Bunny and attracted so many eager fans that the crowd broke down the doors. All North Enders, brothers Dave and Tony Roman grew up on Arlington, while Yogi (Ihor) Klos and Mike Klym spent their early years on Redwood. Described as "the creators of Ukrainian rock'n'roll," the D-Drifters still perform periodically at Winnipeg casinos and other venues.

Ed Evanko

The son of Ukrainian immigrants, Ed Evanko, born in 1941, first sang professionally at Rainbow Stage and, after training and performing in Britain, hosted *The Ed Evanko Show* on CBC Television in the late 1960s. His Broadway career included roles in *Canterbury Tales* and *Rex*, he recorded several albums, and he appeared on a number of television series including *Ryan's Hope* and *Third Rock from the Sun*. After a career in music and theatre that spanned four decades, Ed Evanko entered theological training and returned to Manitoba as Father Edward Evanko to serve as an itinerant Roman Catholic priest in rural communities.

■ Ed Evanko, 1966 • Credit: U of M Archives, Tribune Collection, Personality Files

Burton Cummings

One of the most famous North Enders in recent decades, Burton Cummings grew up on Bannerman Avenue. To some extent, Cummings' musical career began at St. John's High School where he and some schoolmates formed a group called the Deverons. In St. John's perennial Gilbert and Sullivan productions, Cummings gravitated to the lead roles and, because of his obvious talent, was rarely reprimanded for skipping operetta rehearsals to attend garage practices with his band. A regular at Sportsmen's Billiards and the North End Salisbury House – he's now one of the owners of the iconic string of restaurants – 18-year-old Burton Cummings joined The Guess Who in 1965 when the keyboardist position came open. The downtown Walker (Odeon) Theatre and a community centre at Arlington and Bannatyne have been renamed in his honour, and Cummings' loyalty to his North End roots has remained strong.

Harry Freedman

Born in Poland in 1922, Harry Freedman moved to Winnipeg with his family when he was nine years old and attended Aberdeen, Machray, and St. John's. He worked for a period of time as an usher and then an assistant manager at the Palace Theatre on Selkirk Avenue. Although his early interests were in art, Freedman began clarinet lessons at age 18 and went on to play English horn and oboe with the Toronto Symphony Orchestra for 24 years. Beginning in the 1970s, Harry Freedman concentrated on composing classical music. He died in 2005.

Monty Hall

Born Monte Halperin in 1921 in Winnipeg, Monty Hall achieved world-wide fame as the host and co-producer of *Let's Make a Deal* and has been inducted into the Order of Canada and the Order of Manitoba. Hall grew up in the North End (later in Elmwood) while working as a young boy in his father's butcher shop. After graduating from St. John's High School, the financial generosity of garment manufacturer Max Freed enabled Hall to earn a BSc degree from the University of Manitoba. Despite his high academic record, the institution's quota system prevented him, as a Jew, from entering the Faculty of Medicine.

John Hirsch

When John Hirsch, age 17, was showed a map of Canada by Canadian Jewish Congress representatives in Hungary and asked him where he wanted to live, he pointed at Winnipeg. It was a place about which he knew nothing but, because it was in the middle of the continent, he assumed it was "safe." Part of a group of Jewish orphans who had been displaced by the Holocaust, the emaciated Hirsch arrived in Winnipeg in 1947 and was taken into the home of Sasha and Pauline Shack. Although he spoke Hungarian and some German, his English was limited to a few swear words. After receiving credit for his Hungarian schooling, John Hirsch attended St. John's High School, graduating at the age of 19, and the University of Manitoba, receiving a BA in English Literature and Philosophy in 1952. His involvement in the Winnipeg drama community became legendary:

■ (LEFT TO RIGHT) Born in Point Douglas, Hunky Bill became Canada's Perogy King. • Credit: Courtesy Mark Konyk

Henry Kalen, 1977 • Credit: U of M Archives, Tribune Collection, PC18-10254-006, photo by Jon Thordarson

John Paskievich, 2010 • Credit: Photo by John Whiteway

the Winnipeg Little Theatre, CBC, Rainbow Stage, Theatre 77, and finally, in 1958, the first artistic director of the newly-formed Manitoba Theatre Centre. John Hirsch died in Toronto in 1989.

Henry Kalen

Although he chose architecture as his profession, Henry Kalen, who was born in 1928 to working class parents in the North End, decided that photography was his passion. More than 400 postcards published by his company from 1973 to 1990 sold over 12 million copies. *Henry Kalen's Winnipeg*, a full-colour collection of photographs of Winnipeg landmarks, appeared regularly on the local best-seller list for several years after it was published in 2000. Following his death in 2004, a second book on which he had been working was completed in his memory by family members and friends. *Henry Kalen's Manitoba* was published in 2008.

"Hunky Bill" Konyk

"The man who made perogies famous," "Hunky Bill" Konyk was born in 1931 on Euclid Avenue in Point Douglas and attended school at Norquay, Aberdeen, and St. John's. He worked for CP Telegraphs in Winnipeg until 1956, then for two years in Chicago as a freelance sports reporter. Konyk returned to Winnipeg to work for radio station CKY until 1966 before moving to Vancouver. It was then that he began shipping Ukrainian food – including Naleway perogies – from Winnipeg and marketing them under the Hunky Bill label. Although Bill Konyk speaks accent-free English and is far from fluent in Ukrainian ("I know enough to get me into trouble," he chuckles) he developed the sometimes-controversial Hunky Bill character ("Hello Marushka!") for television commercials promoting the plastic perogy makers that bear his name. A 1982 B.C. Board of Inquiry dismissed a complaint from the Ukrainian Canadian Professional Association that the use of the word "Hunky" was offensive to people of Ukrainian origin, and a subsequent appeal to the B.C. Supreme Court upheld the decision.

Perogy Races

Kern-Hill Furniture's Andy Hill tells how Hunky Bill periodically visited the Main Street furniture store to stage perogy-making races in competition with older women to see who could make more perogies faster. The "Babas," ostensibly protesting the use of a plastic device to shape and seal the doughy delicacies, relied on the traditional manual approach, and crowds of 40 to 50 spectators gathered around. Kern-Hill remains the Manitoba distributor of Hunky Bill merchandise.

■ Probably one of the North End's most colourful personalities, Nick Hill became famous for his fast-paced radio commercials and their inevitable concluding catchphrase "C'mon down!" Hill and his business partner John Kernicki first opened Manitoba Television at Dufferin and Derby in 1953, moved to Main and Flora, and then relocated to a former North End Furniture store at 843 Main Street. The name of their business changed to Kern-Hill Furniture. Eventually Hill bought out Kernicki, and at one point, Hill found a legal loophole that enabled him (to the consternation of co-operative movement advocates) to establish the business as a co-op. Nick Hill was a strong supporter of Rainbow Stage, Big Brothers, and the YMHA. Nick Hill died in 2003, and his three sons carry on the business, which has relocated to 660 Nairn Avenue. Number One Son Andy continues the tradition of the "C'mon down" radio spots and, as he did with his father, uses a stopwatch (now upgraded to digital), no script, and a mile-a-minute delivery that continues until the exact moment that time runs out. "There's no such thing as retakes," Andy adds. • Credit: Mural by Michel Saint Hilaire and Mandy van Leeuwen, photo by Mandy van Leeuwen

Morley Meredith

Morley Meredith (Margolis) graduated from St. John's High School and attended the University of Manitoba with the intention of studying medicine. While at university, he performed regularly as a recitalist and recorded for the CBC. His New York debut was in 1956, and he sang in leading roles in *Gentlemen Prefer Blondes* with Carol Channing and *Christine* with Maureen O'Hara. Before his death in 2000 at the age of 77, Meredith had sung 40 roles in 31 seasons at the Metropolitan Opera.

John Paskievich

Born in 1947 in Austria and displaced by the Second World War, John Paskievich came to Winnipeg at the age of five with his family and lived in the North End. A graduate of the University of Winnipeg, he studied photography and film at Ryerson Polytechnic in Toronto. Paskievich has published two books of black and white photographs depicting ordinary North End Winnipeggers going about their daily lives: *A Place Not Our Own* (1978) and *The North End* (2007.) His first film, *Ted Baryluk's Grocery* (1982), done with Michael Mirus, uses still photos to explore the lives and aspirations of an aging immigrant storekeeper and his daughter.

Bert Pearl

One of the most popular shows on CBC radio from the late 1930s until well into the 1950s was *The Happy Gang*, a zany lunchtime variety show hosted by Bert Pearl. Its familiar opening, embedded in the memories of generations of listeners, featured the sound effect of a door knock, Pearl's voice asking "Who's there?" the choral response "It's the Happy Gang!" and Pearl's welcoming "Well, come on in!" Bert Pearl was born in 1913 and attended Aberdeen and St. John's. After *The Happy Gang* folded in 1959, Pearl went to Hollywood to write for Jimmy Durante and later was the musical director for Winnipegger Gisele MacKenzie. He died in Hollywood in 1986.

■ (ABOVE) Bert Pearl, 1972 • Credit: U of M Archives, Tribune Collection, Personality Files

(BELOW) David Steinberg (front centre) age 10. • Credit: David Steinberg official website.

David Steinberg

The son of a rabbi, David Steinberg, who was born in 1942, grew up near the intersection of Manitoba and Charles. He moved to Illinois as a teenager, attended the University of Chicago, and became part of the Second City Comedy Troupe. Steinberg's credentials in comedy are extensive, including appearances on *The Smothers Brothers Comedy Hour* (where his irreverent "sermons" reportedly contributed to the cancellation of the series) and *The David Steinberg Show*

(which helped launch the careers of John Candy and Martin Short.) David Steinberg's directorial work has included the feature film *Paternity* and episodes of *Seinfeld*, *Friends*, and *Curb Your Enthusiasm*. He has released four solo comedy albums, won two Emmys, and directed more than 300 commercials.

■ (LEFT) Jack Silverberg fulfilled his dream of becoming a teacher. • Credit: Courtesy Abe Anhang.

(RIGHT) Sybil Shack, 1966
• Credit: U of M Archives, Tribune Collection, Personality Files

Education

Arnold Naimark

Considered one of the foremost educational administrators in Canada, Arnold Naimark has had a distinguished career in education and medicine. He was physiology department head at the University of Manitoba's Faculty of Medicine in the 1960s, Dean of Medicine in the 1970s, and President and Vice-Chancellor of the University of Manitoba from 1981 to 1996. His community contributions have included serving as chair of the North Portage Development Corporation and on the boards of CancerCare Manitoba, the Sanatorium Board of Manitoba, and many other provincial and national bodies. He has been awarded the Orders of Manitoba and Canada.

Sybil Shack

Born in the family home behind a grocery store in 1911, Sybil Shack's career as an educator included classroom teaching in rural Manitoba and Winnipeg as well as serving as a principal in a series of Winnipeg schools between 1948 and 1976. An advocate for women's rights, Shack was the author of *Armed with a Primer*, *The Two-Thirds Minority*, and *Saturday's Stepchildren*. She was named a member of the Order of Canada and installed in Winnipeg's Hall of Fame. Sybil Shack died in 2004.

Jack Silverberg

After facing many challenges in his early years, Jack Silverberg went on to become one of the most legendary teachers in the history of St. John's High School. Born in 1910 in Polonska, Russia, his childhood memories included having to be careful walking down the street because of the chance of physical attacks, and having to hide under the floor of their home to escape being killed by Jew-hunting gangs. His father left for Canada in 1912 to prepare the way, and, in 1914, the family travelled across Europe (sometimes bribing border guards along the way) to reach Antwerp. Unfortunately, the day they were to board the ship for Canada, World War One began, and they had to trek all the way back to Polonska and wait eight years to try again.

As he grew up, young Jack Silverberg dreamed of becoming a teacher, but was told by school board officials in the 1930s that "his kind" (Jews) were not wanted. After graduating with a BA degree and completing teacher training at Normal School, Silverberg and several other Jewish teachers who could not find work in the public system opened a private school. A year later, he was accepted by the Winnipeg School Board. He became a teacher of mathematics and English at St. John's High School, where he was to stay for over twenty years. In an era when mathematics credits were required to enter university, Jack Silverberg's ability to explain algebra and geometry was the key to success for many students. For those who needed extra help or weren't enrolled in his classes, Silverberg provided private lessons after school and during summers.

He became the first Jewish principal in the Winnipeg public school system (at David Livingstone School) and served as assistant principal of Luxton School and Daniel MacIntyre Collegiate. After retirement, he was the principal of Joseph Wolinsky Collegiate for several years. Jack Silverberg died in Israel in 1987.

Law

Maxwell Cohen

Maxwell Cohen, born in Winnipeg in 1910, grew up on Machray Avenue east of Main Street, the most affluent area of the North End, and attended Machray School and St. John's Tech. He graduated in law at the University of Manitoba in

■ (LEFT) Samuel Freedman, 1978 • Credit: U of M Archives, Tribune Collection, Personality Files

(RIGHT) Sid Green, 1977 • Credit: U of M Archives, Tribune Collection, Personality Files

1934 and went on to study at Northwestern and Harvard. He began teaching at the Faculty of Law at McGill University in 1946 and was Dean of Law at McGill from 1964 to 1969. Cohen chaired five Canadian royal commissions (including the Special Committee on Hate Propaganda) and served as Canadian representative to the United Nations. He later became a judge at the International Court of Justice in The Hague. Maxwell Cohen died in 1988.

Samuel Freedman

Samuel Freedman, who arrived in Winnipeg in 1911 at the age of three and grew up on Stella Avenue and Aikins Street, described his family's financial position as "honourable poverty." They were poor, but so were most other North End families at the time. He attended Strathcona, Aberdeen, Isaac Newton, and St. John's Schools. A friendly and unpretentious man, Freedman graduated in law from the University of Manitoba in 1933 and established a number of precedents for Jewish Manitobans: the first Jewish president of the Manitoba Bar in 1951, the first Jewish judge in 1952, the first Jewish chancellor of the University of Manitoba in 1959, and the first Jewish Court of Appeal judge in 1960. From 1971 until 1983, he set the same precedent as chief justice of the Manitoba Court of Appeal. Samuel Freedman died in 1993.

■ Mary Kelekis with portraits of family members. 2010
• Photo by Russ Gourluck

Public Service

Sidney Green

Like many North End babies in 1929, Sid Green was born at home. He continued to live in the same house at 716 Selkirk Avenue for the first 22 years of his life. As a young law student, Green articled with Joe Zuken, and he began his political career as an unsuccessful NDP candidate in the Winnipeg South federal riding in 1962. Later that year he was elected to Metro Council, and in 1966 became the NDP MLA for the provincial Inkster constituency. After failed bids against Russ Paulley and Ed Schreyer to become the party's leader, Green became a cabinet minister in the Schreyer government. Always an outspoken and independent thinker, Sid Green resigned from the NDP caucus in 1979 and formed the Progressive Party in 1981. The Progressives, with Green as leader, were unable to gain any seats in subsequent general elections, and the party was dissolved in 1995. Sid Green's memoirs, *Rise & Fall of a Political Animal*, were published in 2003.

Mary Kelekis

A member of the family behind the iconic restaurant, Mary Kelekis has found time in her busy career for extensive volunteer involvements, including being a founding member of Folklorama and the first woman president of the Manitoba Restaurant Association. Kelekis has served as the Vice-President of the

■ Saul Miller, 1973 • Credit: U of M Archives, Tribune Collection, Personality Files

(RIGHT) Anne Ross was the Executive Director of Mount Carmel Clinic for 37 years • Credit: Jewish Heritage Centre, undated photo

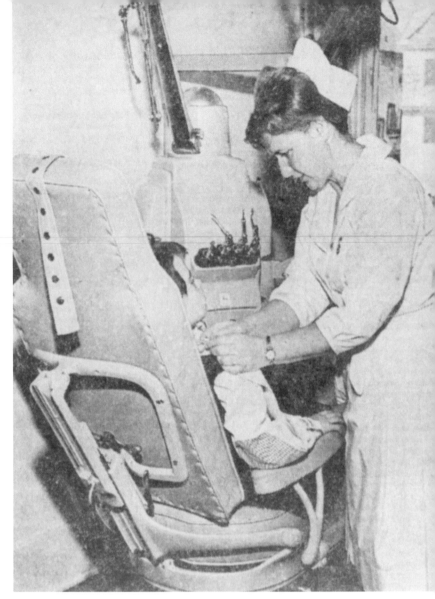

Children's Aid Society, the first woman president of the YMCA in Western Canada, and an honorary member of the Misericordia Foundation Board. She was presented with the Order of Manitoba in 2000 and, in 2002 she received the Queen's Anniversary Medal and the Canadian Confederation Medal.

Saul Miller

Born in 1917, Saul Miller grew up in the North End, where his parents operated the People's Book Store on Main Street, and attended Peretz School and St. John's High School. As an adult, he lived in West Kildonan, where he served as a school trustee and subsequently as mayor. Miller was the Member of the Legislature for Seven Oaks from 1966 to 1981, where he served in a number of ministerial positions in the Schreyer government, including education, urban affairs, health, and finance. A sincere and soft-spoken man, Saul Miller died in 1993.

Bernard Ostry

Bernard Ostry lived on Machray Avenue as a child, attended Luxton School, and graduated in 1942 from St. John's Tech. Although he lived a block away from Sylvia Knelman and the two attended some of the same classes at school, it wasn't until the pair were studying in London, England that they became close and decided to marry. A graduate of the London School of Economics, Ostry held senior positions as a civil servant and administrator, including serving as Ontario's Deputy Minister of Industry and Trade and CEO of TVOntario. He died in 2006.

Sylvia Ostry

Born in Winnipeg in 1927, Sylvia Knelman lived on Polson Avenue and St. Cross Street, attended Luxton and Machray Schools, and graduated in 1943 from St. John's Tech. She went on to study at McGill and Cambridge. Among her many accomplishments, Ostry was Canada's chief statistician (1972) and the first woman deputy minister in Canada's federal civil service (1975). She has received 18 honorary doctorates from across Canada.

Anne Ross

Chana Glasz (later Glass) was born in 1911 in a small Russian village and arrived in Winnipeg in 1921, several years after her father had come to Canada to earn money to send for his wife and children. She grew up on Aberdeen Avenue, attended Peretz School, and, unable to afford the cost of becoming a doctor, studied nursing at the Winnipeg General Hospital – the only Jewish student in a class of 60. She and William Ross (Cecil Zuken) were married in 1937.

Anne Ross became the first full-time employee of Mount Carmel Clinic in 1948, a career that lasted 37 years. As executive director, she implemented a holistic approach to health care that established Mount Carmel as a model across North America and frequently brought her into conflict with governments, doctors, and politicians. She wrote three books: *Pregnant and Alone* (1978); *Teenage Mothers, Teenage Fathers* (1982); and *Clinic with a Heart: The Story of Mount Carmel Clinic* (1998). Anne Ross died in 1998.

Sylvia Todaschuk

After being orphaned as an infant in rural Manitoba and growing up in poverty, Sylvia Todaschuk has become a successful entrepreneur and community leader. Todaschuk Sisters' Ukrainian Boutique, which she opened on Selkirk Avenue in 1985, is one of many expressions of the diverse cultural heritage of the North End as well as a tribute to Todaschuk's own background. In addition to her extensive volunteer involvement with the Ukrainian Canadian Congress, Folklorama, and the Ukrainian Professional and Business Club of Winnipeg, Sylvia Todaschuk has taken a number of leadership roles in North End affairs and

was a founding member of the North End Community Renewal Corporation. She served as president of the Selkirk Avenue BIZ for more than two decades, initiated historical walking tours, and helped organize the creation of murals along the avenue.

Abe Yanofsky

A chess prodigy at the age of 12 – he was the provincial champion and ranked fourth in Canada – Daniel Abraham "Abe" Yanofsky grew up on Manitoba Avenue. He was Canada's first Grandmaster. After his father's death, the 13-year-old boy became the family provider by working during the day and attending school at night. A lawyer by profession, Abe Yanofsky served as Mayor of the City of West Kildonan from 1961 to 1970 and a City of Winnipeg Councillor from 1971 to 1986. He died in 2000 at the age of 74 at the Seven Oaks Hospital, an institution he was instrumental in founding.

Ben Zaidman

Like many North End children during the Depression, Ben Zaidman, born in 1922, worked to help his family financially. He sold *The Winnipeg Tribune* on street corners, delivered groceries and blocks of ice, and left school when he was 15 to work in rural stores and send money home to his family. After

■ (LEFT) Sylvia Todaschuk is known to many North Enders as "the Queen of Selkirk Avenue," • Credit: Courtesy Rosemarie Todaschuk

Abe Yanofsky, 1971 • Credit: U of M Archives, Tribune Collection, Personality Files

■ Nellie Merkel and Ben Zaidman, 1940
• Credit: Courtesy Harriet Zaidman

serving in the RCAF from 1941 to 1946, Zaidman returned to his family's Flora Avenue home and married the girl next door, his childhood sweetheart Nellie Merkel. Ben Zaidman was an electrician, worked in the CNR Transcona Shops, and was a leader in union activities. He was elected to the Seven Oaks School Board in 1968 and served for three decades, including four terms as chairman. In addition to his community contribution as a school trustee, he helped in the establishment of the City of West Kildonan's library and accepted leadership positions with B'Nai Brith, the General Monash Branch of the Royal Canadian Legion, and the Manitoba Public Schools Finance Board. Ben Zaidman sincerely believed in the importance of learning, and, after twenty years of determined study, he graduated in 1989 with a BA in history from the University of Manitoba. In 1999 the School Division named its educational resource centre on Jefferson Avenue in his honour. Ben Zaidman died in 2008.

Science and Medicine

Earl Hershfield

The son of Dr. Sheppy Hershfield, Dr. Earl Hershfield became an internationally-respected authority on the control of tuberculosis. He served as the medical director of the Sanatorium Board of Manitoba (now the Manitoba Lung Association) and was instrumental in having the treatment of tuberculosis change from surgical lung removal to drug treatments. After tuberculosis was virtually eliminated from developed countries

■ Dr. Harry Medovy • Credit: Health Sciences Centre Archives

in the 1970s, Hershfield did research and consultative work in emerging nations. The story of his achievements is told by Maurice Mierau in *Memoir of a Living Disease: The Story of Earl Hershfield and Tuberculosis in Manitoba and Beyond.*

Harry Medovy

Harry Medovy, who was born in Russia in 1904, arrived in Winnipeg with his parents at the age of 10 months. Young Medovy's father was one of several dairy farmers in the West Kildonan area. His given birth name, "Gershon," was anglicized to "Harry" by the principal when he enrolled in Aberdeen School at the age of five and remained with him for life. After graduating from St. John's Tech and the University of Manitoba's medical school, Medovy was the Head of Pediatrics at the Children's Hospital of Winnipeg from 1954 until his retirement in 1970. Affectionately known as "Hurricane Harry" because of the speed with which he moved through medical rounds, Dr. Medovy was admired by thousands of students whom he mentored. He was an advocate for the immunization of children against infectious diseases, a promoter of nutritious diets, and an early opponent of cigarette smoking. Medovy wrote *A Vision Fulfilled: The Story of the Children's Hospital of Winnipeg*, an affectionate history of his beloved institution, and a residence at Health Sciences Centre is named for him. He died in 1995.

Louis Alexander Slotin

The death of Dr. Louis Slotin is a story of heroism and a life cut sadly short. Slotin, who had attended Machray School and graduated from St. John's Tech, enrolled in the University of Manitoba at the age of 16 and obtained bachelor's and master's degrees in science. After completing his PhD in England and working in a position in Chicago that involved research with a cyclotron, he became one of the scientists involved in Los Alamos, New Mexico with the Manhattan Project, the code

■ Dr. Louis Slotin's quick action saved the lives of other scientists. • Credit: Archives of Manitoba, Jewish Historical Society Collection, 3184

name for the process of developing the first atomic bomb. One tragic day in May 1946, Slotin was conducting an experiment on the hand-assembly of the firing mechanism of a bomb, something at which he had become particularly adept, and the momentary slip of a screwdriver triggered a chain reaction. His quick action to terminate a connection saved the other scientists in the room from lethal exposure to radiation, but Slotin himself was fatally exposed and died nine days later at the age of 36. Ironically, just prior to the incident, he had been planning to leave the Los Alamos job to return to the University of Chicago. More than 3,000 people attended his funeral, which was held on the lawn of the Slotin family home on Scotia Street. The story of Louis Slotin was published in 1955 in the novel *The Accident* by Dexter Masters and in the August-September 1995 issue of *The Beaver* in the article "Dr. Louis Slotin and 'The Invisible Killer'" by Martin Zeilig.

The World of Sports

Ben Hatskin

■ Ben Hatskin, 1974 • Credit: U of M Archives, Tribune Collection, Personality Files

Although Ben Hatskin played for six seasons with the Winnipeg Blue Bombers after receiving one of the first American football scholarships to be awarded to a Canadian, he became best known for his involvement with the World Hockey League and the Winnipeg Jets. Born in 1917, Hatskin attended Ralph Brown and Aberdeen Schools before graduating from St. John's Tech. His business ventures, including a stable of racehorses, a box factory, and a jukebox distribution service, flourished on his drive and determination. In 1966 Hatskin founded the Winnipeg Jets. Originally part of the Western Canada Junior Hockey League, the Jets joined the newly-established World Hockey Association in 1971. Probably Hatskin's most memorable achievement – and an event that remains a highlight in Winnipeg hockey history – was the signing of the legendary Bobby Hull in 1972. Ben Hatskin died in 1990.

SHEPPY IN ACTION; Dr. Sheppy Hershfield, former YMHA hurler, turned the clock back Sunday when he demonstrated some old-time form while brother Leible watched closely to see if the stuff was still there. In the background, Tony O'Sipa was also reviving memories.

SEPT. 10-67

Leible Hershfield

A natural athlete, Leible Hershfield (the younger brother of Dr. Sheppy Hershfield) was outstanding in virtually any sport he played. He was initially recognized for his track and field achievements at Isaac Newton High School, and later became involved in soccer, softball, and other sports. Leible Hershfield was the Director of Physical Education for the YMHA from 1936 to 1942 and was named Outstanding Jewish Athlete of the first half of the 20th century in 1969. He was inducted into the Manitoba Sports Hall of Fame in 1981 and died in 1999.

Leible Hershfield shared his memories in a book titled *The Jewish Athlete: A Nostalgic View*.

Fred Ingaldson

One of the most remarkable players in Manitoba basketball history, Fred Ingaldson, who was born in 1932 in Pontiac, Michigan, first played organized basketball at Isaac Newton High School. After graduation, he played at the junior level in Manitoba and at the college level in the USA, and then moved on to become a member of Canadian Olympic teams in 1960 in

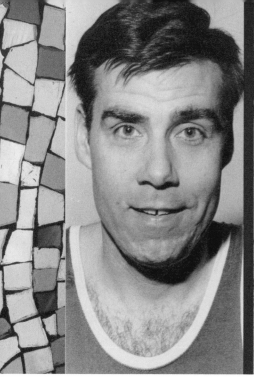

Rome, 1964 in Tokyo, and 1968 in Mexico, as well as on the Canadian basketball team in the 1967 Pan American Games in Winnipeg. Ingaldson was inducted into the Manitoba Basketball Hall of Fame in 1983 and the Canadian Basketball Hall of Fame in 2002.

Joseph Keeper

An outstanding middle distance runner during the 1920s, Joseph Keeper set a Canadian record for the ten-mile run in 1911. A member of the Norway House Cree First Nation, Keeper was born in 1886 in Walker Lake and attended residential school in Brandon, where he developed his interest in long distance running. He moved to Winnipeg in 1910, where he joined the North End Athletic Club, and participated in the 1912 Stockholm Summer Olympics. After joining the Royal Canadian Army in 1916, Keeper received a Military Medal and was one of several Aboriginal soldiers who served as dispatch carriers. Joe Keeper died in 1971 and was inducted into the Manitoba Sports Hall of Fame in 1984.

Charlie Krupp

A legendary softball catcher with YMHA teams during the 1920s and early 1930s, Charlie Krupp was also an outstanding

■ Joseph Benjamin "Joe" Keeper (1886-1971)
• Credit: http://www.halloffame.mb.ca/honoured/1984/jKeeper.htm. Accessed April 22, 2010.

soccer player and participated in various other sports. He became best known, however, as a coach, an executive member, and a generous contributor to amateur sports. The Charlie Krupp Memorial Stadium on McPhillips Street is named in his honour.

Billy Mosienko

Born in 1921, Billy Mosienko grew up in the North End with 14 siblings. During his stint of 14 years with the Chicago Black Hawks, he played in five All-Star games and was credited with

■ Billy Mosienko smiles from the wall of the bowling lanes.

258 goals and 282 assists in 711 games. During a Chicago-New York game in 1952, "Mosie" (as he was nicknamed) scored three goals in 21 seconds – an achievement that might never be matched. He finished his hockey career as a player and then a coach with the Winnipeg Warriors of the Western Hockey league between 1955 and 1960. Billy Mosienko was named Manitoba's Athlete of the Year in 1957 and was inducted into the Hockey Hall of Fame in 1965. In addition to the landmark Main Street bowling establishment that he founded, the former Keewatin Arena was renamed the Billy Mosienko Arena in 1991, and the Billy Mosienko Hockey Tournament has been held since 1982. Dubbed "the Pride of the North End," Billy Mosienko died in 1994.

Writing

Max Freedman

Unable to afford to enrol in courses at the University of Manitoba, Max Freedman spent four years in the library of the institution, reading as many books as he could. The librarians, admiring the determination of this young man, often guided him in his pursuit of learning. The self-described "graduate of the University of Manitoba Library," obtained his first job in journalism after three chief Winnipeg librarians recommended him to *The Edmonton Bulletin*. Following his war service, Freedman joined the *Winnipeg Free Press* as the paper's Ottawa correspondent, then its Washington correspondent, and finally as senior editorial writer. In 1953, he became the Washington correspondent for the *Manchester Guardian*. His syndicated *Chicago Daily*

■ Vince Leah, 1966 • Credit: U of M Archives, Tribune Collection, Personality Files

News column was carried by more than 100 newspapers. Six years younger than his brother Samuel, Max Freedman died in 1980 at the age of 65.

Vince Leah

Born in 1913, Vince Leah attended Ralph Brown and Isaac Newton Schools and joined the staff of *The Winnipeg Tribune* at the age of 16 as a copy boy. He was a sportswriter for *The Tribune* for 50 years and, after that newspaper folded in 1980, he was a columnist for the *Winnipeg Free Press*. Credited with naming the Winnipeg Blue Bombers, Leah was known to generations of Winnipeggers as "Uncle Vince" for his work in founding three hockey leagues and in organizing, coaching, promoting, and managing soccer, basketball, lacrosse, and baseball for thousands of youngsters. He was the author of eight local history books, including a history of the Blue Bombers. Vince Leah died in 1993. Two Winnipeg streets and a recreation centre in West Kildonan have been named in his honour.

John Marlyn (Vincent Reid)

Hungarian-born John Marlyn portrayed the hardships of immigrant life in North End Winnipeg during the 1920s in his 1957 novel *Under the Ribs of Death*. Marlyn grew up in the North End, attended the University of Manitoba, and later lived and worked in Ottawa. The novel, Marlyn's first, tells of the struggles of Hungarian immigrant Sandor Hunyadi, who changes his name to Alex Hunter in a futile attempt to fit into the dominant British culture and become a "real Canadian." Marlyn, who died in the Canary Islands in 2005, also wrote science fiction novels under the pseudonym of Vincent Reid.

Sheldon Oberman

Affectionately known as "Obie," Sheldon Oberman was a prolific writer of diverse works for children and adults. Born in 1949, Oberman graduated from St. John's High, backpacked in Europe and South Africa, worked in a kibbutz in Israel, and returned to Winnipeg to become a teacher for 20 years at Joseph Wolinsky Collegiate. His twelve books included elements of Jewish, African, Inuit, Greek, and French-Canadian culture. Sheldon Oberman died in 2004 at the age of 54.

Val Werier

Val Werier's parents fled to Canada in 1908 from Russia. He was born in 1917 and attended William Whyte, Machray, Aberdeen, and St. John's schools but couldn't afford to go to university. An aspiring journalist, Werier began by submitting unsolicited articles to *The Winnipeg Tribune* and was eventually hired as a reporter in 1941. He remained with *The Tribune* until it closed in 1980 – with a hiatus of three years of war service – and has continued since then as a freelance columnist with the *Winnipeg Free Press*. Described as "the conscience of the community," Val Werier was a champion of disadvantaged people and an advocate for social justice for more than six decades. He was an early crusader for environmental issues, the preservation of Winnipeg's heritage buildings, and the development of The Forks.

■ Val Werier, 1975 • Credit: U of M Archives, Tribune Collection, Personality Files

Alycia's Restaurant, 2009
• Credit: Photo by Russ Gourluck

CHAPTER 4

BORSCHT, BAGELS AND BANNOCK

TASTES OF THE NORTH END

■ The KUB bakery moved from the house next door to an adjoining new building around 1953. • Credit: Courtesy Olga Kucher

■ K.U.B. Bakery began in a house at 626 Stella.
• Credit: Courtesy Olga Kucher

NORTH END BAKERIES

Over the ages, bread has come to be regarded "the staff of life," a basic and even essential part of every meal. In addition to being a staple food, bread has acquired a range of religious and cultural connotations, particularly in Slavic cultures. It's appropriate that some of the earliest and most enduring business ventures in North End Winnipeg were bakeries that offered a cornucopia of baked goods based on traditional European recipes.

KUB Bakery

When Alex Kucher and three business partners (A. Andry-chuk, N. Doskuch, and L. Stroyich), all Ukrainian in origin, established a small bakery in 1923 a house at 626 Stella Avenue, in a largely Ukrainian neighbourhood, it was appropriately named the Ukrainian Bakery. A few years later, when Kucher bought out his partners, he and his son Bill decided to rename it Kucher's Ukrainian Bakery, or K.U.B. for short. Originally the bakery produced only bread, but when its operation was taken over by Bill Kucher, buns and sweet goods were added. Alex worked the overnight shift to have fresh baking ready for the morning, and his wife Polly, son Mike, and daughter Olga all helped out during the day.

The bakery was purchased by Ross Einfeld in 1982 after the death of Alex Kucher, and Einfeld modified the name to KUB by removing the periods. KUB continued to produce a variety of breads, but it was best known for its rye bread, an almost mandatory part of traditional Winnipeg socials. During the 1980s, KUB had as many as four Winnipeg locations, and the Stella Avenue bakery baked only rye bread – 8,000 loaves of it daily. In fact, although KUB makes approximately 100 kinds of baked goods, rye bread still accounts for more than 90 percent of the company's sales.

In April 2008 a $3-million fire levelled the iconic building. Initially Einfeld hoped to rebuild on the site, but the residential zoning of the property ruled that possibility out. Business continues at the company's Transcona location, and Ross Einfeld hopes that KUB will be able build on another site in the North End.

Gunn's Bakery

When Morris Gunn left Poland for Canada in the mid-1920s, he promised his fiancée Florence Grodzenczik, whose parents owned the bakery where Morris worked, that he would send

■ Morris and Florence Gunn rented a former grocery store and delicatessen at 247 Selkirk Avenue to open their bakery in 1937. The building on the right is the Queen's Theatre, later the Hebrew Sick Benefit Hall. • Credit: Archives of Manitoba, Jewish Historical Society Collection, 2843

for her as soon as he had earned enough money for her passage. He arrived in Winnipeg, found a job at Buchwald's Bakery on Salter Street, and in 1930, Florence joined him. They were married shortly after her arrival, and their first child, Betty, was born two years later.

Morris Gunn continued to work at Buchwald's, but he and Florence dreamed of opening their own bakery. In 1937, their dream came true. They rented a small building, formerly a delicatessen, on Selkirk Avenue, moved into the back part, and opened Gunn's Bakery in the front. That same year, their first son, Bernie, was born at home, and in 1942 their second son, Arthur, arrived. By then, the family and the business had outgrown the small building in which they lived and worked, so

Pronouncing KUB

When talking about KUB Bakery, some Winnipeggers pronounce the name "cub" while others favour "koob." Olga Kucher, whose father and brother devised the name, pronounces it "cub."

the Gunns moved their family to a rented house at 231 Selkirk. Soon after, they were able to purchase the building at 247 Selkirk where the bakery was located and where it continues to operate more than 70 years later. There have been several additions since then, most notably a 1979 addition on the west side of the original building, and the 1,800 square-foot bakery is now 10,000 square feet. The section that used to be the entire bakery is now the cake decorating room.

Just as the location of Gunn's has remained the same since 1937, so have a number of other features. It continues to be a family business. Bernie and Arthur now own and operate the bakery and are familiar faces to many regular customers. Bernie – prevented by allergies from becoming a baker – trained as an accountant and worked for a number of organizations, including the Manitoba Museum, but he continued to look after the financial aspects of Gunn's over the years. When Morris Gunn died in 1973, Bernie joined the bakery on a full-time basis. Arthur – known by many as Fivie, his Jewish name – is a Master Baker.

■ City Bread bakes the favourite rye bread of many Winnipeggers. • Credit: Photo by Russ Gourluck

When Gunn's opened in 1937, it offered authentic European-style baking, and that tradition continues. Bagels, and rye pumpernickel breads, poppy seed rolls, and buns filled with apples, blueberries, cherries, and prunes continue to be baked using Morris Gunn's own recipes. Virtually all of the products are made from scratch and most are still formed by hand.

The first kosher bakery of its type in western Canada, Gunn's continues to be a strictly kosher site. Inspected by rabbinical officials as often as three times daily, Gunn's uses no animal products. The shortenings are vegetable-based, and the cheese used in the store's vegetarian lasagna contains no rennet. It's specially made for Gunn's and packaged under close supervision. Items like meat pies and sausage rolls, staples in many other bakeries, are not among Gunn's offerings. The popular cream cheese that Gunn's sells to accompany its bagels was formerly produced by People's Co-op, but since that dairy closed, it has been based on a kosher cream cheese from Kraft, with some extra touches added to enhance the flavour. Because of the limited availability of kosher meat in Winnipeg, Gunn's recently began selling frozen kosher meat from Toronto, sealed in cryovac to ensure there is no contact with other products.

Just as the physical size of Gunn's has expanded, so has their list of baked goods. There are now more than 300 products (displayed with colour photos and descriptions on the company's website.) There are now more than 25 kinds of bagels, and items like apple jacks, biscotti, and croissants have joined the traditional offerings.

A large wholesale market has developed, along with a catering service. With a total staff of approximately 70 (representing a range of ethnic backgrounds), the bakery operates 24 hours a day in the spacious back area, and many of the products are destined for grocery stores, restaurants, delis, and coffee shops.

A visit to Gunn's, especially on a Friday or Saturday morning, is like a trip back to the historic North End. In the crowded front section of the bakery, customers line up as they look over displays of tempting goodies, often stopping to chat with others as they wait their turns. Some come to stock up for the weekend or a summer trip to the cottage. Others know that certain breads – like the formidable three-pound rye loaf – are available only on Fridays.

Although computers and labour-saving bakery machinery have streamlined the operations, the old world appeal of Gunn's hasn't changed, and the bakery continues to attract customers from across the city.

City Bread

If security officials at Winnipeg's Richardson International Airport are used to seeing loaves of City Bread rye bread, it's not surprising. The distinctive kosher rye, so much a part of the tradition of Winnipeg's North End, is one of the most popular "take-home" items for transplanted Winnipeggers as they wing their way home.

Originally located at 312 Stella Avenue and known as the Working Man's Bakery, City Bread was purchased from the original owners in 1950 by brothers Hymie and Morris Perlmutter and two other partners (who were both bakers) Max Bakal and Max Applebaum. Both Perlmutters had previously worked at City Bread – Hymie as a driver and Morris as a bookkeeper – and their father, David, had been a baker there since the 1930s. Eventually, Applebaum sold his share to another Perlmutter brother, Jack, also an employee of the bakery. When the Stella Avenue property was expropriated for the Lord Selkirk Housing Development, the bakery business moved to its current location at 238 Dufferin Avenue.

City Bread was sold in 1975 to Max Goldman, the owner of Northwest Bakery, and the building was expanded considerably. The business is currently owned and managed by Goldman's son, Harvey.

■ The Donut House is a Selkirk Avenue fixture.
• Credit: Photo by Russ Gourluck

The Donut House

A violent incident in November 2008 left Erhard Meier afraid to return to his North End business. Meier, the long-time owner of The Donut House at 500 Selkirk Avenue, was badly beaten by three thugs, one armed with a baseball bat, as he got out of his van behind his store around midnight. Meier, aged 73, received a broken arm, a fractured knee, and severe lacerations to one ear before neighbours dashed out to intervene. Interviewed a few weeks after the incident by Winnipeg media, the still-shaken man explained, "I felt so safe here. I never even thought something like this would happen to me," but, he added, "I built this business up and I just don't want to walk away from something like this." Reflecting on the incident several months later, Erhard Meier acknowledged that he was "beaten up pretty badly," but he was back at work and his son was taking over the business.

Meier purchased the Donut House in the mid-1970s from the original owners, Sam Gillman and Al Slotin. As the name suggests, the bakery specializes in donuts, but Meier reports that cinnamon buns and beef rolls are also big sellers. Along with a wide range of breads and bagels, the Donut House offers an extensive variety of cakes and pastries, including hard-to-find almond tarts and icing-topped lemon slices. In addition to the Selkirk Avenue location, Donut House products are sold at a popular kiosk at the Garden City Shopping Centre.

"That was a meal"

Frank Humniski, who grew up on Stella near KUB, reports that people in the neighbourhood knew that bread was available right from the oven at certain times each day. He recalls buying hot loaves, wrapped in brown paper by Mr. Kucher, and taking it directly home to be eaten with fresh "real" wieners from Manitoba Sausage. "Boy, that was a meal," he laughs. His father, Mike, jokingly adds that people sometimes ate half the loaf before they reached home.

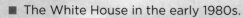

■ The White House in the early 1980s.
• Credit: Jewish Heritage Centre, JM 2309

■ From Left, Sam, Abe, and Ben Hochman at the Oasis Delicatessen counter, 1980 • Credit: Courtesy Ben Hochman

CORNED BEEF ON RYE: NORTH END DELICATESSENS

Delicatessens, whether they were authentically kosher or simply "kosher style," were literally part of the European flavour of the North End. While some served a variety of traditional Jewish dishes, the corned beef sandwich was probably the best known menu item.

When asked about competition from high-profile donut shop competitors, Meier simply smiles and says "We still have a good clientele for our donuts. They say they're the best in the city."

Oscar's

A North End institution that later moved downtown, Oscar's Delicatessen still carries the name of its original owner, Oscar Berman. Oscar's opened in 1930 on the street level of the Globe Apartments at 1236 Main Street (at St. John's) moving in the mid-1970s a few doors south on the same block to 1204 Main Street near Mountain Avenue (the former site of St. John's Pharmacy.) After Berman, Oscar's had a series of owners, including Issy Jacobson and Joe Donin; brothers George, Asher, Myer, and Samuel Ludwig; and Jim and Harold Shukster. In 1979, Larry Brown became a partner in the business with the Shuksters, and the downtown location at 175 Hargrave Street opened three years later. In 1992, Brown purchased the Hargrave deli. Until 1997, both locations remained open, but a decline in the Main Street business (particularly after the closing of the nearby car dealerships and banks) led to the decision to shut down the Main Street store.

Although Oscar's is now a downtown eatery, catering largely to busy business lunchers, the basic North End menu items – including the perennial corned beef sandwich – remain, but there are many additions, including salads, soups, hot dogs, and hamburgers. There are no french fries. Larry Brown chuckles when he mentions that the Greek salad is the most popular menu item because "the only thing close to salad at the Main Street restaurant prior to 1982 was a couple of slices of tomato on a corned beef sandwich." Oscar's still has a take-out service, and it's often visited by out-of-towners who order corned beef to take home. And some older customers still remember when corned beef sandwiches were two for 15 cents.

Simon's

Like Oscar's, Simon's Delicatessen was named for its first owners – Alex Simon and his son Monty. When Fred Solomon bought the deli in 1962 he pragmatically decided to keep the name because of an almost-new neon sign over the sidewalk that had cost $500 or $600. "I said, 'You know what? Let's call it Simon's.' It didn't bother me!"

Solomon owned and operated Simon's (at 1322 Main at Machray – previously the site of Robinson's Bakery) for close to 40 years, until he retired in 2001. He was there at 6:00 a.m. and worked seven days a week for 25 years, assisted by his wife and his mother and father. During that period, Simon's closed only three days a year – for Rosh Hashanah and Yom Kippur – but then they began closing occasionally so the Solomon family could go on vacations.

Simon's menu offered much more than corned beef sandwiches, featuring boiled beef, veal cutlets, gefilte fish, blintzes, and home-made soups (including borscht) that could be taken home by the gallon. "Everything was home made," Solomon points out. Much of the cooking was done by his mother, Rose Solomon, using her own recipes. Fred Solomon often made 1,000 to 1,500 sandwiches in a day, and one business placed an order for 500 sandwiches every Christmas for 25 years. All of the advertising was word of mouth. "In 40 years I never spent one dollar on advertising," Solomon proclaims.

The Oasis

Abraham Hochman arrived in Winnipeg in 1928 from what was later known as Poland, and earned a living as a fruit peddler with a horse and wagon. A few years later, his wife and four daughters followed him to Winnipeg, where their daughter Clara and son Gordon were born. Twins Sam and Ben were born in 1936.

Chicago Kosher

Located at 358 Flora Avenue, Chicago Kosher Sausage Manufacturing was established around 1919 by Jacob Averbach with three business partners. By 1929, Averbach was the sole owner and was joined by his son Abraham. Commonly known as "Chicago Kosher," the plant made salami, wieners, bologna, and garlic sausage, but probably the best-known product was the corned beef that generations of Winnipeggers enjoyed at delicatessens across the city. Chicago Kosher was sold to Schneiders Meats in 1972 and its operations were eventually incorporated into the Schneiders St. Boniface plant.

The Best Corned Beef Sandwich

There are two essential ingredients in a real corned beef sandwich: rye bread and corned beef. Everything else (hot mustard, regular mustard, tomato slices, or whatever else strikes the eater's fancy) is an embellishment.

Consultation with the owners of three of the North End's most legendary purveyors of corned beef sandwiches shows unanimity on the bread of choice. Larry Brown of Oscar's, Ben Hochman of the Oasis, and Fred Solomon of Simon's all name City Bread rye. Hochman is adamant on that choice: "There are many bakeries that have great rye breads, but there's only one that can match with corned beef in a sandwich – and that's from City Bread."

The corned beef at all three of these iconic delis generally came from Chicago Kosher until that business was sold to Schneiders in 1972. Schneiders continues to follow the Chicago Kosher recipe, but the process has been expedited. The brisket used to be immersed in brine from 10 to 14 days, but now the brine is pumped in and it's finished in 24 hours. In Larry Brown's opinion, "The corned beef is still excellent, but it's not as good as it used to be." And the Schneiders version is not kosher.

All three owners agree that corned beef should be served at room temperature to bring out the full flavour, especially from the fat. Ben Hochman reports that Oasis sandwiches contained four ounces of corned beef and that it was sliced very thinly to ensure that it was juicy.

In 1936, the family opened Hochman's Food Store, a fruit and vegetable store at 906 Main Street. The store, heated in the winter by a pot-bellied stove, featured a huge display of fruit in the front window, and Ben and Sam were working there by the time they were 12 years old. As time went on, the Hochman business expanded to include the nearby former Grosney's Delicatessen. Renamed the Oasis Delicatessen, the new integrated business was both a fruit store and a delicatessen. The Oasis made its own chopped liver, dill pickles, coleslaw, potato salad, knishes, and (while kosher briskets were available) corned beef. When horseradish was being ground, the door between the store and the kitchen had to be kept tightly closed to keep customers from crying. The store catered to European tastes, offering a wide selection of herring, and pickle brine as a beverage.

Shelves in the 2,500 square foot store displayed imported canned goods from around the world, including Russia, Norway, Sweden, Iceland, Poland, Israel, and Germany. Immigrants during the 1950s and 1960s occasionally brought visitors from home to the Oasis, and some were moved to tears when they saw products made in their own countries that they couldn't buy at home. Abraham Hochman spoke seven languages and was often able to converse with them.

One display at the Oasis that is still remembered by older Winnipeggers is a pile of bulk eggs at the front of the store, stacked pyramid-style in the way that supermarkets often display

■ From left, Ben, Abe, and Sam in front of the Oasis lunch counter, 1980. • Courtesy Ben Hochman

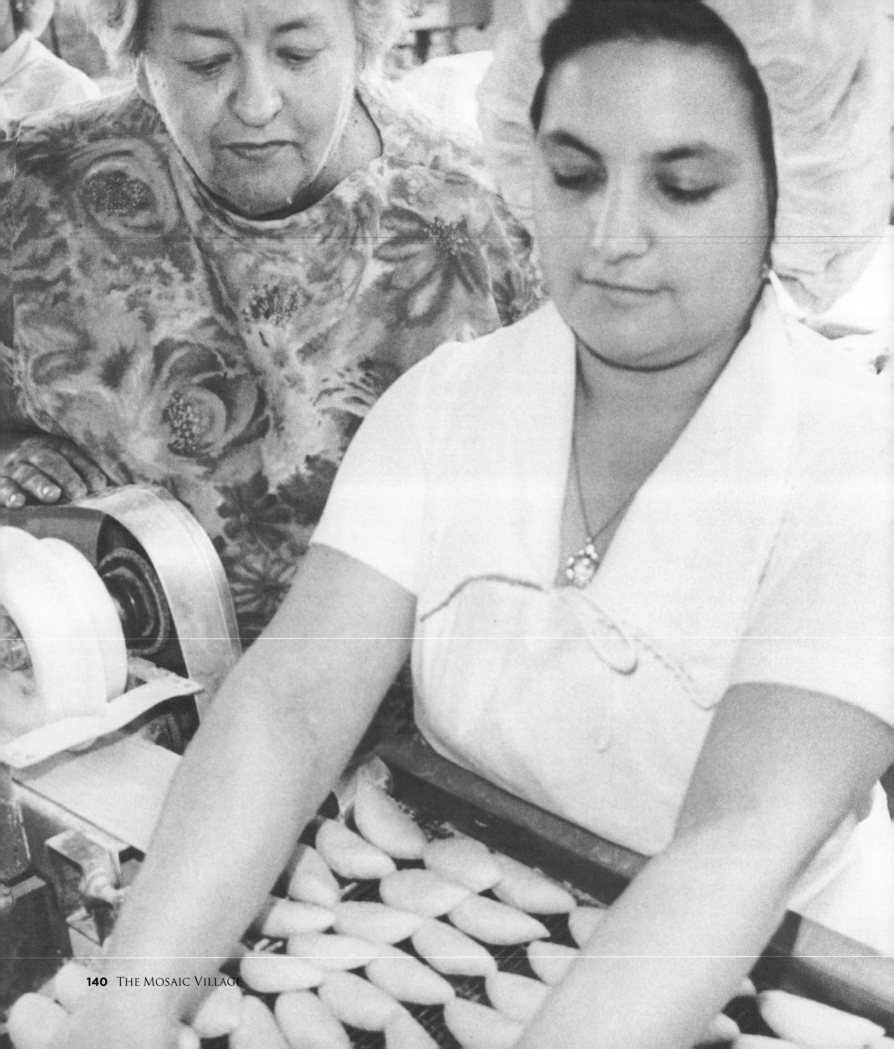

apples and oranges. Regular customers brought empty egg cartons, and some – perhaps early recycling devotees – brought extras for others to use. Hochman describes the eggs as "huge – the size of two standard eggs" and recalls that occasionally an egg in the display would "have an accident." "That would be a real problem," he laughs, "because you'd have to clean them all."

The 18-stool lunch counter often turned its occupants over three times within a 90-minute lunch period. The most popular items were corned beef sandwiches and pie. The Oasis made few baked goods, but their pies – fresh fruit, banana cream, and lemon – were so popular that some customers phoned in the morning to reserve a piece for lunch time.

The Oasis was sold by the Hochman's in 1984.

Elman's Kosher Deli Foods

Samuel Finkleman started his business by making horseradish in the basement of his family's College Avenue home. His daughters stuck labels on the jars and delivered them to customers in their coaster wagon. "Happy" Finkleman had emigrated from Poland in the mid-1930s and brought with him a pocketful of recipes for various condiments, including horseradish. He specialized in that product, adding ground beets for Passover in accordance with Jewish tradition, and it continues to be a popular item. One former Winnipegger, a doctor who has lived in San Francisco for 25 years, has had a case of 12 jars of beet horseradish shipped to him by air every Passover as a gift for his friends – a complex and costly process requiring FDA approval and FedEx refrigeration.

The business eventually moved to Boyd Avenue (the factory was the garage behind the Finkleman home) and to the present 647 Jarvis site in the late 1980s. Elman's (a variation on the family name) began to expand when Samuel's son Manny became involved and added hot mustard and a variety of pickles.

Today, Elman's products are sold from the Lakehead to Vancouver and include pickled eggs, sauces, poultry stuffing, and several versions of herring. Two of the most traditional products are made from vinegar-free recipes: sauerkraut and Baba's Barrel

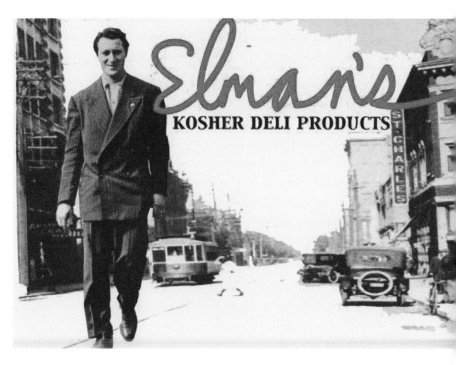

Cured Dills (in a cloudy brine). To conform to kosher standards, the poultry stuffing is made separately from products like horseradish (because of the leavening in the stuffing.)

Manny Finkleman died in 2004 and Elman's is now owned and managed by his partner, Millie Krause.

Naleway Catering

Ann Naleway was an enterprising woman. The daughter of a Ukrainian immigrant who made kubasa in his Point Douglas store, she mixed up packages of cereal in the family bathtub, packaged it, and sold it to corner grocery stores. Family members confide that the product, which was similar to Red River Cereal, wasn't very good, but that Naleway was so persuasive (and attractive) that store owners bought more boxes even though their previous stock hadn't sold. During the 1930s, she used a machine that she purchased for $150 to make potato chips, which she marketed to beer parlours in spite of the fact that women weren't allowed inside.

From 1942 until approximately 1950, Ann Naleway operated Ann's Grill in the Sutherland Hotel on Main Street. It had a varied menu, and her Ukrainian foods were so popular that she was often asked to cater weddings. The catering aspect of the business grew to the point in the mid-1950s where Ann and her husband Leon – they had met when he ate at Ann's Grill - built a banquet hall at 214 Selkirk Avenue and moved into the house next door at 216 Selkirk.

Their son Bob Naleway remembers that Naleway Catering often did three or four weddings on a Saturday in the 1950s and as many as seven or eight by the 1960s. Ann Naleway, who had a beautiful soprano voice, was pleased to sing at wedding receptions on request. The menu included turkey, chicken, roast beef, and veal cutlets, as well as Ann Naleway's signature meatballs. She insisted on fast service – her staff could serve 300 meals in 20 minutes – and on hot food. Several other prominent caterers and restaurateurs in the city, including Marion Staff of Alycia's, began their careers with Naleway.

After catering a wedding for a Dominion Store supermarket manager, Naleway Catering began wholesaling coleslaw and potato salad to Dominion supermarkets, and a whole new dimension of the business opened up. Before long, Eaton's,

Safeway, Woolco, and other retailers were carrying a host of Naleway products, including perogies and holubchi. Perogies were originally made by hand by as many as 20 women, but by 1973 mechanical perogy-makers were used. The hall on Selkirk Avenue closed in 1964 and Naleway Catering moved to larger premises on Fife Street.

By the 1970s, Bob Naleway was operating the business, and frozen Naleway perogies were sold across Canada. A weekly Nordair flight to Toronto saw half an aircraft blocked off to airlift 20,000 pounds of perogies to be sold in Miracle Mart supermarket delis. Bob Naleway describes the flights as "half passengers, half perogies."

Ann Naleway died 1982 at the age of 73. There are currently two businesses in Winnipeg with the Naleway name. Naleway Foods Ltd. on Hutchings Avenue produces and wholesales a range of food products and, since 1995, is no longer operated by the Naleway family. Naleway Catering at 1411 Main Street is operated by Rob Naleway, Ann's grandson and Bob's son, and carries on the family tradition of catering to social events.

■ Manitoba Sausage (shown in the 1950s) was founded in 1912 at 691 Dufferin Avenue. • Credit: Courtesy Ken Werner

RINGS OF KUBASA: NORTH END STEAKS

Just as there are multiple spellings and pronunciations for the European names of garlic sausage, there are many different recipes. Like perogies, ownership of the garlicky delicacy is claimed by several ethnic groups.

Manitoba Sausage and Winnipeg Old Country

With a joint history of nearly a century, Manitoba Sausage and Winnipeg Old Country Sausage are part of the tradition of North End Winnipeg and of Manitoba.

Manitoba Sausage was founded in 1912 at 691 Dufferin Avenue by the Vogt family, and members of the family continued to be the owners until the mid-1970s. Louis Werner, who had been a Manitoba Sausage employee for 41 years and was in charge of production, left the company in 1977 and co-founded a competing business, Winnipeg Old Country Sausage, at Jarvis and McGregor in 1979. In 1982, Werner and his business partners purchased Manitoba Sausage and combined the two businesses under the name of Winnipeg Old Country. The company continues to own the Manitoba Sausage name and use it on some products. Both plants were utilized until 1984, and then all of the operations were consolidated in the Dufferin Avenue facility. Louis Werner died in 1997 at the age of 76 after 61 years of work.

Ken Werner remembers that when he turned 15 his father Louis announced, "Summer holidays are over. Now you come to work." He worked every summer until he completed high school and then, planning to stay for only six months, went to work with his father. He didn't leave. Today Ken Werner is the owner of Winnipeg Old Country Sausage and his daughter and her husband are part of the management. Ken still chuckles at the comment that one of his grade 12 teachers made when he graduated from West Kildonan Collegiate. "Why did you bother staying in school to grade twelve just to go count sausage?"

"Bologna's our big thing," Ken Werner explains. "We make roughly 300,000 pounds a year of it." There's only one kind – bung bologna made with pork and beef. Most of the recipes are the same handwritten ones that Louis Werner passed down to his son. The smokehouses are new, but the sawdust they contain is nothing exotic or sophisticated. It's softwood sawdust from a local lumberyard, just as it's been for decades. The second biggest seller is bacon – 1,800 pounds a day – most of it destined for the restaurant industry.

But if there's one product that has made Winnipeg Old Country Sausage famous and has become an essential part of the operation of several landmark Manitoba restaurants, it's

■ Ted Wojcik, who co-owns Wawel (pronounced VOV-Ell) Meat Market at 423 Selkirk Avenue with his brother Mark, smiles as he explains that people call him Mr. Wawel. The store was actually named in 1964 by its three original owners for a castle in Krakow, Poland. In 1966 Ted's father Kasmir became a part owner in 1966, and then Ted and his brother took over the ownership in 1982. Housed in a building previously occupied by a tinsmith and later Tasty Bread, Wawel offers store-made Polish-style garlic sausage, ham sausage, salami, wieners, blood sausage, and other products. Wojcik reports that many of their customers used to live in the North End, but now most come from outside the area, especially at Christmas and Easter. • Credit: Photo by John Marczyk

In Search of the
Best Kubasa

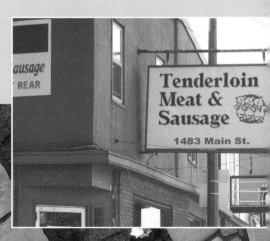

Social Platters

$1.40 per person

Includes various kinds of cold cuts on

the wieners. They can be found on the legendary hot dogs of Kelekis on Main Street and the Half Moon and Skinner's in Lockport as well as at hundreds of other Manitoba eateries. These are the authentic, European-style wiener, with a snappy "natural lamb casing" (a euphemism for sheep intestine) and, like the bologna, are made with pork and beef – no chicken, no MSG, no by-products.

The plant has been upgraded on the inside and refurbished on the outside, and Ken Werner has no plans of moving the business and its 45 employees away from Dufferin Avenue.

The Place for Kubasa

Winnipeg's North End is the home of a number of manufacturers of garlic sausage and a variety of other smoked meats. Most have Ukrainian or Polish connections. Some have been in business for decades, while others are relative newcomers. Many Winnipeggers have their own favourite place to purchase kubasa and are usually willing to defend their choices.

Like many words (and surnames) that originate in the Cyrillic alphabet, there are multiple spellings and pronunciations for this one. An online search uncovers, among others, "kielbasa" and "kovbasa." Fortunately, the *Oxford Canadian Dictionary of Current English* lists only one spelling – "kubasa – but it does provide three pronunciations: "co baw SAW," "COO buh saw," and "ko BASSA."

Hunky Bill recommends a way to test kubasa for quality. He says, "Buy a ring of garlic sausage, weigh it, leave it in the fridge for a week, and then weigh it again." If it has lost a significant amount of weight, the reason, according to Konyk, is "too much bullshit, crap, and water."

■ North End burger destinations

HOT DOGS, NIPS, AND PEROGIES: NORTH END RESTAURANTS

Memories of good food and good companionship are a big part of North End nostalgia. Although some of the area's best-known eating places have moved away or shut down, others remain to attract customers from all over the city.

■ It began with a pushcart. • Credit: Photo by Russ Gourluck

C. Kelekis Restaurant

Earl Barish, previously of Dickie Dee Ice Cream fame and now the President and CEO of Salisbury House, describes Kelekis as "my first entrepreneurial effort." At the age of seven or eight, Earl went to Kelekis every day after school to take out the garbage, help clean up, and do odd jobs. His compensation was a hot dog, fries, and a drink. He viewed this as an opportunity to go to work and get a reward and believes the experience helped steer him in the direction his career has taken. Some 60 years later, Barish jokes that he's still doing odd jobs and cleaning up for a restaurant – but now it's Salisbury House.

Chris Kelekis emigrated from a Greek settlement in Turkey with his wife Magdalene and, after living in Montreal and Edmonton, settled in Winnipeg in 1918. Kelekis started in the food industry in the 1920s by selling peanuts and popcorn from a pushcart. By the 1930s he had converted a Model T truck into a wagon. With his daughters' help, Kelekis visited outdoor events to introduce Winnipeggers to Kelekis chips (as

French fries were then called). Hot dogs and corn on the cob came later.

The first Kelekis Restaurant opened in 1944 at 929 Main (near Euclid) and a year later construction was underway at a second location at 1100 Main (near Redwood) where it continues to operate. The two buildings were identical and each featured a convenient window at the front where customers were able to order food to take with them. This is believed to be one of the first instances of takeout food in Winnipeg.

Some older Winnipeggers are convinced that the chips always tasted better if they were bought at the window. Ben Hochman, whose family owned the Oasis Delicatessen across from the Main and Selkirk location, reports that the lineups at the window were sometimes so long that people stood on the road and risked being hit by cars. Audrey Boyko, who grew up in nearby Point Douglas in the 1940s, explains that chips came in 5-cent and 10-cent sizes and that the same size of brown

paper bag was used for both. She and her playmates, after some diligent research, determined that buying two 5-cent bags usually resulted in more chips than one 10-cent bag. The difference, they found, was approximately eight more chips.

The 929 Main Street location was eventually closed in 1956 (the building remains) a year after the 1100 Main Street site was expanded. The takeout window was eliminated in 1977 as part of a complete renovation. One of the main attractions of Kelekis – besides the food – is a collection of photographs of entertainers, athletes, and politicians who have visited the restaurant. A house rule is that a family member must request a photo from the celebrity. Unsolicited photographs are never displayed on the Wall of Fame.

Another tradition, which most Winnipeggers understand intuitively, is that Kelekis hot dogs are to be held in hands when eaten. Hapless federal Liberal Leader Stephane Dion invited nation-wide snickers in 2007 when, surrounded by media and his shocked entourage, he used a knife and fork.

Chris Kelekis passed away in 1957, and C. Kelekis Restaurant – the "C" stands for Chris – continues to be family owned and

■ White House founders Ruth and Ed Abosh in front of the White House, ca 1940 • Credit: Archives of Manitoba, Jewish Historical Society Collection, 2765

operated. Chris and Magdalene Kelekis had six daughters (Chryse, Fotina, Sophie, Evelyn, Isabel, Mary, and Becky) and one son (Leo), and all of them worked at the restaurant over the years. The remaining children – Chryse, Mary, and Becky – are now the owners. Mary, ever-present at the front counter is uncannily able to greet customers by name even after years of absence.

The White House

Norm Silverberg describes going to the White House as "a ritual" and recalls that, "Everybody went there on a Sunday night." The popular Selkirk Avenue dining spot drew people not just from the North End, but from all parts of Winnipeg. And one of the main attractions was barbecued baby back pork spareribs. When the White House was founded in 1938 by Ed Abosh and Walter Bell, an order of ribs was 75 cents.

The original Selkirk Avenue site of the White House became a Hungarian club. • Credit: Photo by Russ Gourluck

One of the keys to the unique White House ribs was the cooking method. George Gershman, whose sisters Ruth and Annette married Abosh and Bell, explains that the spareribs were never parboiled – that, he says, would make the meat "mushy." Before cooking, the ribs were pierced and sauce was added and allowed to penetrate. The oven used at the White House had been purchased second-hand from the Manitoba Club (which, ironically, Jews were not allowed to join at the time) for $100.

Another key is the barbecue sauce used on the ribs. A number of recipes with widely varying ingredients have been published over the years – one includes chili powder, cayenne, white sugar, and vinegar; another, in the same newspaper column, calls for honey, butter, Tabasco sauce, soya sauce, dry mustard, and brown sugar. Virtually all recipes claiming to duplicate the original White House sauce list ketchup, and a fundamental difficulty is that the original sauce used inexpensive Ben-Hur Ketchup, which has been unavailable for years.

Abosh and Bell sold the restaurant in the late 1940s. It moved from Selkirk Avenue to Grant Avenue in the 1970s

The "Salamander" oven used at the White House was purchased for $100 from the Manitoba Club. The flames cooked from above.
• Credit: U of M Archives, Tribune Collection, 18-4847-55

White House Coleslaw

THE DRESSING:

1 cup (240 ml) white vinegar
¾ cup (180 ml) corn oil
1/3 cup (80 ml) white granulated sugar
1 teaspoon (5 ml) kosher salt
½ teaspoon (2.5 ml) pepper
½ teaspoon garlic (2.5 ml) powder
1 teaspoon (5 ml) dry mustard

Combine above ingredients in a small pot, bring to a boil, and let it cool.

THE VEGETABLES:

2 to 3 pounds (900 to 1350 g) of finely sliced cabbage
1 or 2 shredded carrots
3 or 4 sliced green onions

Pour the dressing over the vegetable mix in a large bowl and toss. Cool before serving.

■ Gus Damianakos enjoys the Selkirk Avenue neighbourhood. • Credit: Photo by Russ Gourluck

and remains in operation. It is open evenings only and offers just pickup and delivery service. Bottled barbecue sauce can be purchased to take home.

Although Ruth and Annette Gershman never tasted the White House's famous spareribs – they kept strictly kosher homes – they contributed the original recipe for the restaurant's distinctive coleslaw. That recipe is printed below, courtesy of their brother George.

The Windmill

Although the Windmill Lunch has achieved international exposure by appearing in a reported seven shot-in-Winnipeg motion pictures, owner Gus Damianakos is convinced that the food is what makes the Selkirk Avenue eatery so popular.

The Windmill has a long history in two neighbouring locations. It was opened in 1947 at 496 Selkirk (now part of the site of The Donut House) by Rita Winrob, her husband Sam, and her parents Hilda and Dave Ludwig. They served breakfast, daily lunch specials, and dinner to the customers who sat in the five booths and at the lunch counter. One of their specialties was corned beef sandwiches made with City Bread rye and Smith's corned beef. The Windmill remained open into the evening to welcome patrons who walked across the street after the last show at the Palace. After a couple of years, the Ludwigs became the sole proprietors.

The restaurant had a series of different owners until it was purchased by Damianakos in 1970, and in the meantime had relocated to 518 Selkirk. The main section has a ten-stool lunch counter and five booths, but in 1979 Damianakos bought the adjoining building and added a dining room that doubled the Windmill's capacity. He reports that his busiest years were from 1975 to 1985, when the Windmill stayed open until 9:00 p.m., drawing customers who dropped in after shopping at stores like Oretzki's, Clifford's, and Misha Pollock's. Now it's open from 6:00 a.m. until 7:00 p.m. seven days a week.

Gus Damianakos, who arrived from Greece in 1963, is not just the owner, he's also the cook, and he's proud that everything served at the Windmill is homemade, including the perogies and the clubhouse sandwiches with real roasted turkey. Some of the regular customers come from other parts of the city, but many live nearby, and Damianakos is proud to say that he gets along well with people from the neighbourhood. "You treat them nice, they're nice to you," he explains. If customers can't pay for their meals, the understanding owner simply says, "I'll see you tomorrow," confident that they'll pay him when they can. One man came back three years later to settle his debt.

■ The Main and Matheson Salisbury House on opening day in 1963 • Credit: Salisbury House of Canada Ltd. photo. Courtesy Pat Panchuk

Sals

"It was like a family," Pat Duseigne reflects as she talks about her career of 35 years at the Main and Matheson Salisbury House. When she began working there in 1974, she lived in the North End; however, even after moving to Transcona, she was willing to ride the bus for an hour each way to stay at the location she preferred. She retired in 2009.

Duseigne and the other staff members, many with twenty or more years of experience at that location, knew their regular customers so well that they'd often put their orders on the grill when they saw their cars drive up. Duseigne laughs, "Once in a while they'd fool us by ordering something different, but we'd say, 'Your order's done already. You can't change your mind.'" Everyone, staff and customers, knew everyone else by their first names.

The "North End Sals" as it's often called, first opened on July 1, 1963, and like most Salisbury House outlets in those days, it was open 24 hours. Now its hours are from 6:30 a.m. to 10:00 p.m. Most of the customers are regulars – one group in the morning, another at lunch time, and another in the evening. Many are seniors, who sit along the back wall – they call it their "Wailing Wall" – to discuss the day's news and solve the world's problems. When one passes away, others chip in money for a charitable donation. Duseigne recalls that she first met some customers when they were teens, and watched as they came in

■ After nearly 50 years, the North End Sals remains a popular gathering place. • Credit: Photo by Russ Gourluck

The North End Skillet

One of the special menu features at all Salisbury Houses in the summer of 2009 was a North End Skillet. In addition to the usual hashbrowns, cheese, and scrambled eggs, it had the added North End flavor of fried onions and kubasa. It was topped by a perogy with a dollop of sour cream.

The North End –
The Place for Perogies

■ Alycia's offers traditional Ukrainian food. • Credit: Photo by Russ Gourluck

with their boyfriends or girlfriends, then their spouses, and then their own kids.

The regulars that Duseigne remembers include athletes Bobby Hull and Al Sparks, Lieutenant Governors Yvon Dumont and Philip Lee, politicians Gary Doer and Gord Mackintosh, and musicians Tom Jackson, Wayne Walker, Randy Bachman, and Burton Cummings – now an owner of Salisbury House. "He was my Number One. I loved Burton," she confesses.

Alycia's Restaurant

"Everyone called her Alycia. She answered to Alycia," Sharon Staff smiles as she talks about her mother. "Many customers didn't even know her real name."

When Marion Staff's husband died in 1971, she needed to find something to do and decided to purchase a restaurant at the corner of Cathedral and McGregor. Known at the time as Alice's Restaurant, it had just six tables with seating for 24 customers. The major appliances were a regular household fridge and stove. Staff had grown up in Vita, the only sister of seven brothers, and had learned to cook at an early age. Her working career had included several years with Naleway Catering. So, her daughter Sharon explains, "She started making just what she knew how to make – perogies, borscht, and other Ukrainian dishes." To add to the Ukrainian flavour, she renamed the restaurant "Alycia's" (pronounced Al - EE - Sha's).

Marion Staff died in 2004 and today Alycia's is operated by Sharon and her husband Roger Leclerc and family. There have been several expansions to boost the seating capacity to 120, but the restaurant still has a homey atmosphere, with its assortment of non-matching chairs, and tables covered with coloured table cloths and clear plastic. Alycia's produces an astounding thousand dozen perogies a day, and even more at Christmas, Easter, and during Folklorama. Each one is pinched shut by hand and made with real – not instant – potatoes. In a typical week, Alycia's uses a ton of potatoes. The most popular variety by far is cheddar cheese and potato, but on Tuesdays specialty perogies with sauerkraut or with cottage cheese are made. Many of the perogies are sold for takeout at the attached deli, while others are eaten (boiled, deep-fried, or pan-fried; alone or in combination with holubchi, kubasa, and all the trimmings) in one of the restaurant's several rooms.

Alycia's was one of the late John Candy's favourite eateries, and he regularly had borscht and holubchi flown to him in Los Angeles by private jet. According to Sharon Staff, "hundreds and hundreds of guest books" have been signed by people from all over the world, many of them visiting celebrities. She acknowledges that Alycia's location makes some new customers hesitant to park their cars and walk in, but there are no plans to move. Marion Staff believed that the only place for a Ukrainian restaurant is the North End.

Perogies from the church

Carrying on a fund-raising tradition of many Ukrainian churches, Holy Trinity Cathedral at 1175 Main Street offered all-you-can eat perogies on the last Friday of each month from September to May 2009 for just $8.00. Other churches have perogies-to-go, often made by genuine Ukrainian Babas.

Alycia's Borscht

Courtesy Sharon Staff and Roger Leclerc

THE INGREDIENTS:

3 or 4 medium-size beets

1 medium onion, finely chopped

2 medium potatoes, grated

¼ head of green cabbage, grated

Salt, pepper, parsley, and dill to taste

2 tablespoons (30 ml) sugar

2 tablespoons (30 ml) white vinegar

14-ounce (398 ml) can of beans with pork

14-ounce (298ml) can of tomatoes, cut into small pieces

14-ounce (298ml) can of yellow beans

10-ounce (284ml) can of consommé or chicken soup base

Whipping cream (optional)

THE PREPARATION:

The ingredients should be added in the order listed to accommodate different cooking times. The beets should be pre-cooked for ease of peeling, then chilled and grated.

Place onion, potatoes, and cabbage in a large pot, cover with water, and cook until all are tender.

Add the pre-cooked beets, salt, pepper, parsley, dill, sugar, and vinegar and bring to a boil. Then simmer for a few minutes before adding the beans with pork, tomatoes, yellow beans, and consommé. Continue to simmer for 10 or 15 minutes. The whipping cream can be added just before serving and heated if desired, but do not boil. The flavour of the borscht will improve if allowed to sit overnight. It can be frozen. Serves 6 to 10 people.

■ Obee's Steam Bath (shown in 1979) became a North
End icon. • Credit: U of M Archives, Tribune Collection, 53-4269-2,
Jim Wiley photo

CHAPTER

5

"I'LL MEET
YOU AT..."
NORTH END
LANDMARKS

■ Aerial views of Main Street looking north and south from Higgins in 1956. • Credit: Archives of Manitoba, Winnipeg-Streets-Main 1956 2, N15579

LANDMARKS OF YESTERYEAR

Some of the best-known landmarks of the North End no longer exist, their buildings demolished or their sites converted to other uses. They do, however, live on in photographs, written accounts, and the memories of people who once knew them.

■ The Main Street Farmers' Market (shown in 1958) brought city and country people together. • Credit: Archives of Manitoba, Winnipeg-Markets 1

The Farmers' Market

Most of the people at the market were immigrants like my parents and the jabbering of mixed languages filled the air like music. Even as a child, I marvelled at the neat rows of vegetable stands strung together on opposite sides creating narrow pathways. Each stand offered fruits and vegetables in a profusion of colours and smells. There were ripe, red strawberries, dimpled rosy raspberries and plump blueberries in bins next to shades of green lettuce, celery and cucumbers, with splashes of orange carrots and red tomatoes. Colourful homemade jams in jars decorated the rough wooden shelves, while my gaze was drawn downward by the pungent odour of pickles in barrels. Eating green peas or fresh carrots was better than ice cream.
—*Libby Simon*

Just as farmers in Europe hitched up their horses and wagons to sell fresh produce to city-dwellers at open-air markets, the Winnipeg's North End developed its own tradition of markets in the early 1900s. One of the earliest farmers' markets was established in the area of Dufferin and Derby by David Morosnick. Probably the best known and longest standing market was first established in 1930 by Isaac Zeilig on the west side of Main between Flora and Stella.

The Main Street market offered bedding plants in the spring, fresh produce in the summer, and pickles and preserves in the fall. During the winter, root vegetables, frozen fish, and, of course, Christmas trees were sold. There were chickens and ducks – dead or alive – fresh eggs, and, in Nellie Zaidman's words, "nice fresh, floppy fish." Goods were displayed on permanent wooden stalls, and haggling, in a variety of languages, was customary. In the early days farmers sometimes began their slow journeys to Winnipeg on mud or gravel roads in the middle of the night, their horse-drawn wagons laden with produce, hoping to arrive early enough to secure one of the stalls.

George Smith, whose uncle Don Smith first operated Smitty's Chip Stand from a wagon on the same block, recalls that the Anglo-Saxon farmers were usually allotted the first row of stands. Smitty's eventually had its own building, which later operated as the North End Chip Shop and is now known as Angelo's. Ben Hochman from the nearby Oasis remembers that when chips were seven cents a bag, Smitty gave books of matches instead of pennies as change.

Many vivid childhood memories of the market revolve around the chickens that were sold there. Tom Halprin's remembers a time when he was 10 or 11 years old and his mother, with Tom in tow, bought a live chicken, and took it to a nearby building to be koshered by a *shochet*. The grotesque image of the running headless fowl remains in his mind more than six decades later. Steve Kiz, who lived on Pritchard west of McPhillips, made the long trek home from the market pulling his coaster wagon with a live chicken inside a cage. His mother sometimes kept a chicken alive for a couple of days before using a block of wood and an axe to behead the bird and immersing it in boiling water to remove the pinfeathers. Ben Zaidman recalled once taking home a live chicken in a streetcar and said it wasn't uncommon to see live fowl being taken home by public transit.

Audrey Boyko's mother bought dry cottage cheese by the cup, scooped into a brown paper bag. She wonders how sanitary it was or if it was government inspected, but, she reflects, "We were never sick from it."

Mary and Vera's Pytel's mother got up early every morning and went to the market for a different reason. She was one of many city women who were picked up there by farmers' trucks to do a day's work in the fields: seeding, weeding, and picking. It was hard work as they laboured bent over under a blazing sun, and the pay in the 1930s was 50 cents a day. After her first day of work, she bought a bushel of potatoes with her pay; after

■ Drewry's Club Room (shown in 1942) was the beginning and ending point for "brewery tours."
• Credit: Archives of Manitoba, Foote Collection 244, N1844

the second day, a bushel of cucumbers. These were enough to feed her family and to share with others who lived in the same terrace. "We never had an empty table," they recall.

In 1956, the market was taken over by a co-operative. At the time there were 58 stalls, each 12 by 16 feet, and the daily rental fee was about $1.50. Concerned about the shortage of parking and stall space at the Main Street location, the co-op purchased a 132,000 square foot site at Nairn and Stapleton and developed ambitious plans that included a parking lot for 200 cars, an enclosed building, and even a restaurant and a major supermarket. The market officially moved in May 1960, but the new location simply didn't have the appeal of the Main Street site and eventually closed down.

Drewry's Brewery

Drewry's (later Carling's) Brewery on the west bank of the Red River just north of the Redwood Bridge, has special memories for North Enders in at least two different ways.

For youngsters, the brewery annually created a Winter Wonderland of outdoor skating with music and of magical Christmas decorations that Tracy Konopada describes as "the most wonderful thing of all. It was so beautiful with Snow White and the Seven Dwarfs. It was magical!"

For adults, Drewry's, like other Winnipeg brewers, hosted events that were euphemistically called brewery tours. In reality, these were opportunities for participants to drink some free

A 1949 aerial view of Drewry's Brewery • Credit: Archives of Manitoba, Winnipeg-Buildings-Business-Drewry's Brewery 4, N16514

beer. The "tours" actually took place in the club room and never ventured into any other parts of the operation.

Drewry's, a local family-owned brewery, was founded in 1882 by Edward L. Drewry after he purchased the decade-old Redwood Brewery. Drewry was a prominent Winnipegger who served on the Winnipeg City Council in 1883-84 and was a Conservative MLA representing North Winnipeg from 1886 to 1889. He sold the brewery in 1924 to Western Canada Breweries. In 1953 Drewry's became Carling Breweries (Manitoba) Ltd., and, after a series of purchases and consolidations, was renamed Carling O'Keefe.

Economy Drugs

"Dave Stern took me in. I don't know why," Harry Kaplan reflects as he tells of his apprenticeship and subsequent partnership at Economy Drugs. He describes Dave Stern as "the wise visionary" and himself as "a young smartass."

The year was 1950, and Kaplan, freshly graduated from St. John's Tech, had applied to serve his mandatory two-year apprenticeship before being accepted into the School of Pharmacy at the University of Manitoba. This involved being a soda jerk, running errands as a delivery boy, dusting the bottles in the dispensary, and soaking in the wisdom of drugstore cowboys who freely offered their views on any and all topics. Harry Kaplan returned to Economy Drugs after graduating in pharmacy and became a partner in the business in 1963.

Dating back to the late 1920s, Economy Drugs was a North End fixture at Main and Redwood. When Harry Kaplan arrived, the store was 1,200 square feet. Benny Ruben owned the building and rented the storefronts to various tenants. Nate Sarbit had a grocery store on the corner at Redwood, then, further south, there was Max the barber, Mainwood Beauty Salon, and Economy Drugs. Kelekis was south of the drug store, and the area that later served as a parking lot at Aberdeen was Speed Service Station. As time went on, Economy took over the entire building.

In 1953, Economy Drugs did only about $120 in business in a typical day. What Kaplan terms "the explosion" began in 1963 when the business became Economy Discount Drug Store. It had been giving discounts on purchases for years – a practice its competitors didn't appreciate or imitate – but when the word "discount" was added to the company name and the price cuts became open, business thrived. From 1963 to 1973, Economy Discount Drugs had the highest volume of sales of all pharmacies in Manitoba. At it peak, Economy employed eight pharmacists – several of them former owners of other drug stores that Economy had bought out.

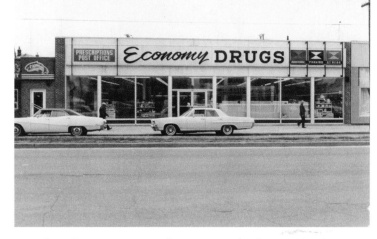

■ When Economy Drugs began openly discounting its prices in the 1960s, its sales soared. • Credit: Courtesy Harry Kaplan

At its peak, Economy Drugs had as many as eight pharmacists. Pictured from left are Dave Stern, Merk Merkel, Archie Orlikow, and Harry Kaplan.
• Credit: Courtesy Harry Kaplan

Economy Drugs became a Shopper's Drug Mart in 1973, and Dave Stern became the Manitoba Vice-President of Shopper's. Stern died in 1994.

The Olympic Rink

Located at the corner of Charles and Church, the Olympic Rink was a barn of a building that seated approximately 1,000 people in its creaky wooden bleachers. It had natural, not artificial, ice that was periodically flooded by the Winnipeg Fire Department, and, with the end doors left wide open, the ice could freeze solid in half an hour. Spectators sometimes joked that when the temperature was 40 below zero outside, it was 50 below inside the rink.

The Olympic Rink was a busy place, with its ice rented out to a number of men's hockey leagues, including a large Sunday night Catholic League that involved many of Winnipeg's most skilled players, who took time off from their regular teams to represent their churches on Sundays. Many of the youth hockey leagues organized by the legendary Vince Leah played at the Olympic. Gord McTavish, who was the manager of the rink during the 1950s, reports, "Uncle Vince was there all the time." Although hockey was an all-male sport in those days, an after-school girls' figure skating club made extensive use of the ice. During the off-season when the ice had melted to expose the soil underneath, the Olympic housed lacrosse games. Free skating on Sunday afternoons offered skate rentals for a quarter.

During the 1950s, the Olympic Rink was used extensively for junior hockey and, in the 1960s, as an eight-sheet commercial curling facility. After the City of Winnipeg turned down the opportunity to purchase the facility as a recreational centre, the property was sold to a developer. The building was demolished in 1969 to make way for an 11-storey apartment building appropriately named the Olympic Towers.

■ Oretzki's Department Store gradually expanded as the business grew. • Credit: Archives of Manitoba, Jewish Historical Society Collection, 2842

Ortezki's Department Store

While George Gershman was a high school student in the late 1930s, he worked at Oretzki's Department Store on Saturdays for 25 cents an hour. One year he sold so many pairs of bedroom slippers just before Father's Day that Louis Oretzki treated him to a 40-cent veal cutlet dinner at the White House. Pearl (Rosenberg) Globerman's job as a 16-year-old was to stand on the sidewalk in front of the store and invite customers to go inside and look around. Young Harry Kaplan's first job at Oretzki's was wrapping parcels and tying them with string. His co-worker was an elderly man whose persistent demands to work faster made the boy so nervous that his nose bled. Kaplan later delivered parcels and remembers one assignment where he was dispatched from the store on his bicycle just before the

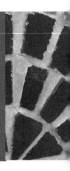

Wolch's Department Store

Although Ortezki's was generally considered the largest department store in the North End, Wolch's Department Store at 881 Main Street (just north of Euclid) was a close second. Like Oretzki's, Wolch's sold mostly clothing and shoes. George Smith, who grew up in nearby Point Douglas, recalls that Wolch's prices were somewhat higher than Oretzki's.

■ Oretzki's in 1981 • Credit: Jewish Heritage Centre, JM 2302

6:00 p.m. closing time to deliver "a huge box" to a nursing home on Roslyn Road. He got home around 8:30 that evening and was to discover later that he wasn't paid beyond 6:00 p.m. He graduated to the position of shoe salesman after an apprenticeship spent rearranging shoes in a stuffy basement stockroom and, like other shoe sellers, was paid 25-cent "spiffs" for selling slow-moving styles. He recalls that he once proudly sold a man a shiny pair of dress shoes to wear to a wedding and feared for his job when the customer returned a week later to point out Kaplan had given him two left shoes.

Oretzki's Department Store was first established in 1911 when Harry Israel Oretzki (known to all as "H. I.") bought - and lived in - a house at 493 Selkirk Avenue and built a store addition on the front. As the business grew, he and his brothers purchased neighbouring houses and expanded the store. Phyllis (Oretzki) Springman, the daughter of H.I.'s younger brother Louis, explains that Oretzki "wasn't our true name," but was

derived from the town of Oretz in Russia. Her father fled from there at the age of six after witnessing the killing of other family members by Russian troops.

Although Oretzki's was often referred to as "the Eaton's of the North End," the store didn't carry as wide a range of merchandise as the iconic Portage Avenue store. However, like Eaton's, Ortezki's maintained a generous "goods satisfactory or money refunded" guarantee. Customers who spoke languages other than English were delighted to find clerks who could converse comfortably with them. Sid Green, who grew up in a predominantly Ukrainian neighbourhood and worked at Oretzki's as a student, recalls, "I could sell most clothing in Ukrainian."

Concentrating mainly on clothing, shoes, dry goods, and toys, Oretzki's outfitted generations of North Enders. Morley Rypp remembers his family's once-a-year visit to the store to pick out each child's annual pair of shoes. Norm Silverberg relates that he and his brother got a new pair of tan-coloured Sisman Scampers shoes every summer. The x-ray device that

was intended to assist with shoe fittings but incidentally became a source of entertainment for toe-wiggling children is long gone, but often remembered.

As the popularity of shopping centres rose and the attraction of Selkirk Avenue declined, Oretzki's sales dwindled. The store closed its doors forever in 1986.

The Children's Hospital of Winnipeg

It was the dedication of a quiet but determined young nurse from England that led to the establishment of a hospital in

Winnipeg devoted exclusively to the care of children and their families. Annie Bond arrived in Winnipeg in 1903 and was appalled to see the crowded and unsanitary living conditions of families in the North End that contributed to the death of one out of every eight infants before reaching one year of age. With the support of community volunteers, Bond coordinated the opening in 1909 of the Children's Hospital of Winnipeg. It was situated in a rundown house at 23 Beaconsfield Street in Point Douglas and initially had one nurse, one "maid-of-all-work," an on-call team of physicians and surgeons, and enough space for only 15 patients. A former woodshed was the outpatient department.

The hospital was filled to capacity as soon as it opened, and a fundraising campaign to build a newer and larger Children's Hospital began almost immediately. With the assistance of a group of local businessmen that included hardware magnate James H. Ashdown, a park-like three and a half acre site on the Red River and bordered by Aberdeen, Main, and Redwood was purchased. In 1911, the new three-storey facility was ready to admit more than 100 patients. Within months, a small chapel and a laundry were added, and a nurses' residence was completed in 1918. By 1920, the Children's Hospital of Winnipeg was

■ The second Children's Hospital near Aberdeen and Main (shown in 1924) later became the Holy Family Home. • Credit: Archives of Manitoba, Winnipeg-Hospitals-Children's N3352

admitting 2,000 patients annually. The Children's Hospital of Winnipeg continued to operate on that site until a new $4-million building on Bannatyne Avenue was completed in 1956.

Obee's Steam Bath

When the European Block was completed at Mountain and McGegor 1914, it offered a service that was appreciated by Winnipeggers from all parts of the city, but especially those from the North End. The top two floors of the building had rental apartments, but the bottom two housed bath tubs and steam baths. At a time when many North End houses and apartments didn't have bathtubs, the European Baths, as they were then called, became a place where people were able to go for their weekly ablutions.

■ Old Ex Arena, 2009 • Credit: Photo by Russ Gourluck

In 1943, the building was purchased by Harry Oberman, and the bottom floors became Obee's Steam Baths. Although by then most homes had more extensive plumbing, Obee's remained a popular destination for men to socialize and play cards, conduct business, perhaps have a few drinks, and enjoy a relaxing steam bath.

Oberman's son, Jack Oberman, continued to look after the business until it was gutted by fire in 1989. The landmark building acquired a new lease on life in 1991 when it was converted to family housing units by the Winnipeg Housing Rehabilitation Corporation. The building was extensively renovated and a house next door was demolished to provide green space for the children of residents.

Old Exhibition Park

When Mike Humniski was a boy in the 1920s, one of his neighbours on Stella Avenue who kept cows arranged for them to be picked up every morning and walked along the back lanes to the Exhibition Grounds to graze for the day. A few years later, Sophie Shinewald, whose family lived at 943 Selkirk Avenue, found that the hubbub from the Ringling Brothers Circus at the Exhibition Grounds across the street made it difficult to concentrate while she studied for her grade twelve exams. Later known as the Old Exhibition (or simply Old Ex) Grounds, the open fields included baseball diamonds, a grandstand, and, at one point, a banked motorcycle and car racing track. The use of the area to accommodate returning soldiers after World War One probably accounts for nearby street names like Artillery and Battery.

Today that area, somewhat smaller than in the past, is known as the Old Exhibition Athletic Grounds and is bounded by

Sinclair on the west and Flora Place on the north. In addition to playground equipment for children, the City of Winnipeg-owned property includes outdoor hockey rinks, baseball diamonds, football and soccer fields, the Old Exhibition Arena, and the indoor North Centennial Pool. Charlie Krupp Stadium – home of North End Nomads football – is nearby.

■ The Queen's Theatre (shown ca 1920) was formerly a Presbyterian Church and later became the Hebrew Sick Benefit Hall • Credit: Archives of Manitoba, Jewish Historical Society Collection, 2941

The Hebrew Sick Benefit Association

Not long after the first Jewish immigrants arrived in Winnipeg, they began forming mutual aid societies. Known in Yiddish as *landsmanshafin*, these organizations provided free loans to help families and individuals establish businesses, as well as offering sick benefits, life insurance, and emergency financial help. Between 1906 and 1925, 36 such groups were formed in Winnipeg, some of them named for the towns in Europe from which their members had come.

One of the best known, the Hebrew Sick Benefit Association (HSBA), was founded in 1906, and, a year later, the organization purchased the former St. Giles (North) Presbyterian Church at 239 Selkirk Avenue. From then until the early 1930s, the facility was known as the Queen's Theatre and its stage hosted some of the best musical and dramatic acts from the Yiddish theatre circuit. The gravity of a performance, however, didn't deter youngsters like Sheppy Hershfield and his friends from waiting for just the right moment to roll an empty pop bottle down the sloped floor until it bumped against the base of the stage.

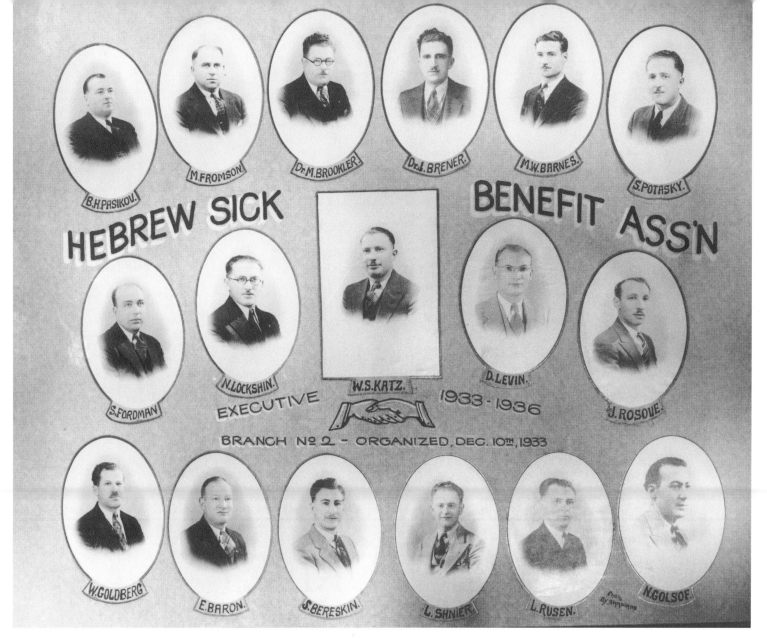

HEBREW SICK BENEFIT ASS'N

B.H.PASIKOV. M.FROMSON. Dr.M.BROOKLER. Dr.J.BRENER. M.W.BARNES. S.POTASKY.

S.FORDMAN N.LOCKSHIN. W.S.KATZ. D.LEVIN. J.ROSOVE.

EXECUTIVE 1933-1936

BRANCH N⍛ 2 – ORGANIZED, DEC. 10ᵀᴴ, 1933

W.GOLDBERG E.BARON. S.BERESKIN. L.SHNIER L.RUSEN. N.GOLSOF.

Photo By Shapiros

■ (ABOVE) The Hebrew Sick Benefit Association was established in 1906. • Credit: Archives of Manitoba, Jewish Historical Society Collection, 46

■ (BELOW) The former HSBA Hall had a new owner in late 2009, but the initials "HSB" remained on the stair railings. • Credit: Photo by Russ Gourluck.

The building later became the Hebrew Sick Benefit Hall (colloquially referred to as "the Hebrew Sick") where countless wedding receptions and other social events were held. Esther Korchynski, whose aunt catered many of the affairs held there, describes the hall as "the hub of Jewish activities." Extensive use of the hall continued until some of the city's synagogues added banquet halls of their own. In addition to its banquet facilities and financial services, the HSBA operated a cemetery on north McPhillips Street and held holiday services.

Eventually the building became a bingo hall and, in 2002, the HSBA as an organization was absorbed in the amalgamation of three synagogues to form Congregation Etz Chayim.

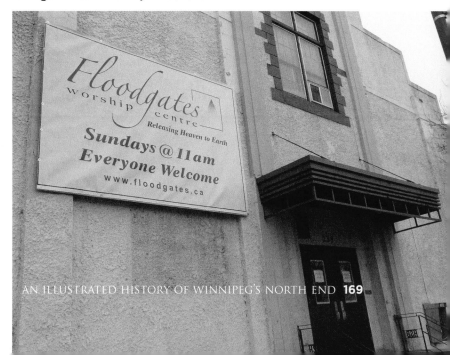

Floodgates
worship centre
Releasing Heaven to Earth
Sundays @ 11am
Everyone Welcome
www.floodgates.ca

A slushy Main Street looking south to Redwood • Credit: Photo by John Marczyk

ENDURING LANDMARKS OF THE NORTH END

Although a few buildings in the North End have received official designations for their architectural features, the historical value of most of the continuing landmarks in the area exists not in the buildings themselves but in the events and activities that they have housed.

■ ■ ■ ■ ■ ■ ■

McGregor Armoury

Originally intended as a military drill hall for North Winnipeg, the building known as McGregor Armoury was designed in 1913 by Winnipeg architect H. E. Matthews. Considering that the design was based on a standard Department of Militia and Defence plan bureaucratically labelled "Type D Alternate," the yellow brick building includes some interesting architectural features, including corner towers with decorative brickwork and Tyndall stone windowsills. In keeping with the military culture of the day, there were separate bowling alleys and shooting galleries for Officers and Men, and separate Men's, Officers', and Sergeants' messes, each with its own kitchen. Some of the original interior features included 13-foot-high arched windows on the north and south sides, internal balconies, oak woodwork, and decorative ironwork. Although there have been many renovations through the years, the original marble washroom stalls remain.

The building has been used by a number of different military units since it opened, beginning with the 106th Winnipeg Light Infantry, whose recruits were trained there in bayonet fighting during the First World War. Dents in the main floor at the west end remain to show where bayonet dummies were tied down. After the war, a surge in public school enrolment saw overflow classes from Ralph Brown School held in the Armoury. When the Second World War began, the Armoury was used as a recruiting centre, and tents were pitched in the north fields to accommodate the crowds of volunteers.

Through the decades, the building has been the home of the Royal Canadian Horse Artillery, the Royal Canadian Army Service Corps, the 13 Provost Company, and the Canadian Women's Army Corps. Since 1965, McGregor Armoury has been the home base of the Fort Garry Horse.

The building continues to be used for army and air cadet activities and for reserve training. A former caretaker's apartment on the third floor now houses the Fort Garry Horse Museum and Archives, and the tank and reconnaissance vehicles erected as monuments in the field to the north have become play structures for neighbourhood children.

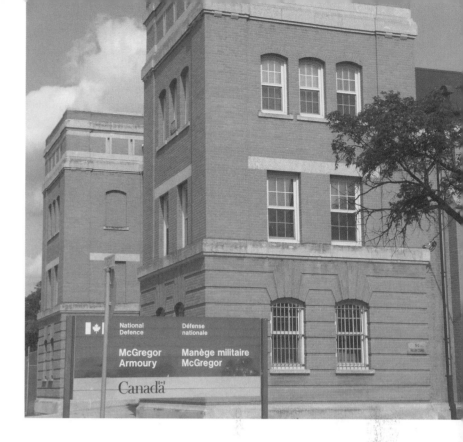

■ McGregor Armoury in 2009 • Credit: Photo by Russ Gourluck

Mount Carmel Clinic

The early Jewish community in Winnipeg demonstrated a strong commitment to taking care of its own people through the establishment of such services as an orphanage and an old folks home in the North End. The most visible and enduring aspect of that commitment is Mount Carmel Clinic.

Named for a mountain located near Jerusalem known as a place of beauty and a symbol of God's favour to His people, Mount Carmel Clinic was established in 1926. Its primary purpose was to provide free medical care to recent Jewish immigrants, many of whom arrived in poor health and with little money, as well as to avoid accusations of being a burden on the public system. It provided a place where immigrants could be treated by Jewish doctors familiar with their cultural and religious values and able to converse in their own languages.

The clinic's first location was in an old house, the former home of Rabbi Chaim Herson, at 263 Pritchard Avenue. The kitchen served as the pharmacy, and a volunteer group of Jewish doctors, dentists, and pharmacists supplemented the efforts of one full-time nurse. The second, which opened in 1929, was a new building, funded by the Jewish community, at 120 Selkirk Avenue, east of Main. The current site at 886 Main Street officially opened on September 24, 1982.

■ The second Mount Carmel Clinic was at 120 Selkirk Avenue. • Credit: Jewish Heritage Centre, JM 2309

Mount Carmel Clinic has a history of innovation – and of controversy – in health care. It became the city's first walk-in clinic by not requiring appointments, operated a day hospital for children, and, in the 1960s and 1970s, ventured into the political minefields of birth control and therapeutic abortion. The mandate of the clinic expanded to provide services for people from all ethnic groups in the general North End area. Its services grew to include a day hospital, social work, psychiatry, nutrition, dental care, a day nursery, and family planning. Much of the leadership of Mount Carmel Clinic in groundbreaking health care initiatives can be attributed to Anne Ross, who served as the Executive Director for 37 years, beginning in 1948. Ross advocated a holistic approach to treating patients and their families that went beyond physiological symptoms to take emotional and economic factors into account as well.

Mount Carmel Clinic continues to evolve to meet changing needs. The Anne Ross Day Nursery, in its own building adjacent to the Clinic, can accommodate 45 children. Recent initiatives include a cross-cultural counselling program, diabetes and Hepatitis C clinics, a teen clinic, and the R.B. Russell Student Health Clinic. In 2006-2007, there were more than 139,000 points of contact at the clinic, including over 13,000 physician visits, 81,000 patient encounters with clinic nurses, 36,557 filled prescriptions, over 3,500 dental visits, and more than 1,200 cross cultural counseling sessions.

The saga of Mount Carmel Clinic is related in two books: *Clinic With a Heart: The Story of Mount Carmel Clinic*, written by Anne Ross, and *Mount Carmel Clinic: A History 1926-1986* by Ross's daughter, Dee Dee Rizzo.

■ The current Mount Carmel Clinic building opened in 1982. Credit: Photo by Russ Gourluck

(RIGHT) A former bank building was renovated in 2009 to house Mount Carmel Clinic's administrative and outreach programs. • Credit: Photo by Russ Gourluck

The Bridges of the North End

The Canadian Pacific Railway mainline and the associated railway yards have served as the unmistakable boundary that separates the North End from the rest of the city. Only a limited number of channels allow passage from one side to the other.

As mentioned previously, the construction of the Main Street underpass in 1904 allowed vehicles and pedestrians to cross the railway tracks. Until then, pedestrians, horse-drawn transportation, and the few automobiles that existed in Winnipeg had to make their way across the level crossing unless, as was often the case, the crossing was blocked by freight cars. Streetcar routes ended south and north of the tracks, leaving passengers to walk between the two points to continue their journeys.

The first Salter Street Bridge over the expansive railway yards was built in 1898 using a superstructure that was salvaged from an earlier Main Street Bridge. It was popularly known at the time as "the overhead bridge." That bridge was replaced in 1932 with a Depression-era project that provided work for

■ The Arlington Bridge was erected in 1912. • Credit: Photo by Russ Gourluck

■ The Redwood Bridge (shown in 1958) opened to allow boats to pass by. • Credit: Archives of Manitoba, Winnipeg-Bridges-Redwood 4, N22031

approximately 700 men. The current bridge, named in honour of veteran City Councillor Slaw Rebchuk, was built in 1984.

The Arlington Bridge was erected over the rail yards in 1912 after its funding was rejected two years in a row by Winnipeg ratepayers. Some sources indicate that bridge was originally designed and built to span the Nile River in Egypt and later sold at auction in Darlington, England by the manufacturer, the Cleveland Bridge and Iron Works.

The City of Winnipeg originally planned to have streetcars cross the bridge, but, after the tracks were laid, only one trial run was made. The steep grades at both ends of the bridge were simply too much for the trolley cars, and the motormen refused to make another trip. For similar reasons, traffic lights at each end of the top of the bridge are synchronized with lights at the bottom to prevent vehicles from being trapped on the steep grade, particularly in icy conditions.

Although major deck reconstruction took place in 1992, the bridge is approaching its 100th year of use. There have been

Down to the Roundhouse

Mike Humniski and other CPR employees who lived near the Arlington Bridge regularly walked to and from work using a set of steps that led from the middle of the bridge down to the railway yards and the roundhouse.

periodic reports of plans to replace the bridge since at least the 1980s, but the plans have yet to find their way into reality.

The original Louise Bridge was built in over the Red River in 1881 as part of the strategy of Winnipeg City Fathers to entice the CPR to cross through Winnipeg rather than Selkirk, and was used by horses and wagons as well as by trains. A replacement bridge was built in 1911, reusing and widening the railway bridge substructure and replacing the superstructure.

The Redwood Bridge was built over the Red River in 1908, connecting the North End and Elmwood, and was intended primarily for horse-and-wagon traffic and streetcars. It is claimed by engineers to be the oldest remaining as-constructed bridge in the City of Winnipeg.

In its early days, the centre section of the bridge could be rotated 90 degrees to allow the passage of boats, particularly

■ During the 1950 flood, the level of the Red River came close to the deck of the Redwood Bridge. Because the approaches to other bridges were flooded, the Redwood was one of the few that remained open. • Credit: Courtesy Dan Skwarchuk

during times of high river levels. The elaborate mechanical operation was controlled from a tin-clad shed perched high in the girders above the middle of the bridge. Danny Pollock recalls that one day in the mid-1940s when he was about five years old – and all dressed up to go to a birthday party – he wandered away from home and climbed the girders almost to the control house. He was rescued and taken home by the police.

After more than a century of service, the Redwood Bridge is closed periodically to allow for repairs to its foundations and to deal with the deterioration of its steel beams and trusses.

■ For many decades, streetcars made their way across the Redwood Bridge. • Credit: Courtesy Manitoba Transit Heritage Association

St. John's Library in 2009
• Credit: Photo by Russ Gourluck. North Enders rallied to save the St. John's Library. • Credit: Courtesy Gord Mackintosh

St. John's Library

"It was unbelievable that City Council would think of closing the only library in Winnipeg's North End. We were outraged!" says Gord Mackintosh, now the MLA for St. Johns, who was part of a vociferous citizens' coalition in 1993 that opposed plans to close the venerable St. John's library branch at 500 Salter Street.

When it opened in 1915, St. John's was the first branch library of the Winnipeg Public Library and one of three (the William Avenue Main Library, the St. John's branch, and the Cornish branch) funded by the Carnegie Foundation. In its early years, it was frequented by immigrants eager to improve their knowledge and their English skills and by St. John's Tech students eager to improve their marks (or at least to meet with their friends.) Its dark oak woodwork and antique reading tables are reminders of an era when public libraries were hushed and somewhat intimidating places.

The branch remains open – although with limited hours – and a project named "Moving Ahead" involves local residents in developing a strategic plan to revitalize the aging branch. One of the major challenges is declining circulation: 36,000 items a year compared to nearly 100,000 at the Cornish branch in trendy Wolseley and 360,000 at the West Kildonan branch on Jefferson Avenue. Some of the recommendations of the group include more advertising of library services, improved building appearance and access, more accommodating arrangements for fines, and holdings and programming that are specially designed to appeal to the community's diverse cultural groups. Some recent innovations are evening "Story Times" for families, an after-school Homework Club for St. John's High School students (with snacks and tutors), and the involvement of library staff in community outreach events.

POLITICS AND RELIGION

The history of church missions in the core of the city reveal their close association with the CCF and the NDP. In addition to J. S. Woodsworth, who was superintendent of both Stella and Sutherland Missions, Stanley Knowles worked at McLean Mission on Alexander, and Doug Martindale, now MLA for Burrows, was at Stella Mission.

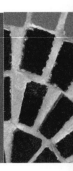

All People's Stella Mission (North End Community Ministry)

Vera and Mary Pytel joined Stella Mission when they were young girls in the 1930s. The two sisters recall that there were many kinds of sports, including basketball, baseball, and hockey (for boys only.) Although the mission was established by the Methodist Church, it was, as the name suggests, open to everyone. Mary and Vera do remember, however, that a Catholic schoolmate they invited to come with them to the mission was afraid to go inside because her parents would be angry.

There were originally two missions in the North End: All People's Mission Stella Avenue (470 Stella at Powers) and All People's Mission Sutherland Avenue (at Sutherland and Euclid in Point Douglas), but they eventually became known

■ Mothers waited for their babies to be seen at the Sutherland Mission in 1921. • Credit: Archives of Manitoba, Foote Collection 1451, N2374

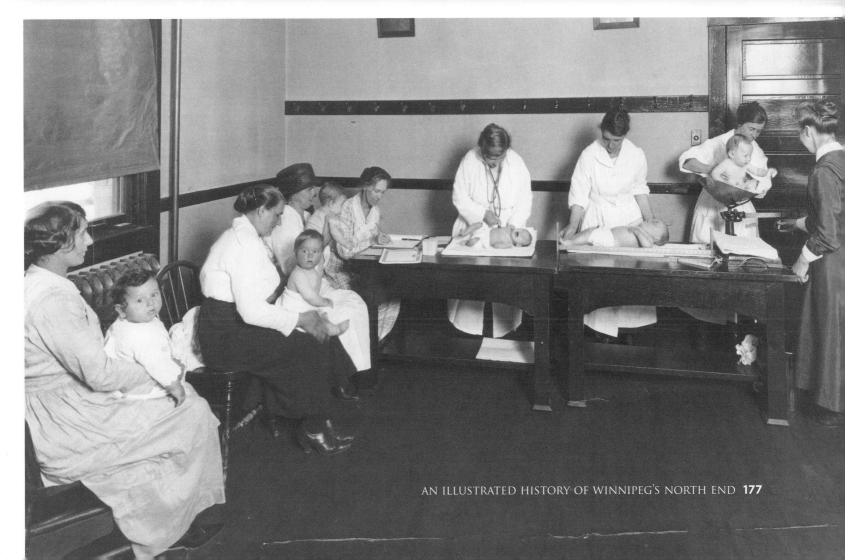

■ (LEFT) All People's Mission offered a range of social and educational programs for newly-arrived immigrants, ca 1910.
• Credit: Archives of Manitoba, Immigration Collection 3, N7928

(BELOW LEFT) The North End Community Ministry (shown in 2009) is affectionately known as "Stella" • Credit: Photo by Russ Gourluck

officially known as the North End Community Ministry. The locals affectionately call it "Stella." Its current programs include computer and telephone access for community members, children's activities, a babysitting service, parenting programs, a monthly feast for children and their families, and free income tax preparation. Sunday worship services, a blend of Christian and traditional Aboriginal practices, begin with a smudge ceremony.

Ukrainian Labour Temple

After more than 90 years, the Ukrainian Labour Temple at the corner of Pritchard and McGregor stands as an enduring symbol of Ukrainian culture and politics in Winnipeg. Built mostly by volunteer labour and financed entirely by donations, the building was constructed in 1918 and 1919 with an elaborate 1000-seat theatre and a print shop. An addition with a larger print shop as well as classroom office and library space was built on the west side in 1926, and a full basement was added in 1948.

more simply as Stella Mission and Sutherland Mission. Both were practical demonstrations of the social gospel, a belief that Christian ethics can solve social problems. Both had basketball courts and swimming pools for recreational programs and offered a range of services to help financially-challenged and newly-arrived North End residents to improve their lot in life.

Now an outreach program of the United Church of Canada, Stella Mission, which recently celebrated its 100th anniversary, is

Constructed at a cost of $72,000, the first and largest Ukrainian Labour Temple in Canada was spearheaded by the Ukrainian Social Democratic Party of Canada (USDP), a group of left-wing Ukrainian-Canadians who had formed their own party because they disagreed with some of the policies of the Socialist Party of Canada. The owner of the building was the Ukrainian Labour Temple Association, later renamed the

■ The Ukrainian Labour Temple is both a National Historic Site and a Provincial and Municipal Heritage Site.
• Credit: Photo by Russ Gourluck

Ukrainian Labour-Farmer Temple Association. In addition to political activities, the organization had its own newspaper and drama group, and the new building was designed to accommodate all of these activities. Although the credentials of the project architect were called into question, the result was a magnificent three-storey neoclassical structure featuring cut stone and fawn-coloured brick. The main entrance includes two hands carved in stone and the Marxist rallying call, "Workers of the World Unite."

Political activities at Labour Temple centred on socialism and trade unionism. The Ukrainian-language newspaper *Robochy Narod* (*Working People*) was published in the basement print shop. Both the USDP and the newspaper were banned by the Government of Canada as radical and anti-war organizations in 1918. The building was raided during the 1919 Winnipeg General Strike by authorities searching for evidence of sedition and conspiracy. Leaders of the organization were rounded up and jailed, along with other left-wingers, during World War Two. A cloak of mistrust and suspicion continued to hang over the Labour Temple though the 1960s as the RCMP maintained files on youth group activities. Even though the organization severed its connections with Communist Party decades ago, its political stance remains left-wing and labour oriented, and there are still Winnipeggers who view the Labour Temple, now operated by the Association of United Ukrainian Canadians, with suspicion.

Although the political aspects of the Labour Temple have received the most public attention, it has also been the home of a variety of educational and cultural activities, including Ukrainian language instruction, brass bands, choral-drama groups, a folk dance school, and theatrical productions. A mandolin orchestra dating back to 1921 is still active – and has even attracted some bluegrass players – as is a mixed choir. Not all of the participants are of Ukrainian origin. As Myron Shatulsky, who has been associated with the Labour Temple for most of his 80 years points out, "You don't need to know the language." Choir members who don't understand Ukrainian lyrics receive explanations in English and learn to sing the words phonetically. The Temple continues to be the site of the annual Lviv Pavilion at Folklorama.

Like many other ethnic organizations, membership in the Ukrainian Labour Temple has declined through the decades, and political passions have mellowed. In 1939, the national Labour Temple Association had 10,000 members and 200 to 300 branches across Canada, but few of the temples remain. In Winnipeg, there were labour temples in Point Douglas, Transcona, East Kildonan, and St. Boniface, and all have now shut down. The print shop, which by 1929 was publishing two newspapers and two monthly magazines for a total annual run of more than two million copies across Canada, has been closed and the equipment sold.

Despite decades of suspicion and even harassment by federal government officials, the Ukrainian Labour Temple was designated a National Historic Site in 2009, recognizing not only the architectural significance of the building but also its role in the social and cultural activities of Ukrainian Canadians. It was declared a Provincial Heritage site in 1995 and a municipally-designated site in 1997.

St. John's Park

On hot, muggy Winnipeg summer days, my mother would pack a blanket, a basket of food, and off we went to picnic in St. John's Park on Main Street. As we spread out on the lush, green grass, she often pulled stems of sweet-smelling, white clover that flourished around us, wove them into a garland and caressingly braided them into my hair like a crown. During the summer months it offered a child's paradise with swings, slides, a sandbox and even a wading pool in which I pretended to be really swimming. When the white coat of winter covered the ground, my brothers and I went tobogganing down the snow-covered banks onto the frozen river.
—*Libby Simon*

■ St. John's Park was one of the city's first public parks.
• Credit: Photo by Russ Gourluck

Situated on the site of an 1814 Red River Colony survey where early settlers once tilled the soil and seeded crops, St. John's Park was one of the first public parks to be established in Winnipeg. Since it opened in 1893 on land donated by brewery magnate E. L. Drewry, St. John's Park has been the site of countless family memories.

Occupying 6.8 hectares, the park now includes a wading pool and play area for children, picnic facilities, and lawn bowling greens.

Point Douglas

Bounded on the west by Main Street, the north by Redwood Avenue, the south by the CPR mainline, and the east by the Red River, Point Douglas was the site of the Hudson's Bay Company's Fort Douglas, which was built around 1813. Both were named for Thomas Douglas, the Earl of Selkirk. Early in that century, the area was used by Selkirk Settlers to grow

■ St. John's Park was the place for pleasant Sunday strolls. • Credit: Courtesy Dan Skwarchuk

wheat, but, after Winnipeg's incorporation in 1873, it became a genteel residential neighbourhood. Embraced by a bend in the Red River, Point Douglas included the residences of some of the wealthiest and most influential people in Winnipeg.

Because of its proximity to the CPR mainline, immigration and industrialization brought major changes to Point Douglas by the beginning of the 1900s. The wealthy established

■ Libby Simon (she's the 5-year-old girl on the far right) and her family posed for family photo in St. John's Park, ca 1940. • Credit: Courtesy Libby Simon; text and photograph originally published in *Geist* magazine, Spring 2008

■ Barber House at 99 Euclid Street was built in 1868 for E. L. Barber. Barber House was declared a Provincial Historic Site in 1987 and restoration began but funds ran out. Recently a local group, Sisters Initiating Steps towards a Renewed Society (SISTARS) has developed a plan that would see Barber House turned into what they affectionately call a "community hub." Barber House would be surrounded by public green space, a laundromat, a coffee shop, and a daycare centre for local children. The project is estimated to cost $2.7 million.
• Credit: Photos by Russ Gourluck

residents (predominantly British in origin) moved to newer and more prestigious suburbs such as Armstrong's Point and Crescentwood, and immigrants (mainly Jewish, Slavic, German, and Scandinavian) moved into the devalued homes of Point Douglas, often cramming dozens of people into houses designed for single families. As happened in the Jarvis Avenue area, industries established themselves in Point Douglas to be close to the railway tracks. These included farm implement manufacturers, foundries, breweries, saw mills, and flour mills.

In 1909, in an attempt to relocate prostitution to one small area of the city (and away from more affluent and politically-influential neighbourhoods), Winnipeg's Board of Police Commissioners designated McFarlane and Annabella Streets as a "Red Light District." Public protests and social reformers had the houses of ill repute (as many as 30 of them) closed down four years later.

The banks of the Red River served as a steamboat dock before the arrival of the railroad in the 1880s and as a Hobo Park during the Great Depression. Rover Street was built up

■ (TOP) The former Ukrainian Hall at 48 Euclid became a centre for Filipino seniors. • Credit: Photos by Russ Gourluck

(BOTTOM) The North Point Douglas Women's Centre, a gathering place for women and families, is one example of grassroots revitalization of the neighbourhood.
• Credit: Photos by Russ Gourluck

after 1950 to form a dike and prevent the flooding that had previously submerged parts of Point Douglas.

While the North Point Douglas area is primarily residential, South Point Douglas, close to the railway tracks, is predominantly industrial. One of the most historic buildings, now occupied by Gateway Packing, was previously Vulcan Iron Works,

Vulcan Iron Works, ca 1910 • Credit: Archives of Manitoba, Foote Collection 1592, N8696

■ The former Vulcan Iron Works building in 2009
• Credit: Photo by Russ Gourluck

iconic Winnipeg lumber company, moved to 5 Sutherland Avenue in 1882.

Because it is one of the oldest neighbourhoods in Winnipeg, Point Douglas is steeped in history. Some of the stately residences of Winnipeg's elite are no longer standing, including the home of John Christian Schultz on Beaconsfield Street. Schultz, who opposed the provisional government of Louis Riel, later served as a Member of Parliament and Lieutenant Governor of Manitoba. The house became the first site of the Children's Hospital of Winnipeg in 1909. Hardware magnate James Ashdown's residence was at 109 Euclid, and the residence of Premier John Norquay (for whom the school in Point Douglas is named) is believed to have been at 108 Hallet Street. Sir William Stephenson, the Canadian master spy, grew up at 175 Syndicate Street.

where the work stoppage that triggered the 1919 Winnipeg General Strike took place. Politician Tommy Douglas's father was a machinist at Vulcan, and young Tommy attended Norquay School. The current Manitoba Hydro station between Sutherland and Rover dates back to the Winnipeg Electric & Gaslight Company in the 1880s. Brown and Rutherford, the

■ One of the most unusual houses in the North End, a stately structure complete with turrets and an iron parapet, is located at 494 College Avenue. "The Castle," as it's generally called, was designed and built by Italian immigrants Ernest Marchetti and Joseph Biollo in 1906 and is included in the City of Winnipeg's Historical Building Inventory. It was owned and occupied for 27 years by Rabbi David Cantor – who is credited with convincing more than 600 families to emigrate from his native Poland – and subsequently purchased in 1947 by Martin Dudzik, a Polish immigrant. Dudzik, who told writer Lillian Gibbons "By trade I am a bricklayer, painter, and artist. I can make anything," added a distinctive weather vane, removed a second-floor balcony, and painted a landscape on the exterior. During the 1950s, the building had seven separate suites.
• Credit: Photo by Russ Gourluck

Bill Konyk was born at 94 Euclid Avenue and describes Point Douglas as "the true North End." He remembers the Ashdown home at Grove and Euclid, a Chinese laundry across the street, and the city garbage collection yard with its Clydesdale horses. Konyk recalls that Mrs. Sparrow (nee Barber) explained that the Selkirk Settlers were instructed by Chief Peguis to look under a horse's belly and told they could claim the land as far as they could see.

As children, he and his friends raided gardens down by the river and dug out potatoes. One brought butter, another brought salt, and the boys baked the potatoes in a hole in the ground. In the winter, they made their own wooden skis and swooshed down the banks of the river.

His mother, Theresa Konyk, who spoke German, Yiddish, English, Ukrainian, Russian, and Polish, acted as an interpreter for the neighbourhood. "Mrs. Konyk, I have trouble I need you talk to them," they would plead.

Young Bill sold newspapers in front of the Oak Theatre at Logan and Main. On his first day on the job he sold three newspapers, earned three cents, and spent the money on jawbreaker candies – at 8 or 9 for a penny – at Krindle's Grocery near Euclid and Granville. He shared them with the other kids in his class at Norquay School during the lunch hour, and they all returned to school with black mouths.

Audrey Boyko, who was born in 1936, grew up in a "huge house" at 180 Austin Street. Formerly the home of a parish priest, it had two sets of stairs leading to the second floor and to the basement. It was later converted to a rooming house.

■ Chesed Shel Emes was established in 1930 as a non-profit organization to prepare deceased Jewish people for burial in accordance with Orthodox tradition. It was Winnipeg's first Jewish funeral home. Until then, family members prepared bodies for burial in their homes or made arrangements with non-Jewish funeral homes. It originally operated in the house at 1023 Main Street (which was converted to a chapel) until the brick addition on the north was completed in 1947. Chesed Shel Emes means "charity of truth" or "charity of true loving kindness."
• Credit: Photo by Russ Gourluck

Other historic landmarks remain. Barber House at 99 Euclid Street was built in 1868 for merchant and newspaper publisher Edmund Lorenzo Barber, and members of the Barber family occupied the house until the late 1950s. The diverse cultural and religious history of Point Douglas is evidenced in several landmarks, including the Ukrainian Hall at 49 Euclid (currently the Filipino Senior Citizens' Hall), St. Andrews Ukrainian Catholic Church at 160 Euclid, and the former Hebrew Immigration Hall at 75 Hallet. The home of the Sutherland All People's Mission (119 Sutherland at Euclid) is currently the Manitoba Aboriginal Cultural Centre.

Joseph Zuken Memorial Park is a tribute not just to Point Douglas but to all of Winnipeg's North End. Named for the now-legendary politician, the park is now the site of Ross House, Winnipeg's first post office. The house was originally located at the foot of Market Avenue and was moved to Point Douglas in 1984. Illustrating the ethnic diversity of the area, the park includes monuments to Ukrainian poet and social activist Markian Shaskhevich, to Sir William Stephenson (whose roots were Icelandic), and to Ukrainian-Canadians settlers as well as those who died in World War Two.

Celebrating a Century: St. John's High School

For many years the only senior high school in North End Winnipeg, St. John's High School can claim some of the best-known and most successful alumni in Canada. After more than four years of planning, the school's centennial reunion took place in mid-June of 2010, celebrating 100 years of history and bringing together an estimated 2,000 former students and staff. A "Centennial Wall," funded by donations, was created in a hallway of the school as a legacy from the alumni to honour the history of St. John's.

■ Graduates of St. John's Technical High School in 1918
• Credit: Archives of Manitoba, Foote Collection 1592, N2691

■ St. John's in 2009 • Credit: Photo by Russ Gourluck

Although St. John's Technical High School accommodated its first students at 480 Salter Street in March of 1912, the school had officially been in existence since 1909 in four classrooms at Luxton School. Increasing demand for high school accommodation in the city had necessitated the establishment of temporary high school departments at Luxton, Alexandra, John M. King, and La Verendrye Schools.

Technical education (also known as Practical Arts) was first offered in Winnipeg in 1909 with experimental manual training classes in grades five, six, and seven. Household Arts for girls had been introduced even earlier, beginning in 1903 at Alexandra School on Edmonton Street with sewing and expanding a year later to cooking. In the school board's 1912 annual report, the director of manual training and technical education explained that "The purpose of the technical school is to enable a lad to discover the line of work for which he is best suited…" The supervisor of household arts courses pointed out that for that program "The aim is to contribute to the refinement and efficiency of girls by giving them high ideals… The training should increase their competency, both as home makers and as wage earners."

St. John's was one of two new high schools that were planned simultaneously and with virtually identical buildings: St. John's in the north part of the city, and Kelvin Technical High School in the south.

Although St. John's was originally conceived as a technical school and seen by some as vehicle to groom the sons and daughters of immigrants to take their place in the workforce, the majority of its students were enrolled in academic programs right from the start. As time went on, technical courses, especially in the Commercial program, gained in popularity.

Remembering the Times

Sophie Shinewald attended St. John's in the late 1920s as a Practical Arts student, where she studied sewing, cooking, and millinery. Although the program was open to both genders, only girls enrolled.

Esther Korchynski, who enrolled in at St. John's in 1948-49, lived in the Isaac Newton catchment area but "I fought to get into St. John's because that's where all my friends were going." Like many students before and after her, she realized that the right choice of options could enable her to attend the school she preferred. She selected a music option program that was offered at St. John's and not at Isaac Newton. Korchynski was in the chorus for *The Gondoliers* and *The Pirates of Penzance* during her two years at St. John's. Because so many students wanted to be involved, each production had two complete casts.

St. John's students, like those of most other schools, devised nicknames for teachers that they didn't dare use in their presence.

■ The St. John's Tigers became one of the original teams when the Winnipeg High School Football League was founded in 1933. Team alumni include Lou Adelman, Larry Fleisher, Norm Hill, Bud Korchak, Rube Ludwig, Len Meltzer, Ted Milian, Lou Mogul, Scott Robson, Vic Rosenblat, Nate Shore, and Chris Walby. • Credit: Archives of Manitoba, Jewish Historical Society Collection, 27

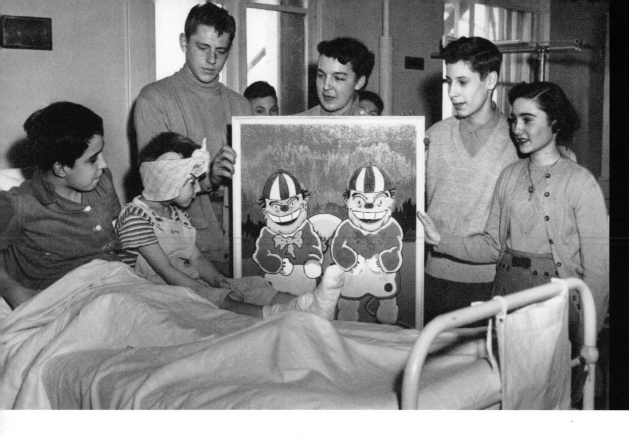

"Pegleg" Johnson, the physics teacher with an artificial leg wasn't likely to be confused with "Sleepy" Johnson, whose voice was claimed to put students to sleep. Another teacher whose nickname has endured, even among students who can't remember her real name, is "Miss Grundy," whose appearance reminded them of the *Archie* comics character.

Lillian Mendelsohn remembers Hank Promislow as a math teacher who "gave up his lunch hour for kids like me who were not good in math to do small group tutoring." He was one of the first men she remembers seeing wearing Hush Puppies. Promislow's colleague Catherine Thexton describes him as "a very influential vice-principal because he knew all of the students and he was always fair with them."

Max Manishen was a popular French teacher for St. John's for nearly 30 years. Lillian Mendelsohn explains that "Pegleg" Johnson had taught her father and was still there when she attended St. John's. William Penn Johnson taught at the school from 1921 to 1967, a total of forty-five years.

When George Gershman attended St. John's in the late 1940s (and had a crush on a Scottish female teacher who taught French) his French-Latin-option class had 44 students and 40 of them were Jewish. On the Jewish High Holidays, the class was empty. Jack Chapman explains that the school remained open on Jewish holidays, but many non-Jewish students stayed away. "A holiday is a holiday," he laughs.

■ For decades, Gilbert and Sullivan productions were annual events at St. John's High School. Burton Cummings (left) was one of countless performers. • Credit: Courtesy Lillian Mendelsohn

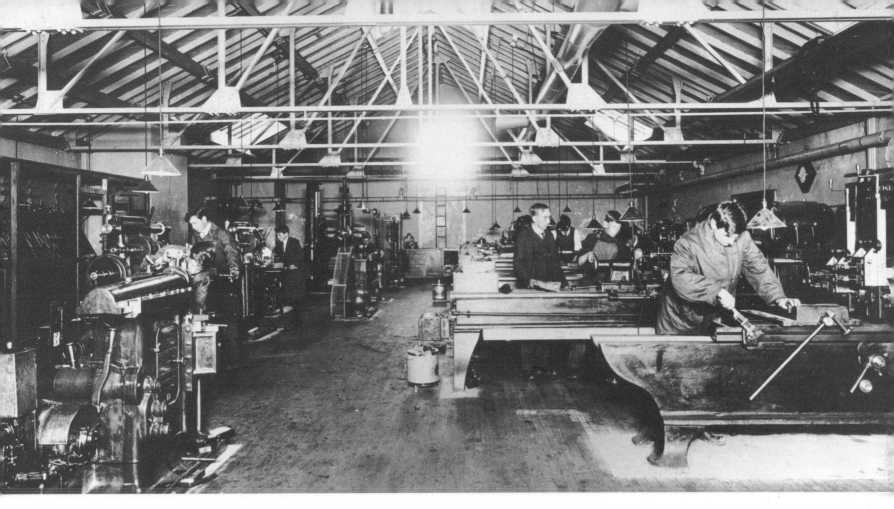

When Esther Korychnski was 11 or 12 years old and attending William Whyte, her aunt Bertha regularly took her to performances in the Celebrity Concert series at the Civic Auditorium. The aunt could afford only inexpensive seats on the main floor near the back. One evening, "a tiny little lady" approached them, explaining that she had trouble hearing and asking asked if Esther would sit in her seat at the front of the hall and allow her to sit next to her aunt. Esther, who had been studying music since she was two, was thrilled to trade places. Her aunt later told her that the woman was a teacher who confided that she didn't really have a hearing problem but made a practice of looking for a child who would benefit from sitting close to the performers. When Korchynski began attending St. John's a few years later she recognized her benefactor as Miss Elsa Handel, who taught at St. John's from 1936 to 1969.

Manly Rusen continues to feel indebted to Jack Silverberg. "He was an outstanding teacher, an outstanding mathematician, and a real character. If it wasn't for him, I wouldn't have become a lawyer because I couldn't get through mathematics in grade twelve." Rusen was tutored all summer in Silverberg's home.

Larry Fleisher describes his history teacher, Mr. Stewart Dack, as "probably the only teacher that had faith in me, that saw my potential." Several years after leaving St. John's, while Fleisher was playing for the Edmonton Eskimos and visiting Winnipeg for a game against the Blue Bombers, he took a cab to St. John's to pay a surprise visit to Mr. Dack. "Mr. Dack was in a downstairs classroom because he couldn't walk up the stairs," Fleisher explains. "I just knocked on his door and walked in. Mr. Dack looked at me, turned to his class, and said, 'My boy's come back.' By then we were both bawling." Larry Fleisher went on to become the Director of the Winnipeg Child Guidance Clinic and served as a Winnipeg City Councillor for 13 years.

Lillian Mendelsohn continues to appreciate her English teachers: Mr. Beer, who taught her how to write a précis and analyze a novel; Mr. Dack, who taught her how to use critical analysis and once set up a panel discussion on feminism; and Miss Beulah Ross, who made Shakespeare come alive. Mr. Burrows, her homeroom teacher in grade 12 was a Latin scholar who occasionally took his classes to Peanut Park to study Latin verbs. Miss Knapp taught her music and biology and loved dance. Mr. Don Hadfield, who had been her junior high music teacher at Machray and taught at St. John's from 1961 to

1966, drew on the musical skills and interests his students had acquired in their churches and synagogues.

Larry Fleisher explains that St. John's major rival in football was Kelvin "because Kelvin had all the rich kids."

Ron Devere, now practising medicine in Austin, Texas, has fond memories of Russ Pastuck's ballroom dancing classes. He continues to enjoy dancing and credits Pastuck with teaching him the importance of life-long exercise.

Len Offrowich, who attended St. John's from 1962 to 1968, insists that the old chemistry and physics labs in the old school building "looked like something out of a 1920's movie set." He remembers the basement shops classes for boys: woodworking with Mr. Wilkinson, metal work with huge coke-stoked furnaces, and Mr. Costantini's drafting class. He also recalls Miss Hyman's art classes, Mr. Burrow's Latin classes, and Miss Handel's library – as well as her detention classes. Dances for senior high students featured live bands (including the Deverons with Burton Cummings.)

Catherine Thexton taught biology at St. John's from 1966 to 1977 and has fond memories of the scores of students she met. She particularly remembers a Major Work class she taught in 1967-1968 and estimates that as many as ten of them became medical professionals, including Manitoba's Chief Public Health Officer Joel Kettner, Winnipeg Regional Health Authority President and CEO Brian Postl, psychiatrist Robert Steinberg, and researcher Gerald Minuk. Thexton, who retired in 1978, maintains an active interest in her former students. One of the projects in some of her classes was giving a flower to each student to examine. She recalls that the flowers were special sources of pride for students during the hippie era

As Times Change

Just as the community it serves has changed in the last hundred years, so has St. John's. The Tigers still play football, and English and math and science and social studies continue to be taught, but, like other schools, St. John's offers some programs and services that might not have been imagined decades ago. Native Studies and English as a Second Language have become important parts of the curriculum, and some of the options available to students as they plan their futures are a pre-employment program, an army reserve co-operative program offered in conjunction with the Canadian Forces, and an apprenticeship option. Some program areas available to students are Business Technology and Computer Education, Human Ecology and Industrial Arts, and Visual and Performing Arts. Some of the services available to students include a teen medical clinic staffed by a doctor and two nurses from Mount Carmel Clinic; an after-school homework club held at community locations; a full-service cafeteria; a Winnipeg Police Service resource officer; and the "Tiger Square" school store that sells St. John's clothing, school supplies, and confections.

Hanging Out at Peanut Park and Salter Drugs

Located, according to Ben and Phyllis (Zelickson) Hochman, "far enough away from the school not to be caught," Peanut Park was a popular gathering place for St. John's students who were skipping classes, having a smoke, or both. Officially named Machray Park by the City of Winnipeg, the small park and playground with the student-ascribed nickname is bounded by Powers, Church, Anderson, and Andrews. Danny Pollock describes it as "a place to go on a sunny afternoon if you didn't feel like going to school." Peanut Park wasn't just a place to skip class, however; Carolyn Rickey recalls that one of her teachers took a class there to sketch houses.

Salter Drugs, on the other hand, wasn't a safe destination for truant students, even for those who tried hiding under the counters. As Lillian Mendelsohn points out, it was one of the first places teachers looked. The drug store was, however, a popular after-school hangout.

■ St. Nicholas Ukrainian Catholic Church was the first Ukrainian church in Winnipeg and in urban Canada. The parish was founded in 1899 and the first church building, located at the corner of McGregor and Stella, was opened in 1901. A second and larger church was built across the street in 1904. The present church building at Arlington and Bannerman was consecrated in 1966. The impressive mosaic of Christ consists of thousands of pieces of blown-glass Italian tiles and the exterior is constructed of Manitoba Tyndall stone. The roof, domes and arches, covered by a glass fibre outer skin, simulate the colour of aged copper. The church seats 825 people.

• Credit: Photo by Russ Gourluck

PLACES OF WORSHIP

Much of heritage of the North End can be seen in its church buildings. Although the demographics of the area have changed, many of the area's oldest religious institutions continue to serve their congregations. Other buildings that were once houses of worship have been converted to different uses.

■ The interiors of churches such as St. Mary the Protectress are elaborately decorated.
• Credit: Courtesy Dan Skwarchuk

A Mosaic of Churches

Polish immigrants were instrumental in the founding of Holy Ghost Roman Catholic Church on Selkirk Avenue in 1899. Most of the Ukrainian immigrants who arrived in the 1890s and early 1900s had belonged to the Ukrainian Greek Catholic Church or the Ukrainian Greek Orthodox Church in the old country. Initially, in the absence of these churches, immigrants new to Winnipeg attended similar services, such as Roman Catholic or Russian Orthodox. Within a few years, however, a number of congregations and buildings were established, particularly in the North End, by the Ukrainian Greek Catholic Church and the Ukrainian Greek Orthodox Church (later renamed Ukrainian Catholic and Ukrainian Orthodox).

■ (OPPOSITE) Baskets of Easter food awaited blessings at St. Andrews Ukrainian Catholic Church (Euclid at Maple) in 1968. • Credit: U of M Archives, Tribune Collection, 34-2073-3

■ (BOTTOM) Holy Ghost Roman Catholic Church (shown in 1960) was built to serve newly-arrived Polish, Slovakian, Ukrainian, and German immigrants and was the first pastoral centre for Polish people in Western Canada. As the other ethnic groups began to establish their own churches, Holy Ghost became primarily Polish. Although Winnipeggers of Polish heritage continue to attend services, growing numbers of Filipino residents in the area have provided an influx of parishioners for the church and students for the school. • Credit: Archives of Manitoba, Winnipeg-Churches-Holy Ghost 1, N10267

■ (ABOVE) Designed by architect Michael Boreskie, the Holy Ghost Parish Centre opened in 1987. The pulpit and altar were specially constructed for use by Pope John Paul II at Birds Hill Park in 1984. A 100-seat chapel behind the main altar is a smaller-sized replica of the original church.
• Credit: Photo by Russ Gourluck

(OPPOSITE) Construction of the basement of Holy Trinity Ukrainian Orthodox Metropolitan Cathedral at 1175 Main was completed in 1952 and that part of the building served as the church for almost a decade until enough money was raised to complete the impressive structure.
• Credit: U of M Archives, Tribune Collection, 42-2610-4, 1961

■ St. Andrews Ukrainian Catholic Church on Euclid Avenue in Point Douglas, 2009 • Credit: Photo by Russ Gourluck

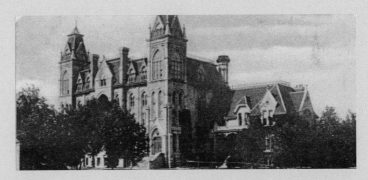

■ The oldest Anglophone educational institution in Western Canada, St. John's College was established in 1866 by Bishop Robert Machray as a theological training institute for Anglican clergy. A three-and-a-half storey brick building located on four acres on the west side of Main at Church was erected in 1884 with classrooms and living accommodations for the 20 students who attended the college at the time. By 1900 it had become a co-ed liberal arts institution affiliated with the University of Manitoba. The college relocated downtown to the corner of Broadway and Hargrave in 1945 and then to the University of Manitoba Fort Garry Campus in 1958.
• Credit: Courtesy Dan Skwarchuk

St. Joseph's Roman Catholic Church at the corner of Mountain and Andrews, 2009 • Credit: Photo by Russ Gourluck

■ (ABOVE) The original St. John Cantius Roman Catholic Church was constructed between 1918 and 1925. When the new church opened in 1971, the old building became a school. • Credit: Photo by Russ Gourluck

■ (BELOW) The Ukrainian Catholic Metropolitan Cathedral of Sts. Volodymyr and Olga at 115 McGregor features stained glass by Winnipeg artist Leo Mol. • Credit: Photo by Russ Gourluck

The former parish hall of St. John's Church was converted into condominium units in 2009. All seven units in the building, located at Main and Church, were sold before the project was completed. • Credit: Photo by Russ Gourluck

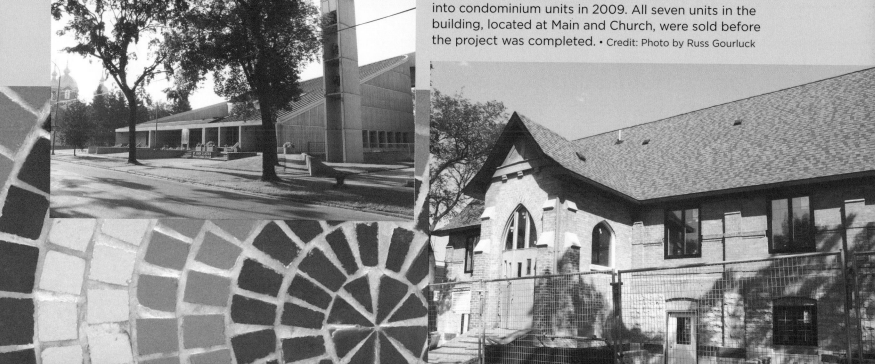

■ Described as the birthplace of the Anglican Church in Western Canada, St. John's Anglican Cathedral has been part of the history of Winnipeg since its first building, a mission house constructed of logs, was built in 1822 on land believed to have been donated by Lord Selkirk himself. It was replaced in 1833 by a second church that was named the first Anglican Cathedral in Western Canada around 1850. A third church was built on the same site in 1862, and the fourth and present Cathedral was reconstructed in 1926 using most of the stone from the third building. • Credit: Photo by Russ Gourluck

198 THE MOSAIC VILLAGE

■ With a busy strip mall next door, Holy Trinity Cathedral stands as an impressive reminder of the heritage of the North End.
• Credit: Photo by Russ Gourluck

■ (BELOW) Springs Inner City Church at 648 Burrows was formerly Robertson Memorial Presbyterian (then United) Church. It was built in 1911.
• Credit: Photo by Russ Gourluck

(BELOW, RIGHT) Bethlehem Aboriginal Fellowship at 294 Burrows was formerly St. Giles United Church.
• Credit: Photo by Russ Gourluck

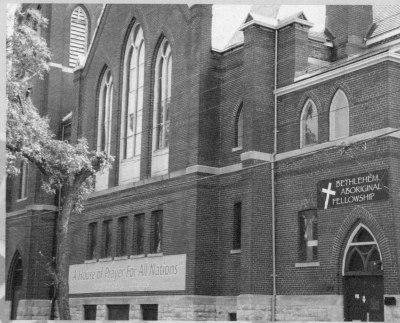

■ Always a symbol of diversity, the churches of the North End continue to show the mosaic nature of the community. • Credit: Photos by Russ Gourluck

A Multitude of Synagogues

Jewish residents of the North End established a number of synagogues, mostly within walking distance of residential areas. In *Journey Into Our Heritage*, Harry Gutkin points out that during the first three decades of the 1900s, 14 synagogues were established in the North End, and all were orthodox. At that time, Shaarey Zedek was the only synagogue in South Winnipeg. That pattern changed with the movement of Jewish families away from the North End. In 2010, Ashkenaze on Burrows, Etz Chayim on Matheson, and Talmud Torah Beth Jacob on Main Street were the only synagogues remaining in the North End.

■ (ABOVE) An Orthodox synagogue, Talmud Torah Beth Jacob is located in the building formerly occupied by the Deluxe (Hyland) Theatre. • Credit: Photo by Russ Gourluck

(LEFT) The former Tabernacle Baptist Church, built in 1906, was purchased by the Ashkenaze orthodox congregation in 1922. At the time it was one of approximately 15 synagogues in the North End. It is the oldest existing synagogue in Winnipeg. • Credit: Photo by Russ Gourluck

EPILOGUE
THE EVOLVING NORTH END

■ Photo by Russ Gourluck

■ ■ ■ ■ ■ ■ ■ ■

THE CHANGING MOSAIC

To many current Winnipeggers, the North End has come to represent crime and violence. Aging neighbourhoods, poverty, and hopelessness have taken their toll.

"Things have changed in the North End."

When Sam Katz was growing up on Cathedral Avenue, he knew every person in every house on the block. Families left their front doors unlocked and kids left their bikes on the lawn. "There was no fear of crime back in those days. It wasn't even a discussion, let alone an issue," the mayor observes. "Today it is, sadly. It's a serious issue, and it has to be dealt with. Things have changed in the North End."

Julie Zatorsky has lived in the same house in the North End since 1949, and she's seen many changes. In the fifties and sixties, most mothers were home all day, the neighbours knew each other, and the kids knew everyone. Now she knows only her close neighbours. "We had a nice neighbourhood and safe streets," she recalls, and in spite of a shooting across the street and a drive-by house shooting nearby, she still believes she has "a pretty good neighbourhood."

Jason McDonald was born in 1973 and, between the ages of five and 18 lived on Selkirk, then on Stella, and then on Bannerman. He and his friends played on the streets and back lanes and in the King Edward schoolyard, played Pacman at

(RIGHT) In 2009 construction began on a new Manitoba Public Insurance Service Centre on the west side of Main between Anderson and Church. Previously the site of St. John's College, the property was occupied by Winnipeg Motor Products (later Park Pontiac Buick) and had been vacant for several years. • Credit: Photo by Russ Gourluck

Pinky's Laundromat, and salvaged sheets of cardboard to practice break dancing. His friends were mostly Caucasian, Filipino, and Aboriginal, and they felt safe. "I'm sure there was crime in the neighbourhood, but we didn't really see it," he comments.

As a teenager, McDonald volunteered at Flora House, a Presbyterian outreach program where he had hung out as a kid, and he began to see some changes. Kids arrived hungry and talked a lot about break and enters. Many parents didn't seem to care. Houses began to look more rundown. And Jason McDonald, who used to walk around Selkirk Avenue day or night without fear, began to feel afraid.

Harry Lazarenko, a resident of Magnus Avenue for more than 40 years, has represented Mynarski Ward, which includes a substantial portion of the North End, since 1974. He remembers the days when nobody locked their doors at night. He now encounters elderly residents who are afraid to leave their homes.

A North Ender who hung around with some of the area's most notorious teens in the 1950s and 1960s observes, "It was tough but not like how it is now. Now it's just crazy. These kids are running around with no souls."

The North End has always been viewed as the "tough" part of Winnipeg, particularly by people who have never lived there. Gambling, bootlegging, theft, and violence, all by-products of poverty, have been part of the North End since the early days. But that image has become larger and more vivid in recent years as the result of some very real increases in violent crime and gang activity. The term "war zone" has become a media favourite, and public impressions of crime issues have been distorted in some instances by media use of the term "North End" when reporting on crimes that occur in the central part of the city, in West Kildonan, and even across the river in North Kildonan.

The Last Kosher Butcher Shop

After 86 years in business, the last kosher butcher shop in Winnipeg's North End closed in early 2008. The closing of Omnitsky Kosher Foods at Main and Polson was attributed to the migration of most of Winnipeg's Jewish population to the south part of the city.

Many North End businesses have closed

■ Pawn Shops and tattoo parlours have become more predominant. • Credit: Photos by Russ Gourluck

(OPPOSITE) A cyclist manoeuvres on icy streets at Aikins and Machray. • Credit: Photo by John Marczyk

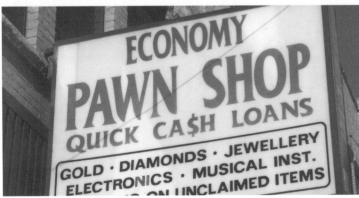

Figures for Point Douglas compiled by the Winnipeg Regional Health Authority in 2003 reveal a median family income of $29,445, compared to $46,698 in the Winnipeg Health Region as a whole, and an unemployment rate that is twice as high as the rest of the city. More than 20 percent of the residents had less than a grade nine education, compared to fewer than 10 percent in the city as a whole.

In 2006, the William Whyte neighbourhood was determined to be one of the lowest-income areas in the city with average household incomes around $26,000, about half of the average for all Winnipeg households. Unemployment among people 25 and over was nearly 16 per cent, and more than half of the adult population had not graduated from high school.

In the midst of changes, there are still many signs of the North End's original immigrant cultures

◼ Credit: Photos by Russ Gourluck

Many North End sites now have an Aboriginal focus

■ Credit: Photos by Russ Gourluck

Changing Neighbourhoods

In 1951, nearly 50 percent of the Winnipeggers of Ukrainian origin and more than 40 percent of those of Polish background lived in the North End. Thirty years later in 1981, less than 20 percent of each group lived in the North End.

Harry Lazarenko estimates that about two-thirds of the population of Mynarski Ward is Aboriginal. MLA Doug Martindale tells that 2006 census figure still showed residents of British and Ukrainian origin as the largest groups in Burrows, but Aboriginals and Filipinos each represented about 20 percent. He knows of only three Jewish families in all of Burrows and foresees a decline in the Ukrainian proportion, with more Aboriginal and South East Asian families moving in. Astrid Lichti, whose family owns Cosmopolitan Florists on Main Street, notes increases in Aboriginal, Filipino, African, and East Indian families in the community.

After Aboriginal Canadians received the right to vote in 1960, journalist Colleen Simard explains, there was an influx of families into Winnipeg. "We're like everybody else. We came to the city wanting a better life, looking for work. It was almost like a wave, like the Polish and Ukrainian immigrants, getting up in the world." But, Simard points out, the analogy is valid only to a point. "Aboriginal people have the extra baggage of residential schools." She talks about family dysfunction, the adoption of Aboriginal children in the "Sixties Scoop," and loss of identity. "I think we're catching up, but it's going to take time."

Simard lives and works in the North End, has a regular column in the *Winnipeg Free Press*, and is the publisher and editor of *Urban NDN*, a community newspaper with an Aboriginal slant. She jokes that when she goes out in evening and sees police cars driving by every few minutes "I feel safe. I feel damn safe." Some Aboriginal people are moving out of the North End, but Colleen Simard stays because "It's community that's important. I have a lot of family here. I know these streets."

Aging Neighbourhoods

Like most areas in the central parts of the city, the North End faces the reality of aging housing, with many houses and apartment buildings approaching or even passing the century mark. At the same time, many long-time residents have reached the stage of their own lives where they are no longer able to continue living in the homes they have known for decades.

Although some of the houses, particularly east of Main Street or on the more northerly streets of the North End, have been purchased by young families who appreciate the charm and quality of older homes and neighbourhoods (and

the attractiveness of the prices), many have been acquired by absentee landlords who are more interested in receiving rent payments than in upgrading or even maintaining the properties.

North End business owner and resident Astrid Lichti insists that there's a "huge difference" between the appearance and condition of owner-occupied homes and those that are occupied by tenants, "especially when the landlords aren't local. They don't care." Lichti isn't alone in claiming that absentee owners – some live outside of Manitoba, others outside of Canada – neglect their properties and hire management companies that do little to ensure that deteriorating houses are maintained. Cultural and language differences often render immigrants from other countries or recent arrivals from northern First Nations particularly vulnerable to exploitation by profit-seeking landlords. The frequent movement of many tenants contributes to the deterioration of the properties.

Harry Lazarenko estimates that about 600 properties in his ward are owned by foreign landlords camouflaged by numbered companies. St. John's Neighbourhood community activist Tracey Proctor says that about half of the houses in her area are occupied by tenants. "I spend a lot of time in my yard in the summer trying to make it look nice. Renters don't have that same interest."

■ (ABOVE) Inkster Boulevard, with its treed boulevards and well-kept homes, is one of the North End's most attractive streets. • Credit: Photo by Russ Gourluck

(RIGHT) Boarded-up and abandoned homes scar many streets west of Main. • Credit: Photos by Russ Gourluck

CONTINUING
BUSINESSES

The spirit of the North End can be found in businesses that have been part of the neighbourhood for ages and are proud to remain.

■ Mike Wolchock and John Latham with classic coaster wagons and lawn mowers, 2009.
• Credit: Photo by Russ Gourluck

Staying in the North End

Brian and Richard Kurtz literally grew up at Valley Flowers. The business was established in 1947 by their father, Jack Kurtz, and family friend Henry Steinhauer, and the building at 368 McGregor near Mountain served both as the flower shop and the residence of the Kurtz family for many years. The Kurtz brothers, who have been involved in Valley Flowers since they were children and now own the business, remember the days when live baby chicks were sold to flower purchasers at Easter time for 25 cents each. Richard Kurtz estimates that 80 percent of their customer base has moved out of the area. Walk-in traffic is now minimal, and most orders are placed by phone, but the Kurtzes have no intentions of moving Valley Flowers out of the North End.

Planting the Seeds of Discovery

When John Marczyk was around 10 years old and went to Pollock Hardware to find parts for science projects, he knew that the owner and his son would help him find them, even if they had to search the basement. "I was there all the time," Marczyk recalls. "It was just one big place to explore. I go to antique places and thrift shops now because the time that I spent exploring Pollock's planted some remarkable seeds of discovery."

In 1966, Ed Lichti and his family bought a business known as Mae Wallis Florist at 994 Main Street near Pritchard but, because so many of their customers had come from distant places, they decided to rename it Cosmopolitan Florists. Most of the people who lived in the area had Ukrainian and Jewish backgrounds and many did all of their shopping on Main Street and Selkirk Avenue. Now, like the owners of Valley Flowers, the Lichtis find that much of their business comes from phone or Internet orders. Luxury items like flowers are purchases that people in the neighbourhood can't afford. Noting that the demographics have changed in the North End, Astrid Lichti mentions that they now frequently ship artificial floral arrangements to remote First Nations communities because fresh flowers can't survive the trip. Astrid helped out in the store as a young child attending Holy Ghost School on Selkirk Avenue ("We're not Catholic, but it was right around the corner.") and has worked there full-time every day of the week for 23 years since she was 16. She and her father Ed live in the North End by choice, and they have no plans of moving because, as she puts it, "We have too much invested."

The story of the survival of Pollock Hardware is a testimony to North End spirit. The landmark North End provider of almost-anything-you-need closed down in December 2007 and its prospects for reopening looked grim. Lois and Wayne Cash, who had owned Pollock's for 14 years, had tried without success for more than a year to sell the business and finally liquidated much of the stock at reduced prices and locked the doors.

Founded in 1922 by Alex Pollock at 1407 Main Street near Atlantic, the business had a series of owners who cultivated Pollock Hardware's reputation as a good-old-fashioned hardware store that stocked hard-to-find items and had staff members who knew their merchandise and took the time to talk with customers.

It was a group of North End residents who gather every Wednesday evening at Lisi's Ranch House on north Main Street who came up with the idea of forming a co-operative to take over Pollock's. They organized an initial meeting on a frigid January evening that, with very little publicity, attracted around 40 people. A subsequent meeting a month later with more publicity attracted 80 to 100 interested people, and membership sales began. That same month, volunteers began taking inventory in the boarded-up and nearly empty store, and, at a community meeting a few months later, the decision was made to form a co-op and purchase the business. Cheques from across Canada and beyond streamed in to purchase $25 lifetime memberships, and Pollock's Hardware Co-op Limited opened its doors in June, 2008. The co-op's initial goal was to sign up 200 members within the first year, but more than 1,000 memberships were sold in less than six months.

Although some of the rare items that helped establish Pollock's reputation over the decades – glass door knobs, out-of-production stovepipes, and parts for decades-old toasters

– were cleared out before the co-op took over, the store takes pride in stocking items that big box retailers don't have. "We focus on specialty things that people will drive across town to get because they know they're not going to find them anywhere else," explains manager Mike Wolchock. He mentions Winnipeg-made galvanized pails that can last a lifetime, Radio Flyer wagons, washboards, wooden drying racks, and clothes lines. In keeping with its environmental philosophy, Pollock's encourages reuse and recycling. Wolchock explains that Pollock's makes a point of having staff members who will answer customers' questions, provide personalized service, and offer advice on making repairs. We sell really good stuff – that's how we compete," says Wolchock.

Like an oasis of tranquility a few steps away from the noise and the occasional meanness of Main Street, De Landes Memorials at 927 Main conceals a small park-like yard with a manicured lawn, shady trees, and flowers. The surprisingly serene area is nestled next to the office and manufacturing building of the headstone provider and features a display of some of its products. Helping to shelter the serene display area is a house, built in 1897, that once contained a Chinese laundry, and was the home of Matt's grandfather, M. C. De Landes, who moved the business to that location in 1943. Matt De Landes, who shares the same initials as his grandfather and father who owned the business before him, has worked there "ever since I was a kid" in the 1960s and 1970s. He remembers wandering along the sidewalk on the east side of Main between Euclid and

Selkirk and visiting Big 4 Sales, the radiator store, a bakery with memorable lemon squares and Snow White Cream Soda, the Blue Boy Restaurant, the UNF (with Pete the barber), Mary the florist, Mr. Kormilo who sold cars, John the shoemaker, his aunt's beauty salon, and the public washrooms. As the third generation owner, De Landes is not considering a move "unless the neighbourhood goes right down to a ghetto." "But," he quickly adds, "it's being revitalized."

Billy Mosienko Lanes at 1138 Main Street became a North End fixture soon after it was founded in 1947 by NHL legend Billy Mosienko. Some North Enders still fondly remember the

■ Billy Mosienko Lanes remains part of the North End scene. • Credit: Photo by Russ Gourluck

place as "Como," a holdover from the years when the business was partly owned by another NHLer, Joe Cooper, and named Cooper-Mosienko Lanes. The days of teenage pinsetters and stubby pencils have given way to automatic pin-setting and automatic scoring. Norm Silverberg bowled there in the early days and recalls that it was especially packed on Saturday afternoons. Current owner Todd Britton reports that the 20 five-pin lanes are "full every night," predominantly with league bowlers.

Arising phoenix-like on the site of the old North End YMCA-YWCA at McGregor and Atlantic, the North End

Wellness Centre, which opened in 2009, has brought a new level of fitness to the North End. With its focus on recreation, social activities, and health programming, the 25,000 square foot (2,322 square metre) wellness centre is an updated replacement for the old "Y," which closed its doors in 1995. The Youth Centre includes an indoor skate park; a climbing tower; an indoor play structure; and youth-sized fitness equipment. In

■ The North End Wellness Centre replaced the YMCA-YWCA • Credit: Photo by Russ Gourluck

(ABOVE) The pool at the North End "Y," 1994
• Credit: Courtesy Judy Wasylycia-Leis

■ Harvey Lipkin (left) and Al Reimer founded Harv-Al in 1947. • Credit: U of M Archives, Tribune Collection, PC18- 4445-001

addition to a gym and basketball court, there's a childcare centre; a community meeting place with a kitchen and café; health care access; employment and life skills training; and community development. Partners in the project are the YMCA-YWCA of Winnipeg, Ma Mawi Wi Chi Itata Centre, and SPLASH Child Care, with the Winnipeg Regional Health Authority as a tenant. Combined public and private sources provided the $5.5 million needed to fund the proect.

A fixture at Main and Machray since 1961, Harv-Al Sportwear is named for its founders Harvey Lipkin and Al Rimer, who had become friends when they worked together as cutters in the garment industry. With Lipkin's background in basketball coaching and Rimer's involvement in baseball, sportswear manufacturing was a good fit, and they established Harv-Al in 1947. Harv-Al made jerseys for decades of Winnipeg high school teams, the Winnipeg Jets during the 1970s, and the Winnipeg Blue Bombers from 1967 to 1989.

■ Selkirk Avenue illustrates the closing of many bank branches throughout the North End. At the same time, "fringe banks" such as cheque-cashing outlets and pawn shops, have become more prevalent. • Credit: Photos by Russ Gourluck

With about 25 employees, the firm now makes jerseys for World Wrestling Entertainment fans as well as for the local market. Harv-Al is now owned by Rimer's nephews, brothers Yale and Mark Singer.

One of the oldest businesses on Selkirk Avenue also has one of the lowest profiles, shipping almost all of its products outside of Manitoba. Ideal Electric Manufacturing, which has been at the same Selkirk Avenue location since 1929, manufactures high-quality decorative lighting fixtures and lamps destined primarily for commercial projects in Canada, the USA, and Central America. It's a fourth-generation family-owned business.

Founded in 1978 by brothers Myron and Peter Kurjewicz, Brothers Pharmacy at 542 Selkirk Avenue at the corner of Andrews was named not only to reflect the kinship of the owners but also to honour the close relationship of the many ethnic groups in the area. Current co-owner Julia Kurjewicz acknowledges that it's not easy for the small drug store to compete with national chains, but Brothers continues to have loyal customers among Polish, Ukrainian, and Aboriginal residents.

As one of the 90 members of the Selkirk Avenue Business Improvement Zone Board for approximately two decades (including several years as president) and as the owner of Todaschuk Sisters' Ukrainian Boutique, Sylvia Todaschuk is very much a part of Selkirk Avenue, She points with pride to the diversity of ethnic groups represented by the businesses along

■ Liberty Photo Studios was one of many photography businesses along Selkirk Avenue. • Credit: Courtesy Joseph Presznyak

the Avenue, but also recognizes that there have been changes. "Selkirk Avenue has changed, but the world has changed too," Todaschuk acknowledges. Because many storefronts are now occupied by educational and social service agencies, parking has become a problem for the customers of the retailers that remain. Business owners are concerned that they are losing potential customers who can't find parking near the stores and are reluctant to park on side streets.

When Joseph Presznyak opened Liberty Photo Studios on Selkirk Avenue in 1968, there were seven studios on Selkirk serving the needs of various ethnic groups. Presznyak, whose own heritage is Hungarian, was able to communicate in German, Croatian, Serbian, and Spanish as well as Hungarian and English. The business closed in 2005 when he retired.

■ The William Norrie Centre, named in 2005 for the former Winnipeg mayor who became Chancellor of the University of Manitoba, houses U of M social work and education programs that incorporate academic and personal supports to increase student success. The building is located on the former site of Oretzki's Department Store. • Credit: Photo by Russ Gourluck

■ Luda's displays a framed magazine cover featuring Ed Koranicki, shown by his daughter Tracy Konopada (left) and her daughter Kristi.
• Credit: Photo by Russ Gourluck

NEW BUSINESSES

For some entrepreneurs, the North End represents opportunity and a place to establish new businesses.

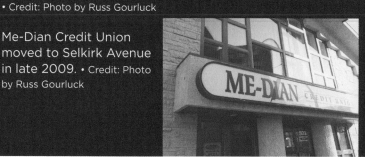

Since being vacated by Oscar's Delicatessen in the mid-1970s, the storefront at 1236 Main has had several tenants, including the Hungarian Goulash House and a Christian biker group. Since 2000, it has housed Food for Thought, a food service business that specializes in frozen foods and catering. Owner Melanie Rushton likes the central location and finds that many of her customers, which include retirees, churches, and schools, are from the area. She and the staff of eight believe that the neighbourhood is changing for the better and plan to remain there.
• Credit: Photo by Russ Gourluck

Me-Dian Credit Union moved to Selkirk Avenue in late 2009. • Credit: Photo by Russ Gourluck

To help serve the financial needs of its members, Me-Dian Credit Union moved to a Selkirk Avenue building previously occupied by Entegra (formerly Holy Spirit) Credit Union. Me-dian, one of Manitoba's smallest credit unions, was previously located on Broadway Avenue, but recognized that many of its members live in the North End. Although, as a closed bond credit union, Me-Dian's membership is restricted to persons of Metis or First Nations descent, its presence on Selkirk Avenue will help to some extent to offset the shortage of banking institutions in the North End.

Located in a former grocery store at the corner of Salter and Aberdeen, Luda's Deli serves up hearty home-cooked food with a side order of North End hospitality. Owner (and cook) Tracy Konopada grew up in the North End and attended St. John's High School. Her father, Ed Koranicki, was the owner of Eddy's Place on Selkirk Avenue. At Luda's (the name is based on the Ukrainian words *nash lyudey*, which mean "our people") some of the most popular menu items are Reuben sandwiches, burgers, home-made borscht, and a special macaroni-cheese-and ground beef soup. But there are some specials that the regulars (who are greeted by name by Konopada as they walk in the door of the 36-seat diner) swear by. One that's not even on the menu is a grilled salami sandwich made with cheese, lettuce, tomato, and raw onions. Others are named for the customers who originally requested them, like the "Ronnie Omelet" (made with whatever Konopada has in the kitchen) and "Wally-sized Fries" (an extra large serving). Konopada explains that she "cooks with love" and ensures that nobody leaves Luda's hungry.

Winnipeg's inner city has been described as a "food desert" – an area where soda pop, potato chips, and chocolate bars are much more prevalent in grocery stores than fresh fruit and vegetables. Although there are supermarkets like Safeway and Extra Foods on major thoroughfares like Main Street and Mountain Avenue, getting there and back often involves taxi or bus rides. Most of the corner grocery stores that used to be found in the North End have faded away, and the few survivors, along with the major convenience stores, don't focus on stocking nutritious foods at reasonable prices.

Neechi Foods Community Store opened at 325 Dufferin Avenue in the early 1990s in response to the expressed need of North End residents for healthy food at an affordable cost. Neechi (which means "friends" in both Cree and Ojibwa) not only sells fresh fruit and vegetables at affordable prices, it's also an Aboriginal specialty store that offers wild rice, wild blueberries, fresh bannock, and local fish. City-wide delivery is available. Because of its special concern for the health of neighbourhood children, Neechi, which won a national award in 2004 for diabetes prevention, has a "kids only" fruit basket where children can purchase pieces of fresh fruit for just 25 cents. An Aboriginal owned and operated worker co-operative, Neechi has become an outlet for hand-crafted moccasins, Aboriginal artwork, and children's books. The co-op exchanges crafts made by local people for credits that can be used in the store.

In late 2009, Neechi Foods announced plans to transform the former California Fruit site at Main and Euclid into a retail, restaurant, and food complex to be named Neechi Commons.

■ "One of our gardeners lost a cabbage the other day. He was quite upset," Annette Champion-Taylor (kneeling, right) tells Tracey Proctor as she checks her strawberries. Vacant lots, leased from the City of Winnipeg for a nominal fee, become community gardens each spring. Small plots in each garden are carefully tended by resident families or individuals using environmentally friendly methods. Vandalism is described as "very minimal."
• Credit: Photo by Russ Gourluck

REVITALIZING THE VILLAGE

North End pride and spirit continue to thrive in the people and organizations that believe in the North End and work together to create a better future.

■ The North End Women's Centre was established in 1984 to provide programs and services to women and their families. It offers community-based solutions to break the cycle of poverty, isolation, addiction, violence, and dependency.
• Credit: Photo by Russ Gourluck

Taking Back the Neighbourhood

Annette Champion-Taylor and Tracey Proctor are passionate about the North End. As a child, Champion-Taylor lived in the area for about three years before her family moved. Then, about 20 years ago, she fell in love with a North End house that was up for sale and bought it. "When most people leave the North End, they don't come back," she laughs. "I came back." She's now the Volunteer and Program Co-ordinator of the William Whyte Residents Association. Her friend Tracey Proctor has been a North Ender for five years and is past chair of St. John's Residents Association.

Since 2008, both have headed up the Neighbour-to-Neighbour Safety Strategy, a partnership that residents formed with police to reduce drugs, gang activities, and the sex trade in high-risk neighbourhoods. The women are optimistic about the future of their community. Champion-Taylor describes how crime peaked around 2007, with open drug deals on the streets, fires ravaging auto-bin garbage containers and prostitutes working street corners against a backdrop of derelict and vacant houses. "It was like an arson zone," she recalls. But the Safety Strategy has helped to reduce criminal activity. They emphasize

that their neighbourhoods are generally safe and quiet during the day. Most gang activity takes place at night and is drug trade-related. Car traffic increases substantially at night as well, as "johns" cruise into the areas populated by sex-trade workers and their pimps.

From their perspective, resident involvement is the key. "Social service agencies and the police can't take care of everything. It all comes down to the individual. Neighbours need to be involved, to step up and say, 'We want better for ourselves.'"

In 2008 the Point Douglas Residents Association accelerated its campaign to reduce crime in the historic neighbourhood.

■ Slum housing was cleared and replaced by Lord Selkirk Park. • Archives of Manitoba, Winnipeg Views 115 and 116, N23007

■ When it was built in the 1960s, Lord Selkirk Park public housing development was seen as a solution to slum housing. But it displaced more residents than it could accommodate and initially offered little hope for families living in poverty. Recent initiatives have focussed on providing opportunities for residents to become self-sufficient. • Credit: Photo by Russ Gourluck

■ Some of the 18 bungalows built in one week in 1993 by Habitat for Humanity volunteers (including former US President Jimmy Carter) are located on the appropriately-named Habitat Place, adjacent to Jarvis Avenue. • Credit: Photo by Russ Gourluck

Working closely with the Winnipeg Police Service and Manitoba Justice officials, community volunteers systematically reported gang activities, prostitution, and drug dealing. In one eight-month period, 30 crack houses were shut down, and the overall crime rate in Point Douglas was significantly reduced.

Better Housing for Better Living

Not all of the efforts of residents committees, which were first formed in 2001, are directed to crime reduction. They also work hard to improve the appearance of their neighbourhoods. Provincial government funding is available for a variety of initiatives, including housing, economic development, recreation, and health. Financial assistance for upgrading owner-occupied and rental housing can be obtained from as many as a dozen sources.

Annette Champion-Taylor and Tracey Proctor describe the challenges faced by the associations and acknowledge that improvements are happening gradually. "There are pockets that are really lovely. Some homes are immaculate, but others are just

■ A United Church minister, Doug Martindale (shown meeting with constituents in 2006) and his family moved to Winnipeg with his family in 1980 from Eatonia, Saskatchewan and chose to live in the North End because of the affordability of housing and because he believed that clergy should live in the community they serve. The Martindales initially lived in the Willow Park East Housing Co-op on Burrows, later moving to St. John's Avenue and then to Machray Avenue. One of the reasons for choosing St. John's Avenue was the proximity of Ralph Brown School, where his children were able to enrol in the Ukrainian Bilingual program. Martindale finds the people in the Burrows Constituency that he's represented in the Manitoba Legislature since 1990 to be unpretentious and friendly He's also found them to be extremely tolerant, even, as he puts it, "of things they shouldn't tolerate like prostitution and crime. People put up with a lot that other people wouldn't." • Credit: Courtesy Doug Martindale

The Welcoming Place

The MLA for St. Johns Constituency, Gord Mackintosh finds the North End "welcoming and warm." Born in Fort Frances, Ontario, Mackintosh attended St. John's Cathedral Boys School north of Selkirk as a boy. After he and his wife Margie married in the 80s they spotted a home on Cathedral and decided that was where they wanted to live. "We chose the North End," he smiles. "Our neighbourhood is one of the best parts of our family's life." Initially Mackintosh became involved in community activism, leading a successful 1993 campaign to halt the closing of the St. John's Library. He'd already "dabbled" in politics, and in 1993 ran successfully for the Manitoba Legislature.

Reflecting on the North End, Gord Mackintosh observes "We've always been the welcoming place for new arrivals. In the North End, your neighbours can be from anywhere in Manitoba, anywhere in the world." Describing himself as "one proud North Ender," Mackintosh praises the diversity of the area in such characteristics as race, family makeup, income, and religion.

Mackintosh talks of the "metamorphosis" that is taking place in the North End as organizations and individuals address the challenges that face the community. He points out that in the last decade organizations have been formed to build homes and clean up neighbourhoods, describing them as "community-driven, grass roots initiatives."

disasters." They tell of slum landlords who own multiple properties and do only enough to meet legal requirements. Champion-Taylor estimates that there are 70 vacant lots where houses have been bulldozed.

Harry Lazarenko tells of the success of a 40-home project built by a private developer along Redwood and Aberdeen and now occupied primarily by Filipino families. He estimates that there are about 1,000 vacant buildings – mainly houses – in the city. Most of them are in the North End, and he expresses frustration that about 400 vacant structures in his ward are still awaiting inspection. He wants to see them torn down and replaced by new homes built by private developers and sold on the condition that the owners live in them.

The North End Community Renewal Corporation, founded in 1998, is committed to social, economic, and cultural renewal in the North End. Its wide-ranging activities include improving the quality and accessibility of housing, job creation and employment programs, crime reduction, and improving the image of the North End.

■ A 90-year-old 11-suite apartment building at 105 Scotia Avenue was converted into affordable condos in 2008. • Credit: Photo by Russ Gourluck

Sandbagging on Scotia

"Finding the North End was like finding my home, Judy Wasylycia-Leis explains. "We gravitated to the North End." When she and her husband Ron moved to Winnipeg from Ontario in 1982, they found that many aspects of the North End appealed to them, including its diverse ethnic makeup, its mixed economic circumstances, and its history of social democratic politics. They were delighted to find that their surname, a blend of her Ukrainian heritage and his Amish-Mennonite background didn't faze North Enders. They enjoy their attractive older home on Bannerman east of Main and their neighbourhood, where periodic house concerts are held. "We're trying to keep it from becoming too trendy," Judy smiles. "We don't want to see it become gentrified."

Since becoming an elected representative provincially and then federally, Wasylycia-Leis has noticed a number of changes in the North End. The traditional Polish, Ukrainian, and German makeup of the area has decreased in terms of numbers, but continues to maintain a strong presence through cultural and religious institutions. The number of Filipino, East Indian, and Aboriginal families has grown significantly.

She's disturbed by stereotypes of the North End that have been "perpetuated and promoted to some extent by the media" in an attempt to associate the area with crime and violence. Many of the challenges the community faces "stem from economic circumstances, from poverty, and from families that can't make ends meet," she comments. The MP is especially proud of what she terms "the North End fighting spirit" and the North End's "history of struggle, of people coming together to make a difference through strength in numbers" as they work together to restore and rejuvenate their neighbourhoods.

HONOURING THE VILLAGE

Although the North End, like all things, is in a continuing state of change, aspects of its distinctive personality have been preserved for posterity by writers and artists.

As the most colourful and, in many ways, the most interesting part of Winnipeg, the North End has been portrayed in a number of artistic modes, usually by people who grew up there. One of the most comprehensive is a collection of biographies of well-known North Enders titled *The Worst of Times The Best of Times: Growing up in Winnipeg's North End* and written by Harry Gutkin with Mildred Gutkin. Published in 1987, the book provides interesting insights into the lives of 18 individuals, ranging from Monty Hall and Allan Blye to Samuel Freedman, David Orlikow, and John Hirsch.

Growing up and living in the North End has been a significant influence on a number of writers, including Jack Ludwig, Adele Wiseman, and Miriam Waddington. John Marlyn's *Under the Ribs of Death* (1957); Sondra Gotlieb's *True Confections or How my Family Arranged my Marriage* (1978); Ed Kleiman's *The Immortals* (1980); Ryszard Dubanski's *Black Teeth: and Other North End Souvenirs* (2005); and Sidura Ludwig's *Holding my Breath* (2007) are accounts of many facets of North End life. The diversity of the area has been portrayed in drama (*Selkirk Avenue* by Bruce McManus), film (Noam Gonick's *Stryker*), and still photography (John Paskievich's *A Place Not Our Own* and *The North End*). Artistic glimpses have included Roman Swiderik's "North End Main Street" and Armand Paquette's "Evening Shopping" and "St. John's Tech."

BIBLIOGRAPHY

Artibise, Alan F. J. *Winnipeg: A Social History of Urban Growth 1874 – 1914*. Montreal: McGill-Queen's University Press, 1975.

Artibise, Alan F. J. *Documents on the City of Winnipeg 1873 – 191. Volume V: The Manitoba Record Society Publications*. Winnipeg: The Manitoba Record Society in association with The University of Manitoba Press, 1979.

Artibise, Alan F. J. *Winnipeg An Illustrated History*. Toronto: James Lorimer and Company, 1977.

Blicq, Andy. *Bloody Saturday: The Winnipeg General Strike* [DVD videorecording]. Winnipeg: Canadian Broadcasting Corporation, 2007.

Bellan, Ruben. *Winnipeg First Century: An Economic History*. Winnipeg: Queenston House Publishing, 1978.

Blanchard, Jim. *Winnipeg 1912*. Winnipeg: University of Manitoba Press, 2005.

Bredin, Thomas F. *The Cathedral Story: A Brief History of St. John's Cathedral, Winnipeg in commemoration of its 50th Anniversary, 1926-1976*. Winnipeg: Peguis Publishers Ltd., 1975.

Bumstead, J. M. *St. John's College: Faith and Education in Western Canada*. Winnipeg: University of Manitoba Press, 2006.

Bumstead, J. M. *The Winnipeg General Strike of 1919: An Illustrated History*. Winnipeg: Watson and Dwyer Publishing Ltd., 1994.

Chafe, J. W. *An Apple for the Teacher: A Centennial History of the Winnipeg School Division*. Winnipeg: [Winnipeg School Division No. 1], 1967.

Chiel, Arthur A. *The Jews in Manitoba*. Toronto: University of Toronto Press, 1961.

Czuboka, Michael. *Juba*. Winnipeg: Communigraphics/Printers Aid Group, 1986.

Dafoe, Christopher. *Winnipeg: Heart of the Continent*. Winnipeg: Great Plains Publications, 1998.

Davies, Bill (director). *The Jews of Winnipeg*. National Film Board of Canada, 2007.

Diamond, Robert T. *Kings of the Diamond*. Calgary: Robert T. Diamond, 2008.

Dubanski, Ryszard. *Black Teeth: And Other North End Souvenirs*. Winnipeg: Signature Editions, 2005.

Ewanchuk, Michael. *Pioneer Profiles: Ukrainian Settlers in Manitoba*. Winnipeg: Michael Ewanchuk, 1981.

Fraser, William J. *St. John's College Winnipeg 1866-1966: A History of the First Hundred Years of the College*. Winnipeg: The Wallingford Press, 1966.

Gibbons, Lillian. *Stories Houses Tell*. Winnipeg: Hyperion Press, 1978.

Goldin, Max. *An Affair with my City: Selected works of Max Goldin*. Winnipeg: The Manitoba Branch, Canadian Authors Association, 1988.

Gotlieb, Sondra. *True Confections or How my Family Arranged my Marriage*. Don Mills, Ontario: Musson Book Company, 1978.

Green, Sidney. *Rise & Fall of a Political Animal*. Winnipeg: Great Plains Publications, 2003.

Grenke, Arthur. *The German Community in Winnipeg 1872 to 1919*. New York: AMS Press, 1991.

Gutkin, Harry. *Journey Into Our Heritage: The Story of the Jewish People in the Canadian West*. Toronto: Lester and Orpen Dennys Limited, 1980.

Gutkin, Harry with Mildred Gutkin. *The Worst of Times The Best of Times: Growing Up in Winnipeg's North End*. Markham, Ontario: Fitzhenry & Whiteside, 1987.

Hamilton, John David and Bonnie Dickie. *A Winnipeg: Album Glimpses of the Way We Were*. Toronto: Hounslow Press, 1998.

Hershfield, Charles Sheppy. *Medical Memories*. Winnipeg: Comet Press, 1973.

Hershfield, Leible. *The Jewish Athlete: A Nostalgic View*. Winnipeg: Leible Hershfield, 1980.

Jewish Historical Society of Western Canada Inc. *Personal Recollections: The Jewish Pioneer Past on the Prairies* Vol. VI. Winnipeg: Jewish Historical Society of Western Canada Inc. 1993.

Jones, Esyllt W. *Influenza 1918: Disease, Death, and Struggle in Winnipeg*. Toronto: University of Toronto Press, 2007.

Kleiman, Ed. *The Immortals*. Edmonton: NeWest Publishers, 1980.

Krawchuk, Peter. *The Ukrainians in Winnipeg's First Century*. Toronto: Kobzar Publishing Company Limited, 1974.

Leah, Vince. *The Best of Vince Leah*. Winnipeg: The Prairie Publishing Company, 1985.

Leah, Vince. *Pages from the Past*. Winnipeg: The Winnipeg Tribune, 1976.

Levine, Allan. *Coming of Age: A History of the Jewish People of Manitoba* Winnipeg: Heartland Associates Inc., 2009.

Lucas, Fred C. *An Historical Souvenir Diary of the City of Winnipeg Canada*. Winnipeg: Cartwright and Lucas, 1923.

Ludwig, Sidura. *Holding my Breath*. Toronto: Key Porter Books, 2007.

Marlyn, John. *Under the Ribs of Death*. Toronto: McLelland and Stewart, 1957.

McVay, Athanasius (editor in chief) and June Dutka (research and text). *St. Nicholas Ukrainian Catholic Church: Celebrating 100 Years: Together for Tomorrow*. Winnipeg: St. Nicholas Ukrainian Catholic Church, 2006.

Medovy, Harry. *A Vision Fulfilled: The Story of the Children's Hospital of Winnipeg*. Winnipeg: Peguis Publishers, 1979.

Mierau, Maurice. *Memoir of a Living Disease: The Story of Earl Hershfield and Tuberculosis in Manitoba and Beyond*. Winnipeg: Great Plains Publications, 2005.

Mochoruk, Jim with Nancy Kardash. *The People's Co-op: The Life and Times of a North End Institution*. Winnipeg: The Wind-up Committee of the People's Co-operative Ltd., 2000.

Paskievich, John. *A Place Not Our Own: North End Winnipeg*. Winnipeg: Queenston House Publishing Ltd., 1978.

Paskievich, John. *The North End*. Winnipeg: University of Manitoba Press, 2007.

Penner, Roland. *A Glowing Dream: A Memoir*. Winnipeg: J. Gordon Shillingford Publishing Inc., 2007.

Redekop, Bill. *Manitoba's Most Notorious True Crimes: Crimes of the Century*. Winnipeg: Great Plains Publications, 2002.

Redekop, Bill. *More of Manitoba's Most Notorious True Crimes: Crimes of the Century*. Winnipeg: Great Plains Publications, 2004.

Rizzo, Dee Dee. *Mount Carmel Clinic A History 1926-1986*. Winnipeg.

Robinson, Guy M. (editor). *A Social Geography of Canada*. Toronto: Dundurn Press, 1991.

Ross, Anne G. *Clinic with a Heart: The Story of Mount Carmel Clinic*. Winnipeg: Mount Carmel Clinic, 1998.

Rudnyckyj, Jaroslav B. *Mosaic of Winnipeg Street Names*. Winnipeg: Canadian Institute of Onomastic Sciences, 1974.

Sharon Home, The. *Building on a Tradition of Caring: The Sharon Home*. Winnipeg: The Sharon Home, 1997.

Silver, Jim. *North End Winnipeg's Lord Selkirk Park Housing Development: History, Comparative Context, Prospects.* Ottawa: Canadian Centre for Policy Alternatives, 2006

Smith, Doug. *Joe Zuken, Citizen and Socialist.* Toronto: James Lorimer and Company, 1990.

Wells, Eric. *Winnipeg Where the New West Begins An Illustrated History.* Burlington, Ontario: Windsor Publications Inc., 1982.

Werner, Hans. *Imagined Homes: Soviet German Immigrants in Two Cities.* Winnipeg: University of Manitoba Press, 2007.

Wilder, Joseph E. *Read All About It: Reminiscences of an Immigrant Newsboy.* Winnipeg: Peguis Publishers, 1978.

Winnipeg Free Press. The Way We Live in Manitoba. Winnipeg: Winnipeg Free Press, 1998.

Yuzyk, Paul. *The Ukrainians in Manitoba: A Social History.* Toronto: University of Toronto Press, 1953.

Zolf, Larry. *Zolf.* Toronto: Exile Editions, 1999.

INDEX